"We have come to expect from Paul Bradshaw the very best in critical historical studies of Christian liturgical practice and the most accurate and balanced accounts of the diversities of current Christian liturgical meaning. Both gifts are brilliantly present in this book. No future consideration of the history or the meaning of the appointment to leadership in Christian communities will be able responsibly to ignore this important book. Even more, the excellent questions that Bradshaw puts to every period of this history—including our own—will be able to form the basis for a lively conversation between the churches, a conversation that may move toward both mutual recognition of ministries and mutual admonition about their potential misuses. This is a fair, honest, important, and genuinely ecumenical book."

—Gordon W. Lathrop
Professor of Liturgy Emeritus
Lutheran Theological Seminary at Philadelphia

Paul F. Bradshaw

Rites of Ordination

Their History and Theology

A PUEBLO BOOK

Liturgical Press   Collegeville, Minnesota
www.litpress.org

A Pueblo Book published by Liturgical Press

Cover design by Ann Blattner. Illustration by Frank Kacmarcik, OblSB.

Scripture texts in this book are the author's own translation.

Excerpts from the *Book of Occasional Services*. Prepared by the Office of Theology and Worship for the Presbyterian Church (U.S.A.), 100 Witherspoon Street, Louisville, KY 40202. Published by Geneva Press, Louisville, KY. ©1999. Used by permission.

© 2013 by Order of Saint Benedict, Collegeville, Minnesota. All rights reserved. No part of this book may be reproduced in any form, by print, microfilm, microfiche, mechanical recording, photocopying, translation, or by any other means, known or yet unknown, for any purpose except brief quotations in reviews, without the previous written permission of Liturgical Press, Saint John's Abbey, PO Box 7500, Collegeville, Minnesota 56321-7500. Printed in the United States of America.

1   2   3   4   5   6   7   8   9

Library of Congress Cataloging-in-Publication Data

Bradshaw, Paul F.
    Rites of ordination : their history and theology / Paul F. Bradshaw.
        pages cm
    "A Pueblo book."
    Includes index.
    ISBN 978-0-8146-6267-0 — ISBN 978-0-8146-6292-2 (ebook)
    1. Ordination (Liturgy)—History.   I. Title.
    BV176.3.B73   2013
    265'.409—dc23   2013029185

Contents

Preface

The aim of this book is to provide as full a history of the theology and practice of ordination as is possible within the limits of a reasonably sized volume. Inevitably, however, some aspects cannot be adequately covered. That is true both of the minor orders and also of the ministries belonging exclusively to women (including that of deaconess). These receive some attention for the period of the first few centuries but it has not been possible to trace their later history in detail. Similarly, no attempt has been made to deal with the disputed question of the ordination of women to the ministries traditionally exercised by men, a subject that has been extensively treated in many other publications, among the more recent being Gary Macy's *The Hidden History of Women's Ordination: Female Clergy in the Medieval West* (New York: Oxford University Press, 2008). After we reach the period following the sixteenth-century Reformation, it has also been necessary to cover the ordination practices of the wide range of Christian denominations more superficially and selectively. It has simply not been possible to provide here a detailed comparative study of all the aspects of so many different rites: perhaps someone else will be inspired to take up this piece of research. Furthermore, while it has been necessary to touch on certain other aspects of Christian ministry in order to understand some dimensions of ordination practice, this is not a history of the ordained ministry as such. Nonetheless, in spite of these limitations, it is hoped that this book will serve as a useful introduction to the various ways that different Christian groups through the ages have understood what it means to ordain someone as a minister and how they have expressed that in their practice.

Some twenty-three years ago I published a collection of English translations of the ordination texts of the ancient Christian churches, together with an extensive introduction—*Ordination Rites of the Ancient Churches of East and West* (New York: Pueblo, 1990), hereafter referred to simply as *ORACEW*. Some of those texts have been reproduced in this book and I have also drawn on parts of the introductory material. But interested readers will still need to turn to that volume itself for other texts for which there was not room and for critical questions associated with the texts that are included here. Finally, I wish to record the special debt of gratitude I owe to the Warden and Fellows of Merton College, Oxford, who elected me as a Visiting Research Fellow for the Trinity term 2011, enabling me to lay the foundations for the book, and to my esteemed colleague Maxwell Johnson, who read the manuscript and offered many useful suggestions.

Paul F. Bradshaw

Abbreviations

AAS	*Acta Apostolicae Sedis*
BCE	Before the Common Era
CE	Common Era
JEH	*Journal of Ecclesiastical History*
JTS	*Journal of Theological Studies*
NPNF	Nicene and Post-Nicene Fathers
ORACEW	Paul F. Bradshaw, *Ordination Rites of the Ancient Churches of East and West* (New York: Pueblo, 1990)
PG	J. P. Migne, *Patrologia Graeca*
PL	J. P. Migne, *Patrologia Latina*
Puglisi	James F. Puglisi, *The Process of Admission to Ordained Ministry: A Comparative Study*, 3 vols. (Collegeville, MN: Liturgical Press, 1996–2001)
SL	*Studia Liturgica*
SP	*Studia Patristica*
ST	Studi e testi

Translations of primary sources not otherwise attributed are the work of the author.

Chapter 1

Historical and Typological Background

Christian ministers are not the direct historical successors of any of the ministries mentioned in the Old Testament, but because successive generations of Christians have drawn upon those texts and used them as images or "types" for their various ministries, in order to help define their essential character, it is important that we consider them before passing on to ministry in the New Testament.

THE OLD TESTAMENT PRIESTHOOD

As we shall see in chapter 3, from the third century onward the ordained ministry was increasingly viewed as a priesthood, and the threefold pattern of bishop, presbyter, and deacon that had emerged in the course of the second century was understood as forming the counterpart of the threefold ministry of high priest, priest, and Levite found in the Old Testament. According to the Pentateuch, Aaron was appointed as the first high priest and his sons as priests (see, e.g., Exod 28ff.), with certain other members of the tribe of Levi as their ministers (Num 8:5-26), thus forming a threefold hierarchy that continued throughout the centuries. Historical-critical scholarship, however, suggests that the true story of the Israelite priesthood was not as simple as that.[1]

The oldest layers of the Pentateuch know of no professional priests. Instead, in the patriarchal narratives it is the family or tribal leader who officiates at sacrificial acts on behalf of his people. Examples include Noah (Gen 8:20), Jacob (Gen 31:54), and, above all, Abraham in his willingness to sacrifice his son Isaac (Gen 22:1-19). Similarly, although the later contributors to the Pentateuch material never portray Moses as a priest (because they regarded the Israelite

---

[1] Much of the material in this section is based on Aelred Cody, *A History of Old Testament Priesthood*, Analecta Biblica 35 (Rome: Pontifical Biblical Institute, 1969).

1

priesthood as stemming from his brother Aaron), Moses nonetheless consecrates Aaron and his sons as priests and offers sacrifice on that occasion (Exod 28–29), in line with the ancient tradition by which tribal leaders exercised that role. Remnants of this remain in the presiding position of the head of the household at the domestic celebration of the Passover meal.

The only partial exception to the rule is the mysterious figure of Melchizedek, described as King of Salem and a priest of the most high God who "brings forth bread and wine" and blesses Abraham (Gen 14:18-20). He fulfills none of the conditions of priesthood that later Israelites would regard as requisite—he is neither a Hebrew, nor a worshiper of Yahweh, nor a member of the tribe of Levi—and the story seems intended to justify the later prerogatives of the kings of Israel to control the cult and receive revenues from it. We may note, for example, the story of David bringing the ark of the Lord to Jerusalem and sacrificing and dancing before it in the procession (2 Sam 6:13-14). The figure of Melchizedek was, however, seized on by the author of the Letter to the Hebrews, who describes Jesus as being "a priest for ever after the order of Melchizedek" (Heb 5:6, 10; 6:20; 7:17, 21), because although he did not come from a priestly family like Melchizedek did, Jesus possessed a priesthood that transcended earthly limitations of time and lineage (see the section below, "Priesthood in the New Testament").

It was only after the settlement in Canaan and the abandonment of the nomadic life that local shrines were established, which then needed resident officials to staff them. Eventually members of the tribe of Levi became the preferred persons to function as these sanctuary attendants, one of whose duties was to cast lots to determine God's will. Why the Levites came to predominate in this capacity is not clear, except that they lacked tribal territory of their own and thus needed to acquire income in some other way. The story in Judges 17 well illustrates this development. Here a man by the name of Micah had consecrated one of his sons as the priest for his household shrine, but when a Levite came by, Micah appointed him as his priest instead, at a salary of ten shekels of silver a year. Similarly, in 1 Samuel 1–2, the sons of Eli function as priests at the prestigious sanctuary at Shiloh. The impression given is that individual worshipers still offered the sacrifices themselves and the officials simply assisted and received a portion of what was offered in recompense.

After the establishment of the monarchy came an element of centralization in these cultic activities. Abiathar, a Levite, became King David's priest in Jerusalem along with Zadok (2 Sam 15:23-37), but in the quarrel over who should succeed David as king, Abiathar supported Adonijah, while Zadok supported Solomon (1 Kgs 1) and thus won a privileged place for Zadokite priests at Jerusalem when Solomon became king (1 Kgs 2:35). Later tradition portrayed Zadok as a descendent of Aaron through his son Eleazar (Num 20:24-29; 1 Chr 6:50-53). The Levites and other priests continued to function in sanctuaries elsewhere after the division of the kingdom, such as at Bethel, Beer-Sheba, Dan, and Gilgal in the north (1 Kgs 12:26-33), but the fall of the northern kingdom to the Assyrians in 721 BCE put an end to these sanctuaries, and the subsequent Deuteronomic reform in the south in the seventh century brought about an even greater centralization of the sacrificial cult in Jerusalem.

This would have left the traditional Levitical priesthood without a place to minister, but Deuteronomy 18:1-8 attempted to legislate a role for the Levites in the Jerusalem Temple, assigning to them a proportion of what was offered there in return for their service. However, with the Zadokite priests firmly in control of Temple, the Levites were forced to be subordinates, resulting in the existence thereafter of two levels of cultic officials. Ezekiel 44:10-31 explains this situation as punishment for the Levites having gone astray after idols and reward for the Zadokite priests for having remained faithful. The Levites were permitted only to take charge of the Temple gates, the slaying of the animals, and other menial tasks, while the Zadokites had the privilege of entering the sanctuary and offering the sacrifices. A further consequence of the reform was that everything concerned with the sacrificial act was now in the hands of these professionals. Individuals who were not priests no longer performed sacrifices themselves.

While the exile in Babylon from 587 onward led to the destruction of the Temple and the temporary cessation of the sacrificial cult, King Cyrus' edict of 539, permitting a return, led to the construction of the Second Temple by the end of the century and to the restoration of its worship. In the pre-exilic period the cultic figure in charge at a shrine had often been called simply "the priest," as in the case of Zadok (e.g., 1 Kgs 4:2; 1 Chr 16:39), although sometimes "high priest" (e.g., 2 Kgs 12:10; 22:4), but it was after the exile that this third tier of cultic official came to prominence, filling the void created by the absence of a king as such. The summit of the high priest's ministry was the Day of Atonement—an annual feast that seems to have come to the fore in this period—when he entered the Holy of Holies to sprinkle the blood of bull and goat and offer incense for the transgressions of the people (see Lev 16).

It also appears that at this time a formal consecration of the high priest at his appointment was established, transferring to him the anointing and other ceremonies that had been the practice with regard to the installation of the monarch, as evidenced by the later strata in the Pentateuch, which direct that Aaron shall be ritually washed, vested, and his head anointed with oil. His sons, too, are to be vested, and the vestments of both Aaron and his sons sprinkled with oil and the blood of a sacrificial ram (Exod 29; Levi 8). Eventually the unction with oil seems to have been extended to the consecration of other priests, as Exodus 40:12-15 directs that the sons of Aaron are also to be anointed. Levites, too, were purified by sprinkling water on themselves, shaving themselves, and washing their clothes (Num 8:6-14).

Israel subsequently found itself part of the empire of Alexander the Great and following his death, under Ptolemaic and Seleucid rule and subject to the ever-increasing pressure of Hellenization. During this period the prestige of the old priestly aristocracy eroded, and new non-Zadokite priestly families achieved prominence and held the position of high priest.

Because there were far too many priests and Levites for all of them to be employed year round in the Temple, they were organized into twenty-four courses or divisions—an arrangement credited to King David in 1 Chronicles 24. Each of these, consisting of several hundred men, came up to Jerusalem in turn to perform a week's service from one Sabbath to the next. During the rest of the year they resided in their hometowns and only rarely exercised any priestly function, such as declaring a leper clean after he had been healed (see Matt 8:4; Luke 17:14). Although they received various tithes and taxes, these were not sufficient to support them, and they were obliged to supplement their income in other ways.

According to the Mishnah (*Ta'an.* 4.2), attached to each of these priestly divisions were groups of pious laymen known as *ma'amadoth* or "standing-posts." When the corresponding division went up to Jerusalem to fulfill its duty, part of the *ma'amad* accompanied it and was present at the daily sacrifices to represent the people as a whole and part remained behind in the hometown or village and came together each day at the time of the daily sacrifices in order to read the account of creation in Genesis, thus associating themselves with the offering at a distance.

ELDERS

The term "elder" (in Greek *presbyteros*) was used by early Christians to designate one of the three orders of ministers that came into being in the second century, and the seventy elders appointed by Moses to govern the people in Numbers 11:16-17, 24-25 were later sometimes appealed to as an Old Testament "type" for this Christian ministry. Because those appointed by Moses are said to have been given some of the Spirit that he had received, this, in turn, encouraged the association of appointment to office with a particular gift of the Spirit. But Christians were using the term *elder* at an even earlier date, deriving it from Old Testament and Jewish use, making it important to understand its meaning in that context.

The tribes of Israel were composed of clans, which in turn consisted of a number of extended families. The heads of these families, clans, and tribes were the people referred to as elders in the Old Testament, the senior men whose age and attributed wisdom gave them respect and authority. Although quite prominent in the Pentateuch narratives and in the early history of the nation, they tend to diminish in importance under the monarchy, as the king appointed officials to take charge of everyday affairs, but they regain significance during and after the Exile (see Jer 29:1; Ezra 5:5; 6:7; 8:1). The word always occurs in the plural as a collective term for a group of leaders, and never as the title of a specific office to which an individual might be appointed. Thus, Moses does not appoint seventy men to be elders to govern the people of Israel but chooses seventy of the elders to carry out this role. In early Judaism, *elders* becomes a generic term to cover various groups of leaders, not solely the official members of the Sanhedrin, and is used in this way by the writers of the New Testament Gospels and

Acts.[2] In Greco-Roman society, older men occupied a similar place of privilege, although the preferred Greek term for a ruling oligarchy as distinct from senior citizens in general was *gerontes* and not *presbyteroi*.

THE SYNAGOGUE

Because the first Christians were Jews and would therefore have attended synagogue, it is natural for scholars to imagine that the pattern of synagogue leadership and administration provided a model for ministry within the earliest Christian communities. There is considerable uncertainty as to when the synagogue first emerged. Some would place its origin immediately after the return from Exile, others centuries later.[3] What is clear, however, is that the term referred primarily to those who assembled and not to a building in which such meetings took place. Although at one time it was thought that the gatherings each Sabbath were for an act of worship, it is now widely accepted that synagogue liturgy as such was a creation of the period after the destruction of the Temple in 70 CE and that prior to that the prime purpose of the assembly was the study of the Torah, although this activity might have been accompanied by prayer.[4]

Within the synagogue, any male with sufficient competency might in theory function as reader, translator, or interpreter of the Scriptures, although inevitably prominence tended to be given to those regarded as sages, mainly of the Pharisaic party. Each synagogue had two officials, both mentioned in the New Testament. One was the *archisynagogos*, "ruler of the synagogue" (Luke 8:41, 49; 13:14; Acts 13:15), a kind of superintendent, although the precise nature of his appointment is not clear. Some scholars have

---

[2] See further, R. Alastair Campbell, *The Elders: Seniority within Earliest Christianity* (Edinburgh: T & T Clark, 1994), 20–44.

[3] See Lee Levine, *The Ancient Synagogue: The First Thousand Years*, 2nd ed. (New Haven: Yale University Press, 2005), 21–173.

[4] See ibid., 134–59; Heather A. McKay, *Sabbath and Synagogue: The Question of Sabbath Worship in Ancient Judaism* (Leiden: Brill, 1994); Pieter W. van der Horst, "Was the Synagogue a Place of Sabbath Worship before 70 C.E.?," in *Jews, Christians and Polytheists in the Ancient Synagogue*, ed. Steven Fine (New York: Routledge, 1999), 18–43.

argued that he was elected for a limited period, perhaps a year, others that the office was permanent and hereditary, and others that he was the patron or principal benefactor of the synagogue. There is also evidence for priests assuming this leadership role in some places.[5] Some have suggested that there could have been more than one such person in each synagogue (note the use of the plural in Acts 13:15), and even that the office could have been held by women.[6] The principal functions exercised by the *archisynagogos* were administrative and presidential, keeping order at the meetings and inviting individuals to perform various tasks. The other official was the *hazzan*, "attendant," mentioned in Luke 4:20 as the one to whom Jesus handed back the scroll after reading the passage from Isaiah and before expounding its meaning to those assembled. (If historically reliable, this passage suggests that not only the Law but also the prophets were being read in the synagogue in the first century.) This person seems to have been a sort of janitor, taking care of the building and its furnishings, especially the scriptural scrolls.[7]

Traditionally, it had been thought that each synagogue was governed by a formally appointed board of elders, but it is now seriously questioned whether this was so at such an early date, and it is considered more likely that in first-century Palestine the elders of the synagogue would have been the same natural elders of the community mentioned in the section above (see "The Elders of the Jews" of Luke 7:3). What might have been the case in the Diaspora is less clear. Similarly, it was also once believed that rabbis would have exercised a leading role in the synagogue, especially in the interpretation of the Law, but that, too, now seems a less likely assumption in the face of Lawrence Hoffman's arguments that the term "rabbi" did not come into use until after the destruction of the Temple, and that although individual rabbis subsequently did appoint disciples, if ever there was any liturgical ceremony associated

[5] See Levine, *The Ancient Synagogue*, 136–37, 415–20; Tessa Rajak and David Noy, "*Archisynagogos:* Office, Title and Social Status in the Greco-Jewish Synagogue," *Journal of Roman Studies* 83 (1993): 75–93.

[6] See Bernadette J. Brooten, *Women Leaders in the Ancient Synagogue*, Brown Judaic Studies 36 (Chico, CA: Scholars Press, 1982).

[7] See Levine, *The Ancient Synagogue*, 435–42.

with this act in the early period, we do not know anything about it.[8]

As said above, it has been popular to suppose that the administrative structure of the synagogue would have provided a natural pattern for the early Christian church to adopt and adapt, with the bishop replacing the ruler of the synagogue, the presbyters its elders, and the deacons the attendant, but that assumption too now seems more questionable. Although the very first converts were Jews, they seem to have met together more often in houses for shared meals than in assemblies modeled on the synagogue, and so it is the Greco-Roman household that now appears to have exercised a greater influence on shaping the practice of Christian congregations in the long term. This would have especially been the case in Gentile communities with no experience of a regular meeting of the synagogue type and who would in any case not have been covered by the exemption from work on the Sabbath granted to Jews in the Roman Empire and so unable to devote part of the day to corporate Bible study as their Jewish counterparts could. For them, of necessity—except perhaps for the leisured few—the communal study of Scripture would have had to be an activity associated with the gatherings for evening meals: early mornings before work could not have provided sufficient time for anything substantial of this kind.

NEW TESTAMENT TITLES

The Twelve

For the writers of the books that make up the New Testament, the events in the life of Jesus and the foundational moments of the first Christian communities belong to the past and not to their present. Particular groups who had apparently assumed leadership roles in the emerging church were known to them through stories that were handed down, just as they were to later generations of Christians. Thus "the Twelve" are figures belonging to memories of the past. As companions of Jesus, they symbolized the leaders

---

[8] Lawrence Hoffman, "Jewish Ordination on the Eve of Christianity," SL 13 (1979): 11–41.

of the eschatological twelve tribes of Israel that would exist in the kingdom of God, and for Luke they had formed the leadership of the church in Jerusalem; but, apart from the replacement of Judas by Matthias at the beginning of Acts, they appoint no successors to themselves. Although later Christians would seek to forge a link between the subsequently emergent episcopate and these men, such a connection is not made anywhere in the New Testament. Among the Twelve, Peter is recalled as having exercised a leading role, but both Acts and Paul also ascribe to James, the brother of the Lord, a prominent position in the Jerusalem church even though he is not listed as having been one of the original Twelve (see Acts 12:17; 15:13; 21:18; 1 Cor 15:7; Gal 1:19; 2:9, 12).

Apostles

The place of James raises the question as to the meaning of the word *apostle* in the New Testament. Although the book of Acts appears generally to equate the Twelve with "the apostles" and so later ecclesiastical tradition has tended to speak of "the twelve apostles," the term is not restricted to the Twelve in the writings of Paul but refers to a much wider circle of people—this extension no doubt occasioned by his own desire to be numbered among them (Rom 1:1; 11:13; 1 Cor 1:1; 4:9; 9:1-5; 15:9; 2 Cor 1:1; 11:5; 12:11-12; Gal 1:1; Eph 1:1; Col 1:1). Thus, he includes James among the apostles (Gal 1:19), Barnabas (1 Cor 9:6) and Andronicus and Junia (Rom 16:7). Even Luke describes both Paul and Barnabas as apostles in Acts 14:14, and Paul also speaks of the existence of other "false apostles" (2 Cor 11:13). Chapter 11 of the *Didache*, too, is familiar with people it calls apostles—apparently itinerant preachers, similar or identical to those called prophets.[9] Subsequent to this, however, the title appears to have died out and we do not encounter it being used for current church leaders in later documents.

The Seventy

Unique to Luke's gospel is the sending out, in addition to the twelve disciples, of a further seventy in pairs "to every city and place" to which Jesus was intending to go (Luke 10:1-17). Various

---

[9] For ministries in the *Didache*, see below, pp. 25–27.

sources for the number seventy (or in some manuscripts, seventy-two) have been proposed, among them the seventy descendants of the sons of Noah in Genesis 10, the seventy elders chosen by Moses to govern Israel in Numbers 11, and the seventy-two translators of the Septuagint mentioned in the *Letter of Aristeas*. Later traditions gave names to each of them, differing somewhat from list to list and drawn to some extent from names mentioned elsewhere in the New Testament. Some modern commentators have suggested that this sending out was meant to prefigure the eventual mission to the Gentiles, but others doubt that Luke would have viewed the Samaritans as the equivalent of the Gentiles. Medieval writers on the subject of orders commonly viewed the episcopate as being derived from the apostles and the presbyterate from these seventy commissioned by Jesus.

The Seven

The appointment of the Seven in Acts 6:1-6 was later interpreted as the institution of the first deacons, but there is nothing in the account itself to suggest such a link, and the earliest evidence for this identification occurs only in the late second century—first in the writings of Irenaeus.[10] It seems to have been the phrase "serve tables" that led later Christians to view those appointed as having been deacons, but there is no reason to understand their role as the equivalent of merely being waiters. The distribution of charity was one of the fundamental aspects of the life of the early Christian community, and the need to appoint some from the Greek-speaking members of the movement as administrators to ensure that the indigent from that same group received their fair share of goods would have been a natural step to take. In any case, their activities do not seem to have been restricted to this particular function: Stephen does great wonders and miracles (Acts 6:8); Philip evangelizes and performs miracles in Samaria (Acts 8:5-7) and he baptizes the Ethiopian eunuch on the road to Gaza (Acts 8:26-40). Some modern commentators have suggested that these individuals were actually Christian prophets and that the author created this plau-

---

[10] See below, p. 37.

sible appointment scene so as to portray their authority as deriving from that of the Twelve and not independent of them.[11]

It is interesting to note that those chosen are described as already being "full of the Spirit and wisdom" (Acts 6:3), which does not suggest that their appointment involved the bestowal of any particular new gifts of the Spirit. Nevertheless, prayer was made for them in their new responsibility and hands were laid on them. After the early chapters of Acts we hear no more about the Seven (except for "the house of Philip the evangelist" being mentioned in Acts 21:8) and no direct successors to them ever emerge.

THE IMPOSITION OF HANDS

The appointment of the Seven is not the only place in the New Testament where the imposition of hands is mentioned in connection with the commissioning of individuals for a particular task or ministry. In Acts 13:1-3, Barnabas and Saul are set apart by the laying on of hands after fasting and prayer for a particular work to which the Spirit has called them, and there are two references to the gesture in the Pastoral Epistles that have usually been understood as related to appointment to office: 1 Timothy 4:14 speaks of a gift received by the addressee of the letter at "the laying on of hands by the eldership," and 2 Timothy 1:6 of the gift of God possessed by the addressee through the laying on of the author's hands. (1 Tim 5:22 instructs the recipient not to be hasty in the laying on of hands, but this may concern a different ritual context, possibly initiation or healing.) Later Christian tradition has generally treated these four occurrences as sufficient proof that the imposition of hands in commissioning ministers was standard practice in New Testament times and that the later use of the imposition of hands in ordination stood in direct continuity with it. It is at least questionable, however, whether this view is correct.

In particular, the author may have introduced the imposition of hands when describing the two instances in Acts in order to emphasize the legitimation of that commissioning by others, just as he added a subsequent imposition of apostolic hands on the Samaritans

---

[11] See, for example, Luke Timothy Johnson, *The Acts of the Apostles*, Sacra Pagina 5 (Collegeville, MN: Liturgical Press, 1992), 110–12.

baptized by Philip in Acts 8:14-25 and on twelve disciples who had only received the baptism of John in Acts 19:1-7—this is highly unlikely to have been standard baptismal practice in his day as it did not continue as a universal custom in connection with that rite. (The coupling of a laying on of hands with "washings" in Hebrews 6:2 may be thought to suggest a baptismal context there, but is too ambiguous to draw any firm conclusion.) Indeed, it has been suggested by some that the commissioning of Joshua, son of Nun, "a man in whom is the Spirit," as leader by Moses through the laying on of hands (Num 27:16-23; see also Deut 34:9) may have provided the model for the description of the Seven's appointment in Acts 6. It has even been proposed that the reference to the imposition of hands on Barnabas and Saul in Acts 13 may also have been influenced by another Old Testament precedent—that of the appointment of the Levites in Numbers 8:10.[12] Even the references to the laying on of hands in the Pastoral Epistles might be related to the need to reinforce the authority of the unusually youthful Timothy rather than a mere reflection of standard practice.

It is interesting to note that apart from the two instances just referred to, the imposition of hands is never mentioned in association with other acts of appointment or commissioning in the Old Testament—neither the consecration of the sons of Aaron as priests in Exodus 29, nor the anointing of kings (see Judg 9:8, 15; 1 Sam 9; 15:1, 17), nor in the recognition of prophets, nor even the authorization of the seventy elders to govern in Numbers 11—so that is unlikely to have been the source of the later general Christian use of it in ordination. On the other hand, it does occur there in relation to other actions: the conferral of blessing (e.g., Gen 48:8-22), on an animal about to be sacrificed (e.g., Exod 29:10, 15, 19; Lev 4:4; Num 8:12; and esp. Lev 16:21, where the guilt of the people is transferred

---

[12] See, for example, Johnson, *The Acts of the Apostles*, 107; Ben Witherington, *The Acts of the Apostles: A Socio-rhetorical Commentary* (Grand Rapids, MI: Eerdmans, 1998), 251. Note that grammatically the subject of the verbs "pray" and "lay hands" in Acts 6:6 would most naturally be the whole company, as was the case in Numbers 8:10, an interpretation accepted by some modern commentators but rejected by others who struggle to explain that it *must* mean the Twelve alone (presumably because later Christian laying on of hands at ordinations only involved ordained ministers and not the whole assembly).

to the scapegoat on the Day of Atonement), and prior to stoning for blasphemy (Lev 24:14).

Similarly in the New Testament, while other places where some sort of appointment is referred to fail to mention the use of the imposition of hands (e.g., Mark 3:14; Acts 1:26), it is frequently spoken of in relation to healing, something with which it is not associated in the Old Testament (see Matt 9:18 // Mark 5:23; Mark 6:5; 7:32; 8:23, 25; 16:18; Luke 4:40; 13:13; Acts 9:12, 17; 28:8). It is also, not surprisingly, found where a blessing is taking place (Matt 19:13, 15 // Mark 10:16). Thus, even though innumerable pages have been published on the origin and meaning of the gesture in relation to ordination, its inherent ambiguity seems to preclude reaching any definitive conclusion as to its precise significance in those few New Testament instances where it might be connected with appointment, still less abstracting from them a fixed interpretation that can then be applied unequivocally to its use in later ordination rites. Furthermore, as we have seen earlier, the suggestion often made that Christians derived the custom from contemporary rabbinic ordination practice also lacks any evidence to support it.

In other words, we cannot safely assume that when this ritual act is first explicitly mentioned in connection with ordination in Christian sources from the third century onward, it must have been either copied from the New Testament references or practiced in direct continuity from the first days of the church, and with precisely the same meaning that it might have had in those days. It is quite possible that when we first encounter it in the ordination practice of subsequent centuries, it signifies no more than the person or persons for whom the accompanying prayer is being made. As Augustine of Hippo observed of the laying on of hands in a different context, that of baptism: "What is it but prayer over a person?"[13] This interpretation is supported by the fact that it is given little prominence in some of those early texts, and not explicitly mentioned at all in others. It does not, at least at first, necessarily imply that something is understood as being transmitted from whoever is laying on hands to those on whom the hands are laid, and without

---

[13] Augustine, *De baptismo contra Donatistas* 3.16.

any corroborating evidence to that effect within the particular text itself, it would be unwarranted to draw that conclusion.

The increasing prominence given to the imposition of hands in ordination from the third century onward seems to be related to a change that took place in the interpretation of the Greek word *cheirotonia*, "the lifting up of the hands," and of its associated verb *cheirotoneo*. In classical Greek usage it had signified the act of election, voting by raising the hand, but early Christianity extended it to designate not just the first half of the process of ministerial appointment but the whole ordination—both election and prayer with the laying on of the hand. Later, however, the word came to be understood as referring to the second action rather than the first—the lifting up / laying on of the hand in prayer—thus giving that gesture greater importance and obscuring the significance given earlier to the act of election as integral to the process.

PRIESTHOOD IN THE NEW TESTAMENT

There are no signs in the New Testament that any members of the Jewish priesthood who might have been attracted to join the new Christian movement were granted any privileged role within it. Instead, it is the risen and glorified Jesus to whom the title of high priest comes to be applied in the Letter to the Hebrews, where Jesus is said to possess a priesthood like that of Melchizedek (see above, p. 2), who is described as being "without father, without mother, without genealogy, having neither beginning of days nor end of life" (Heb 7:3). Not only was Jesus immortal like Melchizedek but his priesthood, too, was based neither on physical descent from a priestly family nor on the Law and was one that was permanently effective (Heb 4:14-5:10; 6:19–7:28). In a complex and rather repetitive argument, the author asserts that while the Jewish priests exercised their function on earth, Jesus' priesthood is in heaven (Heb 8:1-4); while they offered the blood of animals, Jesus sacrificed his own blood (Heb 9:11-14); while the Jewish high priest entered an earthly sanctuary, Jesus had entered a heavenly one (Heb 9:24); while the high priest had to do this year after year on the Day of Atonement, Jesus had done this once and for all (Heb 9:25-28); and while his offerings only dealt with ritual impurity, Jesus' sacrifice took away sin (Heb 10:11-12). Jesus had thus eliminated for ever the need for earthly priests and sacrifices and given his followers confidence to draw near to God to find mercy and grace (Heb 4:16; 10:19-22).[14]

The designation of Jesus as high priest is not taken up explicitly in any of the other New Testament writings, but it is implicit in other passages that speak of thanksgiving or glory being offered to God *through* Jesus Christ (see Rom 1:18; 16:27; Col 3:17), and it finds a place in some other early Christian writings.[15] On the other hand, the New Testament does attribute a priestly character to the Christian people. This is made most explicit in 1 Peter 2:9, where four Old Testament titles that had been applied to Israel are attributed to the body of Christians: they are a chosen race (see, e.g., Deut 7:6), a kingdom of priests (Exod 19:6), a holy nation (Exod 19:6), and God's own people (Hos 2:23). As living stones, they are built up into a spiritual temple and "a holy priesthood to offer spiritual sacrifices that are acceptable to God through Jesus Christ" (1 Pet 2:5). It cannot be emphasized enough that this description does not refer to the ordained ministry or to the exercise of specific liturgical functions within the church. It concerns the relationship between Christians and the rest of the world. Just as Israel had been intended to be a nation dedicated to the service of God and thus a mediator between other nations and God, so now the Christian church assumes that privilege and duty. The same designation of Christians as priests is also found in the book of Revelation (1:6; 5:10; 20:6). Although, therefore, in one sense the priesthood possessed by Jesus was seen as absolutely unique to him, in other respects Christians could be said to share in his priesthood.

As for the nature of the "spiritual sacrifices" that they are to offer, these are to be primarily the ways in which they conduct their lives, so that when the Gentiles see their good works, they too will come to glorify God (1 Pet 2:12). The same idea is put forward

---

[14] See further, Harold W. Attridge, *The Epistle to the Hebrews*, Hermeneia (Philadelphia: Fortress Press, 1989); Craig R. Koester, *Hebrews: A New Translation with Introduction and Commentary* (New York: Doubleday, 2001); Eric F. Mason, *"You are a Priest for Ever . . ." Second Temple Jewish Messianism and the Priestly Christology of the Epistle to the Hebrews*, Studies on the Texts of the Desert of Judah 74 (Leiden: Brill, 2008).

[15] *1 Clement* 36.1; 61.3; 64; Polycarp, *Philippians* 12.2; *Martyrdom of Polycarp* 14.3. For other examples, see below, pp. 41–43.

in Paul's Letter to the Romans: "I beseech you, therefore, brothers, by the mercies of God that you present your bodies as a living sacrifice, holy, pleasing to God, your rational worship" (Rom 12:1). So familiar are these words to so many of us that we fail to notice how striking they would have been to Paul's original readers. A *living* sacrifice would have seemed an oxymoron, as sacrifices were things that were usually killed, and "rational worship" is precisely contrasting the offering of human reason with that of animals.

Even the Letter to the Hebrews, in spite of its emphasis on the unique and ultimate character of the priesthood of Jesus, urges its readers to offer through Jesus "the sacrifice of praise continually to God, that is, the fruit of the lips that confess his name. And do not neglect to do good and to share, for with such sacrifices God is well pleased" (Heb 13:15-16). Here we have the twin aspects of Christian priestly living: worship offered through the words uttered by the lips, combined with deeds of charity and generosity toward others, both actions being described as sacrifices. The expression, "the fruit of the lips," meaning what comes out of the mouth, and here specifically the verbalization of praise, also occurs in Isaiah 57:19 and Hosea 14:2 and had been taken up by the Jewish community at Qumran, who, finding themselves unable to perform the requisite sacrifices in the Temple because they regarded it as corrupt and defiled, were forced to turn to the offering of verbal praise as a temporary substitute for that activity.[16] However, what they regarded as merely temporary became for Christians the permanent replacement for those sacrifices.

[16] See, for example, James VanderKam, *The Dead Sea Scrolls Today* (Grand Rapids, MI: Eerdmans, 1994), 117. But cf. Russell C. D. Arnold, "Qumran Prayer as an Act of Righteousness," *Jewish Quarterly Review* 95 (2005): 509–29.

Chapter 2

Ministry in the Earliest Christian Communities

Nearly all of the older scholarship on the origins of Christian ministry presumed a high degree of uniformity of practice between different communities of believers and tried with considerable difficulty to reconcile the various allusions in the New Testament to ministries and offices. Unfortunately, even some recent studies tend in a similar direction and seek to force the evidence for every early Christian community to fit the same blueprint, be it of synagogue or household. Modern research on Christian origins in general, however, has recognized the basic diversity and pluriformity of the earliest groups of believers, not only in their theology but also in their liturgical and other practices. Hence there is no reason to suppose that their structures of ministry must have been identical to one another or that one particular pattern of ministry must always have changed over time into another, as some older theories did in presuming that charismatic leadership must have come first in all Christian communities and then eventually replaced by an institutional structure. Indeed, there are no grounds to expect that the concept of a wide variety of different gifts of the Spirit being exercised by different members of the congregation (see 1 Cor 12–14) was ever operative outside the churches that came under Pauline influence, and perhaps not even fully operative within them. Just because Paul believed that certain things should be so does not necessarily mean that they were so.[1]

AMBIGUOUS TERMINOLOGY

Besides the tendency to presume a greater uniformity than seems to have been the case, there is a further problem facing those trying to understand the practice of ministry in New Testament times: the

[1] See, for example, Margaret Y. MacDonald, *The Pauline Churches* (Cambridge: Cambridge University Press, 1988), 51–60.

basic ambiguity of the terms used. Thus, the Greek words *diakonos* and *diakonia* are obviously employed in some places in a general, seemingly nontechnical sense to refer to a "minister" (e.g., 1 Cor 3:5; 1 Tim 4:6) and to "ministry" (e.g., Acts 6:1; Rom 15:31).[2] This makes it difficult to be confident that a specific office of a deacon is meant in other places. When Paul speaks of *diakonia* in Romans 12:7, is he referring to service in general or to a specific ministry of service? Indeed, when in the same verse he speaks of "one who teaches," does he mean a designated official or just someone who engages in teaching? Similarly, when Phoebe is called a *diakonos* in Romans 16:1, and Tychicus a *diakonos* in Ephesians 6:21 and Colossians 4:7, are they simply those who serve in a general sense (as seems to be true of Epaphras in Col 1:7) or the holders of the office of deacon? Even Philippians 1:1, where at first sight *episkopoi* and *diakonoi* do look like the titles of two distinct sorts of office holders, could simply be referring generically to leaders who also serve.[3] In short, the only place in the New Testament where we can be reasonably sure that a particular office holder called a deacon is intended is in 1 Timothy 3:8-13.

In the same way, the word *presbyteros* seems capable of different meanings. The normal Greek sense is "an older person," to whom societal norms would expect that respect should be paid because of their age, as seems to be the meaning in 1 Timothy 5:1, 1 Peter 5:5, and Titus 2:2 (where the word *presbytēs* is used instead). The possibility has been suggested that there could also have been a more specifically Christian sense of "one senior in the faith"—a member of a loosely defined group within the community of believers who had been converted longer than the rest (but not necessarily the oldest)—and therefore looked to for guidance and leadership for that reason, like the household of Stephanas in 1 Corinthians 16:15, which is described as being "the first-fruits of Achaia" (i.e., the

---

[2] See also John N. Collins, *Diakonia: Reinterpreting the Ancient Sources* (Oxford: Oxford University Press, 1990), who argued that the word *diakonos* did not necessarily carry the connotation of lowly service, akin to that of a slave, *doulos*, but rather that of a trusted agent or representative.

[3] See Douglas Powell, "Ordo Presbyterii," *JTS* 26 (1975): 290–328, here at 306; R. Alastair Campbell, *The Elders: Seniority within Earliest Christianity* (Edinburgh: T & T Clark, 1994), 123–25.

earliest converts there).[4] This would not be the same as an "elder" in the third, more technical sense in which we find it in later sources, as someone formally appointed as a leader of a Christian community or member of a council of such leaders, although one would expect such people to have been drawn from the other two categories.

The collective noun *presbyterion* in 1 Timothy 4:14 might seem to suggest this latter sense, but it could be one of the others. Other cases are ambiguous too. Are the elders mentioned along with the apostles of the church at Jerusalem (see Acts 15) in this third category or one of the other two, and what was their relationship to the apostles?[5] Likewise, do the elders in 1 Peter 5:1 (and the alleged apostolic author too, who styles himself there as a "fellow-elder") belong in the same category as the older people mentioned in verse 5, or are they different? And the elders who pray over and anoint the sick in James 5:14, the elder who is the author of 2 John and 3 John, and the elders in the heavenly scenes in Revelation, to which group or groups do they belong? The only two passages that explicitly mention elders being appointed are Acts 14:23, "having appointed elders for them in every church . . . ," and Titus 1:5, "you would appoint elders in every city." Although one might not unreasonably presume from the Acts 14 passage that the elders of the church at Ephesus mentioned in Acts 20:17ff., who are said to have been made *episkopoi* by the Holy Spirit to shepherd the church of God (Acts 20:28), were also appointed officials, that does not necessarily follow. Similarly are the elders "who have led well" (*kalōs proestōtes*) in 1 Timothy 5:17, of whom only some labor in preaching and teaching, the same as the *episkopoi* and *diakonoi* mentioned earlier in the letter, or some other broader group?[6]

This brings us to the term *episkopos* and its relation to *presbyteros*. In the ancient Greek-speaking world, *episkopos* was a recognized title for a public official appointed by the ruling power, and the

---

[4] Powell, "Ordo Presbyterii," 305–6. See also C. H. Roberts, "Elders: a Note," *JTS* 26 (1975): 403–5.

[5] See Alistair V. Campbell, "The Elders of the Jerusalem Church," *JTS* 44 (1993): 511–28, who believes that Luke equates the elders with the apostles.

[6] For discussion of some of these, see A. E. Harvey, "Elders," *JTS* 25 (1974): 318–32, here at 326–27, 330–31.

service such officials performed might be called a *leitourgia*. It could also be used of officers of a club or association (known in Latin as a *collegium*[7]). It is not necessary, therefore, to look specifically, as some have, to the Hebrew term *mebaqqer* used for an overseer in some of the Qumran texts, to find a precedent for its adoption by some early Christian communities to denote their appointed officials. Its use in Acts 20:28, however, looks less like an already established name and more like a simile ("the flock over which the Holy Spirit has made you *episkopous*"), although in 1 Timothy 3:1-7 it has clearly become a customary title. Similarly, the terms "pastor" and "evangelist," occurring in Ephesians 4:11, Acts 21:8 (where Philip, one of the Seven, is designated as "the evangelist"), and 2 Timothy 4:5 (where the recipient is admonished to do the work of an evangelist), seem to be descriptions of what certain people do rather than titles of specific offices held.

Noting that in the Pastoral Epistles *episkopos* occurs in the singular and *diakonoi* in the plural, Frances Young proposed that these were the only appointed officers of a congregation in a pattern that had been modeled on the household (see 1 Tim 3:15), the *episkopos* being the equivalent of the steward of the household (to whom he is compared in Titus 1:7) and the *diakonoi* the equivalent of the servants, while the elders mentioned in 1 Timothy 5:17 and Titus 1:5 would have been a natural grouping of leading Christians acting as an advisory council to the *episkopos*. She argued that a similar pattern can also be seen both in the letters of Ignatius of Antioch and in the *Didascalia apostolorum*, where the bishop and the deacons are the ministers of the congregation and the presbyters an advisory council, and she tentatively suggested that increasing conformity to the model of the synagogue may have encouraged this development, with its ruler (*archisynagogos*), attendants, and council of elders, a movement from being God's household to being God's people.[8]

This is an interesting idea, but it leaves some questions unanswered. While in 1 Timothy 4:14 the elders seem to have appointed

---

[7] On *collegia*, see further Philip A. Harland, *Associations, Synagogues, and Congregations* (Minneapolis: Fortress Press, 2003).

[8] Frances Young, "On ΕΠΙΣΚΟΠΟΣ and ΠΡΕΣΒΥΤΕΡΟΣ," *JTS* 45 (1994): 142–48.

the recipient (as *episkopos*?), in Titus 1:5 the recipient is instructed to appoint elders in every city, who are then apparently equated with the *episkopos* (1:7). We also need to remember that houses, even of the very richest Christians, would only have been able to accommodate relatively small congregations to dine there, probably too small to justify a bishop, several deacons, and a whole circle of "elders," leaving few members who did not fall into one or other of these categories. It seems much more likely therefore that the *presbyteroi* in these letters and other texts are not a third group of people at all, and we may note that while the qualities requisite in *episkopoi* and *diakonoi* are listed in the Pastoral Epistles, there is no separate list of equivalent qualities needed in *presbyteroi*. Instead, because older men and/or the first converts in a city were looked to for leadership in the earliest communities, the word had now come to be used simply an inclusive generic title for church leaders—such as *episkopoi*, any prophets and teachers who were there, and possibly the *diakonoi* too—in a similar way that it had been used in the Old Testament and in Judaism.[9] Thus, in 1 Timothy 4:14, the whole leadership in that place laid hands on the recipient, while in Titus 1:5 the recipient was to appoint leaders in every city, each of whom will become an *episkopos* in his own congregation. Since in very large cities, unless the number of believers there was very small, there would presumably have been several house churches, the leaders of each might naturally be called collectively *presbyteroi*, especially if some of them were prophets or patrons, while in other congregations there was an appointed *episkopos*.

ORIGINS

Can we therefore go back behind all this and tentatively reconstruct how these ministries might have emerged? It has long been acknowledged that the earliest Christians commonly met in houses (see, e.g., Rom 16:5; 1 Cor 16:19; Phlm 1–2), but connections were not often made between the pattern of hospitality that this would

---

[9] See Powell, "Ordo Presbyterii," 306: "Nothing leads us to suppose that this is an office additional to that of bishop and deacon rather than a status which comprises both"; also Campbell, *The Elders*, 126–31, though I would dissent from some of his other conclusions.

have called for and the pattern of leadership to which it is likely to have given rise. It is only in recent decades that this has come to the fore, and it has begun to be recognized that the natural leader of these emerging congregations would often, though not necessarily always, have been the one in whose house they met.[10] As some of these houses were owned by women (see Acts 12:12; Col 4:15), it is probable that in those cases they would have exercised leadership.[11] At the same time we must also bear in mind that not all Christian communities would have had a wealthy patron in whose house they could gather, and hence not only their meeting place but also the patterns of leadership they adopted might well have been different from those of a household.[12]

Others who would have assumed prominent roles within those communities would doubtless have been those who were regarded as possessing the gifts of prophecy and teaching, where such existed in the congregation,[13] and it is surely significant that prophets are consistently mentioned second after apostles in lists of God's gifts to the church (1 Cor 12:28; Eph 2:20; 3:5; 4:11). It seems unlikely that any of these would have been formally appointed, but would simply be people whose gifts were given recognition by

---

[10] See, for example, Roger W. Gehring, *House Church and Mission: The Importance of Household Structures in Early Christianity* (Peabody, MA: Hendrickson, 2004); and for the extension of this into the second century, Harry O. Maier, *The Social Setting of the Ministry as Reflected in the Writings of Hermas, Clement and Ignatius* (Waterloo, ON: Wilfrid Laurier University Press, 1991).

[11] See particularly Ute E. Eisen, *Women Officeholders in Early Christianity: Epigraphical and Literary Studies* (Collegeville, MN: Liturgical Press, 2000); Carolyn Osiek, Margaret Y. MacDonald, with Janet H. Tulloch, *A Woman's Place: House Churches in Earliest Christianity* (Minneapolis: Fortress Press, 2006). Much has been made by some of the description by Paul of Priscilla/Prisca as a "fellow-worker" (Rom 16:3-5; cf. Acts 18:1-3, 18, 26; 1 Cor 16:19) and of the possibility that the apostle Junia(s) was a woman (Rom 16:3, 6, 7).

[12] For an attempt to look in this direction, see Bradly S. Billings, "From House Church to Tenement Church: Domestic Space and the Development of Early Urban Christianity—The Example of Ephesus," *JTS* 62 (2011): 541–69.

[13] Mentioned in Acts 13:1; 15:32; 21:9-10; 1 Cor 12:28-29; 14; Eph 2:20; 3:5; 4:11; 1 Thess 5:20; 1 Tim 4:14. On Christian prophets in general, see David E. Aune, *Prophecy in Early Christianity and the Ancient Mediterranean World* (Grand Rapids, MI: Eerdmans, 1983).

their fellow Christians.[14] Nor would there necessarily have been any conflict between a host or patron of the church and these charismatic figures, where both existed in the same congregation. The one would have assumed administrative leadership, presided over its common meals and meetings and its charitable works, the others would have taken a leading role in the interpretation of the scriptures and in the revelation of God's will within the community. Even in the Pauline churches, where those with such gifts seem to have been particularly valued, there appear to have been others exercising leadership alongside them: Romans 12:8 mentions "one who leads" (*proistamenos*) and the same word is found in the plural in a phrase in 1 Thessalonians 5:12, "those presiding over you in the Lord and admonishing you," while in 1 Corinthians 16:15-16 the readers are urged to be subject to those like the household of Stephanas, the "first fruits of Achaia." But, as R. Alistair Campbell has remarked, "Paul's failure to say more about the leaders there were, is more likely to be because their role as household heads was largely unquestioned than because Paul thought them unimportant."[15]

It should not be a particular cause for surprise that the patron or host of the local church, man or woman, would have presided at their regular communal meals. That would have been the natural arrangement within Greco-Roman culture, and we have no evidence to suggest that the Christians thought it necessary to do otherwise. For previous generations of scholars who conceived of the earliest Eucharist as a religious rite composed of specific actions and words instituted by Jesus within the Last Supper (and still today for some), then it naturally followed that they expected its presidency to have been restricted to particular individuals authoritatively designated for that purpose and for it to have been strictly separated from normal eating and drinking at a very early date. But the trend in more recent scholarship is to view the roots of later eucharistic practice as lying within the regular meal customs of the ancient world, in which the householder would naturally preside

[14] On false prophets and teachers, see below, pp. 25–26, 28, 37.
[15] Campbell, *The Elders*, 111. See also ibid., 120–23.

at table.[16] He or she might on occasion have ceded that right to an honored guest, and especially to one of the prophets because of their particular gift of utterance,[17] and such people would certainly have been encouraged to address the assembly after the meal with any words of insight and wisdom that they might have. Some of these prophets were women (see Acts 21:9; 1 Cor 11:5).

At some point in the second or third generation of Christians (we do not know exactly when), some congregations, but probably not yet all, began the practice of formally appointing officers (apparently exclusively, or at least normally, male[18]) to provide specific services for the congregation. To these they gave the names *episkopoi* and *diakonoi*, words that seem already to have been used occasionally in a more general sense, and not as official titles, for those serving the congregation by leading it, as in Acts 20:28 and Philippians 1:1 and probably other instances too. It appears that the practice of formal appointment may have been known to the author of Luke-Acts, because of his reference in Acts 14:23 to Paul "appointing" elders in every city. Although anachronistic for Paul's own communities, it may well reflect the practice of the author's own day, especially as the verb used here, *cheirotoneo*, normally means "to elect by raising the hand"[19] and would more naturally refer to the action of the community (as it does in 2 Cor 8:19) than to that of an individual, differing from the parallel mention of appointing elders in Titus 1:5, where the verb *kathistēmi* is used. Possibly the custom began when some patrons wished to delegate certain responsibilities to others, perhaps especially the management of the

[16] See for example Andrew B. McGowan, *Ascetic Eucharists* (Oxford: Clarendon Press, 1999); Dennis E. Smith, *From Symposium to Eucharist: The Banquet in the Early Christian World* (Minneapolis: Fortress Press, 2003); Paul F. Bradshaw, *Eucharistic Origins* (2004; Eugene, OR: Wipf & Stock, 2012); Hal Taussig, *In the Beginning Was the Meal: Social Experimentation and Early Christian Identity* (Minneapolis: Fortress Press, 2009).

[17] See *Didache* 10.7: "But allow the prophets to give thanks as long as they wish."

[18] See 1 Timothy 3:1-13; Titus 1:6-9. Whether women could be deacons depends whether 1 Timothy 3:11 is understood as referring to deacons' wives or to female deacons. Widows here (1 Tim 5:3-16) are entered on a list to be the recipients of the church's charity, and not to exercise a particular ministry.

[19] See above, p. 14.

community's resources and its charitable work, and they may first have employed their own steward and slaves to do this.

The particular issue lying behind the Pastoral Epistles, probably dating from around the end of the first century, appears to have been that Timothy was apparently rather young to have been given a position of seniority and so potentially liable not to be respected (1 Tim 4:12), especially as here the *episkopos* seems already to have taken over wider functions than administration. In 1 Timothy 4:13 he is to give attention to "reading, exhortation, teaching," and in Titus 1:9 he is expected "to exhort with sound teaching and to refute those who oppose it," while in 1 Timothy 5:17 some of the *presbyteroi* are said to "labor in preaching and teaching." Thus, although "prophecy" is said to have played a part in Timothy's appointment (presumably because either a prophetic voice selected him or a prophet prayed over him), it does not look as if either prophets or other teachers were regular members of the congregation and so able to give this lead in the ministry of the word instead of the bishop. Hence it was thought necessary for Timothy to have received a spiritual gift to do this through his appointment (1 Tim 4:14; 2 Tim 1:6), which is said to have been effected through the laying on (*epithesis*) of hands, by the whole "eldership" in the first passage, and by the alleged apostolic author of the letter in the second (see also 1 Tim 5:22). This gesture of commissioning for a particular purpose is recorded as having been accompanied by prayer in Acts 6:6 and by prayer and fasting in Acts 13:3 (see also Acts 14:23), and might be presumed to be so here too.

THE *DIDACHE*
The date when this church order was composed has been heavily debated, but there is a growing consensus that it may have reached its final form around the end of the first century, even if some of the material in it may be considerably older. Just as in 2 Peter 2:1 and 1 John 4:1, the communities addressed by the *Didache* seem at one time to have experienced the need to distinguish between true and false itinerant apostles and prophets.[20] Tests such as the length

---

[20] See further Aaron Milavec, *The Didache: Faith, Hope, and Life of the Earliest Christian Communities, 50–70 C.E.* (Mahwah, NJ: Newman Press, 2003), 436–90.

of their stay, whether they asked for money, and the congruence of their lifestyle with their teaching are proposed (chapter 11), but it is also anticipated that some prophets and teachers may wish to settle permanently, and if genuine, they can be supported financially (chapter 13). Chapter 15 then directs the whole Christian community to "elect for yourselves bishops and deacons." The verb used is *cheirotoneo*, no further details of the process are given, the candidates are said to be male, and there is no mention of presbyters. It continues: "they, too, minister (*leitourgousi*) to you the ministry (*leitourgian*) of the prophets and teachers. Therefore do not despise them, for they are to be honored among you with the prophets and teachers."

The general consensus of scholars has been to see this as evidence for a situation where charismatic leaders were being gradually replaced by elected bishops and deacons because of a decline in the number of the former or because of the difficulty of distinguishing true from false prophets, and where this transition involved something of a struggle to persuade people to give equal respect to these less obviously gifted replacements. André de Halleux, however, argued that (a) prophets and teachers in the *Didache* constituted one category and not two, (b) they were usually resident and not itinerant, (c) they existed alongside bishops and deacons rather than being replaced by them, and (d) there is no need to view chapter 15 as a later addition to the rest of the text, as many scholars do.[21] While this may be going a little too far, it is possible that the *Didache* does reflect a situation where both charismatic and

---

[21] André de Halleux, "Ministers in the Didache," in *The Didache in Modern Research*, ed. Jonathan A. Draper (Leiden: Brill, 1996), 300–320. See also Jonathan A. Draper, "Social Ambiguity and the Production of Text: Prophets, Teachers, Bishops, and Deacons and the Development of the Jesus Tradition in the Community of the *Didache*," in *The Didache in Context*, ed. Clayton N. Jefford (Leiden: Brill, 1995), 284–312, here at 291, who believed that bishops and deacons existed before the intrusion of prophets and teachers; and Alistair Stewart-Sykes, "Prophecy and Patronage: The Relationship between Charismatic Functionaries and Household Officers in Early Christianity," in *Trajectories through the New Testament and the Apostolic Fathers*, ed. Andrew F. Gregory and Christopher M. Tuckett (Oxford: Oxford University Press, 2005), 165–89, here at 182–84, who argued that the bishops and deacons existed alongside prophets and teachers, providing financial support to their ministry.

elected officials had formerly shared together in the leadership of the community, with different responsibilities, but that with the decline of the former, the latter were now being called upon to fulfill a wider role and take upon themselves functions once exercised by the charismatic leaders, apparently including praying at the community's meals. This would explain the existence of prayer-texts in *Didache* 9–10, an unusual feature in Christianity as in early Judaism, where prayers were not normally written. While prophets were to be free to use their own words (10.7), less gifted leaders might need some written help to prevent them from appearing liturgically incompetent. Nothing, however, is said about these men receiving any financial support from their community (where there are no prophets, the first-fruits that would have been given to them are to be donated to the poor[22]), nor is it completely clear from the text whether each community would have several bishops as well as deacons, or whether there would be only one bishop together with several deacons in each place.

THE *SHEPHERD OF HERMAS*

This work is believed to have originated in Rome and is usually dated around the middle of the second century, although several scholars have contended that it was written much earlier, near the end of the first century.[23] Whatever the truth of this claim, the document certainly reflects a very primitive stage of ministry development. It is not entirely clear whether the *diakonoi* who are mentioned in Similitude 9.26.2 as having "ministered badly" and embezzled funds intended for the relief of widows and orphans are "deacons" as such or whether the term is being used in a more general sense, as *diakonia* is in Similitude 9.27.2; but because *diakonoi* are listed along with apostles, teachers, and bishops in Vision 3.5.1, it seems more likely that specific officials are intended. The author

[22] *Didache* 13.4. See Jonathan A. Draper, "First-Fruits and the Support of Prophets, Teachers, and the Poor in *Didache* 13 in Relation to New Testament Parallels," in *Trajectories through the New Testament and the Apostolic Fathers*, 223–43.

[23] Among them, James S. Jeffers, *Conflict at Rome: Social Order and Hierarchy in Early Christianity* (Minneapolis: Fortress Press, 1991), 106–12; Maier, *The Social Setting of the Ministry*, 55–58.

addresses his remarks "to those who are leaders [*proēgoumenois*] of the church" and "to those in the first seats [*protokathedritais*]" (Vision 2.2.6; 3.9.7). Elsewhere there is mention of *presbyteroi* "who preside [*proistamenōn*] in the church" (Vision 2.4.2-3) and of *episkopoi* (Vision 3.5.1) who have a ministry (*diakonia*) of hospitality (Similitude 9.27.2).[24] The question that arises, therefore, is whether *episkopoi* and *presbyteroi* here are alternative designations for the same group of people, or whether distinctions should be made between them. Harry Maier believed that certain elders out of a larger presbyteral body acted as bishops, each one representing a house church, although there was not as yet a full distinction between *episkopoi* and *presbyteroi*.[25] This is a plausible explanation, but not the only possible one.

It seems that prophets also still exercised some influence on this community, as the need to distinguish between true and false prophets is discussed in Mandate 11 and the author is told to communicate his prophetic visions to the elders in Vision 2.4.2–3, even though prophets are not included in the list of ministers in Vision 3.5.1 ("apostles and teachers and bishops and deacons"), unless they are to be equated with the teachers. Although there is no explicit evidence for the existence of specific conflict between prophetic and presbyteral authority, there are many references to divisions between members, at least some of which were over prominence and involved leaders (Vision 3.9.9–10; Similitudes 8.7.4; 9.31.4–6), and in one place a false prophet is described as "coveting the first seat (*protokathedria*)" (Mandate 11.12), which certainly suggests a lack of harmonious leadership within the church. It is possible, therefore, that some house churches might have been under the leadership of a prophet or prophets[26] and others under that of an *episkopos*. In that case, *presbyteroi* could be being used generically for all church leaders, and *episkopoi* for those of them who

---

[24] The *presbyteroi* in Vision 3.1.8, however, are probably merely older people, in spite of what some commentators have thought: see Carolyn Osiek, *The Shepherd of Hermas: A Commentary*, Hermeneia (Minneapolis: Fortress Press, 1999), 62–63.

[25] Maier, *The Social Setting of the Ministry*, 63–64.

[26] Stewart-Sykes, "Prophecy and Patronage," 176, argued that Hermas himself was both a prophet and, as a householder, leader of a house church.

had been appointed as an individual head of a house church, just as we have suggested that it was in the Pastoral Epistles.

THE FIRST LETTER OF CLEMENT

Dispute over leadership is clearly manifested in *1 Clement*, written on behalf of the church at Rome to the Christians in Corinth and usually dated ca. 96 CE, although both earlier and later dates have occasionally been suggested.[27] The whole letter is a denunciation of those in Corinth who have removed from office some who have fulfilled their ministry blamelessly (44.6). Attempts have been made by various scholars to determine the cause of the dispute, whether it was, for example, charismatic or gnostic Christians who were rejecting the authority structures, a rebellion by the young against the old, a theological dispute, or merely a personality clash, but there is simply not enough evidence to draw any firm conclusions,[28] and, in any case, the letter may reveal more about the situation in the Roman church than it does about the church at Corinth. Maier concluded that there had been "a division within one or two of the Corinthian house churches which has resulted in the creation of an alternative meeting place, the exodus of members who were sympathetic with these persons and, presumably, the exclusion of members who are opposed to them."[29] On the other hand, the author of the letter could have been trying to play down the seriousness and extent of the disruption, which may have involved more than just "a few reckless and arrogant individuals" (1.1; see also 47.6).

The author's argument against removing people from office rests on the importance of not transgressing the respective orders established by God for different people. He asserts that God does not arrange things randomly, but in the Scriptures prescribed the particular times for sacrifices to be offered and where and by whom

[27] See for example A. E. W. Hooijbergh, "A Different View of Clement Romanus," *Heythrop Journal* 16 (1975): 266–68; John A. T. Robinson, *Redating the New Testament* (London: SCM / Philadelphia: Westminster, 1976), 327–35; Lawrence Wellborn, "On the Date of First Clement," *Biblical Research* 29 (1984): 35–54.

[28] Maier, *The Social Setting of the Ministry*, 87–94.

[29] Ibid., 93.

this should be done. "For to the high priest his proper services have been assigned, to the priests their proper office has been appointed, and on the Levites their proper ministries have been laid. The lay person is bound by the laity's ordinances" (40.5). Although this comparison might seem to suggest that the author had in mind a threefold order of ordained Christian ministers, references to bishops and presbyters elsewhere in the letter have been treated by most scholars as synonyms for the same office: the corporate leadership of the church.[30] On the other hand, it may be better to see *presbyteroi* once again as a general inclusive title for church leaders (44.4; 47.6; 54.2; 57.1), with *episkopos* and *diakonos* as the names of the specific offices.

The author not only cites this scriptural precedent in defense of his position but also claims apostolic institution of the ministers. He asserts that the apostles themselves originally appointed (*kathistamon*) their "first fruits" as bishops and deacons—an arrangement that, he says, was no novelty but already prophesied in Isaiah 60:17, which he cites as naming *episkopous* and *diakonous* rather than the *archontas* and *episkopous*, "rulers and overseers," of the Septuagint text (42.4–5). This may perhaps contain a kernel of genuine historical truth, even if those particular titles were not used at as early a date as that. But it is interesting to note that when it comes to maintaining that the apostles intended these offices to be held for life, he seems to speak somewhat more cautiously, saying only that they "afterwards added the codicil that if they should fall asleep, other approved men should succeed to their ministry [*leitourgian*]." The method of their appointment had been "by other men of repute"[31] but "with the consent of the whole church," and so it would be sinful to "eject those who have offered the gifts of

---

[30] Douglas Powell ("Ordo Presbyterii," 296) speculated that the equivalent of the high priest here might be meant to be Christ himself (which would leave the presbyters, bishops, and deacons as corresponding to the priests and Levites), but apart from the not very surprising occurrence of "high priest" as an epithet for Jesus elsewhere in the letter (1 *Clement* 36.1; 61.3; 64), there is nothing really to substantiate this suggestion.

[31] I take this to be a generic expression that might cover notable figures within a particular congregation and/or the leaders of other local house churches. But cf. W. Moriarty, "1 Clement's View of Ministerial Appointments

the episcopate blamelessly and purely" (44.2–4). This expression, which can alternatively be rendered "eject from the episcopate those who have offered the gifts blamelessly and purely," is usually treated by commentators as a reference to their offering of the eucharistic sacrifice, especially in the light of the author's earlier use of the Old Testament priesthood as a "type" of Christian ministry, but Ulrich Volp has suggested that it could mean "bring donations" and so be referring, instead, to their economic and financial responsibilities.[32]

What is particularly interesting is that in the whole of this lengthy and impassioned plea for obedience to God's will, the author never once plays what would surely have been a trump card: a reference to the fact that the expulsion of church leaders is unheard of, and contrary to the practice of all churches. Later Christian writers had no hesitation in making universalistic claims for various liturgical practices that were, in reality, far from being generally observed. Why then did our author draw back from using such an argument? Could it have been because he was well aware that such an assertion could easily be disproved?

POLYCARP'S *LETTER TO THE PHILIPPIANS*

This letter is usually thought to have been written somewhere between the years 110 and 140. It does not use the word *episkopos* anywhere, but is addressed from "Polycarp and the presbyters that are with him." It speaks of the qualities required in deacons and in presbyters (5.2–6.1). Young men are admonished to submit themselves to the presbyters and deacons "as to God and Christ" (5.3), and the presbyters are charged with care of the sick, widows, orphans and the poor (6.1). There is no explicit mention of them presiding at worship or of exercising the ministry of the word.

---

in the Early Church," *Vigiliae Christianae* 66 (2012): 115–34, who examines all the possibilities in detail and concludes that they are "Apostolic Delegates."

[32] Ulrich Volp, "Liturgical Authority Reconsidered: Remarks on the Bishop's Role in Pre-Constantinian Worship," in *Prayer and Spirituality in the Early Church*, ed. Bronwen Neil, Geoffrey D. Dunn and Lawrence Cross, 3 (Strathfield, NSW: St. Pauls Publications, 2003), 189–209, here at 195. See also B. E. Bowe, *A Church in Crisis: Ecclesiology and Paraenesis in Clement of Rome* (Minneapolis: Fortress Press, 1988), 150–52.

The problem we encountered in the *Didache*—the apparent reluctance of congregations to accept the authority of bishops and deacons as equal to that of prophets and teachers—seems to recur in the letters of Ignatius of Antioch, together with a similar reluctance to surrender the independence of individual congregations to a wider oversight. These letters have conventionally been dated soon after the beginning in the second century, and thought to provide the earliest clear evidence for the existence of a threefold order of bishop, presbyters, and deacons, at least in some churches. More recently, however, this dating has been challenged by several scholars, and it has been suggested that the letters may in fact be forgeries, written in the 160s or even 170s.[33] But even those who continue to champion their authenticity now tend to see Ignatius as trying to impose a new pattern on churches that hitherto had not been structured in that way, rather than simply reflecting what was already a well-established arrangement.[34]

Ignatius repeatedly insisted on the necessity of obedience to the bishop, presbyters, and deacons, apparently against opponents who seemingly did not share his position, and so the letters represent a particular view that ultimately came to triumph but which did not achieve supremacy without a considerable struggle against alternative positions and practices. Thus, Christine Trevett argued that Ignatius' opponents, who were continuing to hold their own liturgical assemblies, were under the leadership of those displaying prophetic gifts,[35] with the result that Ignatius himself is forced into the rather contradictory position of claiming that he too has received a charismatic revelation—people should respect episcopal rather than charismatic authority! "I cried out when I was among

---

[33] See the works cited by Volp, "Liturgical Authority Reconsidered," 197; and the response to their arguments in Allen Brent, *Ignatius of Antioch: A Martyr Bishop and the Origin of Episcopacy* (London: Continuum, 2007), 119–43.

[34] For a recent example, see Brent, *Ignatius of Antioch*, 30–43.

[35] Christine Trevett, "Prophecy and Anti-episcopal Activity: A Third Error Combatted by Ignatius?," *JEH* 34 (1983): 1–18. But cf. Stewart-Sykes, "Prophecy and Patronage," 177–82, who sees Ignatius' opponents as more likely those influenced by a Jewish form of Christianity that rejected the authority of the bishop.

you; I spoke with a loud voice, the voice of God: 'Give heed to the bishop and to the presbytery and deacons.' . . . I did not learn it from human flesh, but the Spirit proclaimed this word: 'Do nothing without the bishop'" (*Philadelphians* 7).

The typology used for the three offices in the letters is not completely consistent and, in any case, does not portray a strictly hierarchical sequence. In *Magnesians* 6.1, the bishop is described as presiding in the place of God, the presbyters occupy the place of the college of the apostles, while the deacons are said to be entrusted with the ministry (*diakonia*) of Christ—a role clearly superior to that of the apostles! In *Trallians* 2–3.1, on the other hand, the people are to be subject to the bishop as to Jesus Christ, and to the presbyters as to the apostles, leaving the deacons to be described as ministers of the mysteries of Christ who should be pleasing to all. A similar picture is painted in *Smyrnaeans* 8.1. Moreover, we need to recall that the term *diakonos* did not necessarily connote a position of inferiority but of a trusted representative.[36]

Ulrich Volp has gone further in questioning the status of the bishop in these letters, arguing that it was not until the third century that the episcopal office acquired any specifically liturgical functions and therefore prior to this time others would have presided at worship. He sees the bishop's role here as being that of God's *oikonomos*, "steward" (*Polycarp* 6.1), the person responsible for managing the community's resources, and it is for that reason that he is said to be the one without whom an *agape* ought not to be held (*Smyrneans* 8.2). Volp maintains that Ignatius actually distinguishes the bishop from those who preside, *tois prokathēmenois*, in *Magnesians* 6.2.[37]

I believe he overstates the argument, for if the bishop is only functioning as an *oikonomos* in the Christian community, why is his presence also required for a valid baptism in *Smyrnaeans* 8.2? Volp's answer that he was responsible for ensuring the use of the right kind of water and the correct environment is not very convincing, but he may be correct in discerning the activity of stewardship as constituting the origin of the bishop's office, even if it

---

[36] See Collins, *Diakonia*, esp. 239–41.
[37] Volp, "Liturgical Authority Reconsidered," 198–200.

had now grown beyond that function; and eucharistic presidency was certainly not the exclusive prerogative of the bishop: it is just that Ignatius wants it to be restricted to "one to whom he has entrusted it" (*Smyrnaeans* 8.1)—something that does not appear to be happening. Nor would all bishops necessarily have yet taken a prominent role in the ministry of the word. Although Ignatius' references to "silent bishops" have been variously interpreted by scholars, one possibility is that they are to those who lacked the gift of preaching and teaching, and so ceded this function to others.[38] Finally, we should note that the verb used for making ecclesiastical appointments is *cheirotoneo*, "elect" (*Philadelphians* 10.1; *Smyrnaeans* 11.2; *Polycarp* 7.2).

JUSTIN MARTYR

In the description of Christian worship contained in his *First Apology* written at Rome in the middle of the second century, Justin refers to "those called by us deacons," who distribute the consecrated bread and wine to those present and take it to those who are absent (65.5; 67.5). He also mentions a "reader" (67.4), but it is not clear whether this is the title of a permanent official or just referring to a person who reads, and also a "president" (*proestōs*: 65.3, 5; 67.4–7), who in a discourse admonishes and exhorts the people to live according to what has been read, gives thanks over the bread and wine, and is responsible for receiving and distributing money that is given for the relief of those in need. It is unlikely that *proestōs* was an official title used in Justin's community; instead, it is employed to be intelligible to his non-Christian readers, as it was normally used for the head of a philosophical school. Interestingly, it is the same word as in 1 Timothy 5:17, where some of the elders who have led well (*kalōs proestōtes*) are said to labor in preaching and teaching, but different from *proistamenos* used of a leader elsewhere in the New Testament (Rom 12:8; 1 Thess 5:12) and in Hermas (Vision 2.4.2–3) or *prokathemenos* in Ignatius (*Magnesians* 6.2). Justin may also have chosen it because he was aware that those occupying this role in Christian congregations might be an

---

[38] See Harry O. Maier, "The Politics of the Silent Bishop: Silence and Persuasion in Ignatius of Antioch," *JTS* 55 (2004): 503–19, who lists at the beginning the various interpretations that have been put forward.

episkopos, presbyteros, or even a prophet, and so he needed a generic designation.

THE *DIDASCALIA APOSTOLORUM*

This church order has traditionally been regarded as an early third-century composition originating from Syria, but Alistair Stewart-Sykes has recently argued that it is more like the other church orders in early Christianity, being made up of different strata that were gradually put together over a period stretching from the late first century through to the early fourth century.[39] Scholars have always thought that the presbyters mentioned in this text were rather inactive compared to the bishop and deacons, to whom specific functions are allotted, and Stewart-Sykes claims that mention of them was added in a later layer than that in which the activities of bishop and deacons were described, thus suggesting an evolution in the patterns of ministry from one historical period to another. He notes that there are directions for the appointment of bishops, deacons, and widows, but none for presbyters. The bishop here appears to be the head of a single congregation and not a group of churches, and to be primarily concerned with the administration of the church's charity and the exercise of discipline. There is no trace of opposition from charismatic figures, unlike some of the other sources we have examined, but Stewart-Sykes suggests that the many injunctions given to the bishop not to show deference to persons imply that the office was still subject to pressure from wealthy lay patrons.[40]

The bishop should ideally be not less than fifty years of age and be learned, but if he is illiterate, he should be skillful with words and advanced in years. If in a small congregation it is not possible to find an older man who is suitable, but there is a younger man whose maturity and good conduct are attested by all, then he can receive the imposition of hands and be placed in the episcopal seat (*Didascalia* 2.2). All this suggests a quite early stage in the evolution of the ordained ministry. There is no sign that similar community approbation was required in the appointment to other ministries,

[39] Alistair Stewart-Sykes, *The Didascalia apostolorum: An English Version with Introduction and Annotation* (Turnhout: Brepols, 2009), 22–55.

[40] Ibid., 56–62.

but simply the nomination of the bishop (see 3.12). We shall return to other aspects of this church order in a later chapter.

THE SO-CALLED *APOSTOLIC TRADITION* OF HIPPOLYTUS

Although this church order was once thought to be the *Apostolic Tradition* by Hippolytus and to have originated in Rome in the early third century, it is now increasingly recognized as an anonymous work made up of layers from different places and again built up over the same sort of period as Stewart-Sykes has suggested for the *Didascalia*.[41] Here, in a section that seems to be based on the oldest stratum of material in the work (dating perhaps from the middle of the second century) and that mentions a host or patron who invites the community to eat, the bishop is nonetheless expected to be the one who says the blessing over the food and drink (if absent, he can be replaced in this by a presbyter or a deacon, but not a layperson) and who controls the discourse that accompanies the meal—activities that in normal Greco-Roman society would have belonged to the host/patron. This seems to be an instance of a situation where an older pattern of leadership by the patron in a Christian community was giving way to one exercised by the bishop.[42] Again, we shall return to the later layers of this work in a subsequent chapter.

IRENAEUS

Irenaeus, originally from Smyrna in Asia Minor, was Bishop of Lyons in France in the latter part of the second century. As is well known, his main contribution to the theology of ordained ministry was his development of the concept of apostolic succession, not in the later sense of the unbroken transmission of grace from ordainer to ordinand, but in terms of a line of authoritative teachers in the

[41] See Paul F. Bradshaw, Maxwell E. Johnson, and L. Edward Phillips, *The Apostolic Tradition: A Commentary*, Hermeneia (Minneapolis: Fortress Press, 2002), 13–15.

[42] Ibid., 27–28. See Charles Bobertz, "The Role of Patron in the *Cena Dominica* of Hippolytus *Apostolic Tradition*," *JTS* 44 (1993): 170–84; Alistair Stewart-Sykes, "The Integrity of the Hippolytean Ordination Rites," *Augustinianum* 39 (1999): 97–127, here at 113–15. For the text, see Bradshaw, Johnson, and Phillips, *The Apostolic Tradition: A Commentary*, 144–51.

ancient sees stretching back to the apostles, who had received the "sure gift of truth" (*Adversus haereses* 4.26.2), which thereby guaranteed the orthodoxy of their doctrine against the claims of Gnosticism.[43] But it is interesting to note that even at this date, Irenaeus continued to use the word presbyters in its older sense of church leaders in general, effectively employing it as a synonym for bishops (e.g., *Adversus haereses* 3.2.2; 3.3.1; 4.26.2, 5) and even speaking of the predecessors of Victor, Bishop of Rome, as "presbyters" (in Eusebius, *Historia ecclesiastica* 5.24.14–16). There also existed some who were false presbyters (*Adversus haereses* 4.26.3). On the other hand, he was clearly aware of the more recent sense of the word, so that when paraphrasing Acts 20:17, where Paul sends to Ephesus for the elders of the church, he describes them instead as "bishops and presbyters" from Ephesus and other cities (*Adversus haereses* 3.14.2).

Irenaeus also provides us with the earliest instance of a connection being made between Stephen and his companions in Acts 6 and the diaconate (*Adversus haereses* 1.26.3; 3.12.10; 4.15.1). Nevertheless, the older typology that associated deacons with the *diakonia* of Christ still persisted in some later writings. He also implied the continuing existence of prophets, or at least of some whom he regards as "false prophets" (*Adversus haereses* 4.33.6), and we know from other sources that they continued to play a significant part in Montanist circles, even if they had by now lost their authority to bishops in more mainstream Christian communities.

CONCLUSION

The picture that emerges from all these early sources is of a gradual movement from communities in which leadership seems generally to have been very loosely structured, with the patron of the church, those displaying the gift of prophecy, and other senior converts all taking some part in its community meals, in the interpretation of God's word and in the distribution of charity to the poor, to a later situation in which formally appointed *episkopoi* and *diakonoi* were added to the mix in some places, with the term

---

[43] There is a very substantial bibliography on this topic. For a guide to some of it, see Puglisi 1:11–21.

presbyteroi generally being used more broadly to cover various kinds of leaders. The responsibility of these appointed officials gradually expanded, at speeds varying from place to place, from a primary concern with the administration of the community, and especially its charitable work, to a more dominant role in the ministry of the word and in other liturgical functions, as other leaders slowly faded from the picture or were challenged by the bishop in seeking to expand his own position.

With the letters of Ignatius, whenever they were written, however, we enter new territory in which the writer wants to reserve the term *episkopos* for the chief minister in a city and employ *presbyteroi* for all others who once would have shared that title, thereby seeking to subordinate them and their congregations to the authority of the bishop. His vision appears to have taken considerable time to catch on, and in some places, especially Rome, it does not seem to have established itself until the latter part of the second century, or even later still.[44] In this process the structure became more clearly hierarchical, as we shall see in the next chapter. For this early period, there is little indication of the method by which the church officers were appointed. Some sort of election, or at least ratification by the community of the choice of candidate, appears to have been usual, and prayer with imposition of hands by other community leaders may perhaps be presumed, but our sources do not provide us with details. For that we must wait until a somewhat later era.

---

[44] Allen Brent has argued that a monarchical episcopate as such did not really come about at Rome until the middle of the third century: *Hippolytus and the Roman Church in the Third Century: Communities in Tension before the Emergence of a Monarch-Bishop*, Supplements to Vigiliae Christianae 31 (Leiden: Brill, 1995). See also Stewart-Sykes, "The Integrity of the Hippolytean Ordination Rites," 102–6.

Chapter 3

Ministry and Ordination
in the Third and Fourth Centuries

CLERGY AND LAITY

Although the Greek word *laos*, "people," was at first used to refer to all members of the church, even as early as *1 Clement*, as we saw in the previous chapter, the notion began to emerge that God had arranged for there to be different orders (*tagmata*) in the church (41.1) and that "the laity," *laikoi* (40.5), constituted a distinct one of these. A similar idea was picked up by Tertullian at the beginning of the third century, who drew on the Latin expressions used in Roman society to differentiate the *ordo*, the magistrates and officials, from the *plebs*, the general populace, in order to distinguish the ordained ministry from the rest. "It is the authority and honor of the church sanctified to God through the joint session of the Ordo that has established the difference between the Ordo and the Laity."[1] His terminology was not immediately adopted, however. Cyprian and other third-century writers seem to avoid the use of *ordo*, although they do speak of *ordinatio*, "ordination."[2] It is only in the fourth and fifth centuries that *ordo* and "holy orders" become more common to designate ordained ministers, although some writers did regard laypeople, too, as constituting an order: Jerome

---

[1] *De exhortatione castitatis* 7.3. For further explanation of this passage, see Douglas Powell, "Ordo Presbyterii," *JTS* 26 (1975): 292–95; Roland Minnerath, "Le présidence de l'eucharistie chez Tertullien et dans l'Eglise des trois premiers siècles," in *Le Repas de Dieu/Das Mahl Gottes*, ed. Christian Grappe (Tübingen: Mohr Siebeck, 2004), 271–98, here at 271–76.

[2] See Pierre van Beneden, *Aux origines d'une terminologie sacramentelle: ordo, ordinare, ordinatio dans la littérature chrétienne avant 313* (Louvain: Spicilegium sacrum Lovaniense, 1974), esp. 46–49.

speaks of five orders in the church—bishops, presbyters, deacons, faithful, and catechumens.[3]

The term "clergy" (*clerus* in Latin) is derived from *klēros* in Greek, which had originally meant a "lot," both in the sense of the token used in a lottery and in the sense of an allotment of land, but was adopted by Christian writers from Clement of Alexandria onward (*Quis dives salvetur* 42) as a designation for ordained ministers. The reasons for this are not entirely clear. It may have been influenced by the fact that priestly duties were allocated by lot in the Old Testament (e.g., 1 Chr 24:5; 25:8), especially as the *Apostolic Tradition* uses the expression "to give lots" in its ordination prayer for a bishop apparently to mean "to assign ecclesiastical duties" (3.5; see also 30A.2). Equally, the word had been used in the New Testament to denote an allotted place or salvific inheritance received from God (e.g., Acts 26:18; Col 1:12), and also to denote those entrusted to one's charge (1 Pet 5:3, "not lording it over those allotted," *tōn klērōn*). In the second century, Ignatius describes martyrdom as his inheritance, *klēros* (*Romans* 1.1; *Trallians* 12.3), and the phrase "the *klēros* of the martyrs" in the sense of the company of martyrs occurs twice in the accounts of the martyrdoms at Lyons (Eusebius, *Historia ecclesiastica* 5.1.10, 26). This understanding of the word as a place assigned to one by God seems to have led Irenaeus to use it to denote an allotted place in the episcopal succession from the apostles (*Adversus haereses* 1.27.1; 3.3.3), and may well have contributed to its usage for those allocated by God to ordained ministries.

Later on, Augustine connected its adoption to the election of Matthias by lot in Acts 1:26 (*Enarrationes in Psalmos* 67.16), while Jerome (*Epistula* 52.5) related it to the Levites who possessed no land because the Lord was their lot (Num 18:20), an interpretation derived from Philo (*De specialibus legibus* 1.131, 156). This explanation became enormously popular in later centuries, and was used to justify the special status, privileges, and rights of the clergy. At first, however, it was not clear which of the ordained ministers were to be accounted as "clergy." Sometimes the term was used inclusively of all ordained ministers, at other times to denote or-

---

[3] See S. *Hieronymi Presbyteri Commentariorum in Esaiam Libri I–IX*, ed. Marc Adriaen, Corpus Christianorum 73 (Turnhout: Brepols, 1963), 198.

dained ministers other than the bishop. The *Apostolic Tradition* even excludes deacons from "the counsel of the clergy" because they lack the "common spirit of the presbyterate" (8.3–4). Later writers, however, tend to speak of "bishops and clergy."

PRIESTHOOD

Prior to the beginning of the third century no Christian text uses the title "priest" (*hiereus* in Greek, *sacerdos* in Latin) directly to designate a particular individual or group of ministers within the church. Instead, sacerdotal terminology is applied both to Christ—usually as "high priest," following with the language of the Letter to the Hebrews (e.g., Justin, *Dialogue with Trypho* 116.1; Irenaeus, *Advesus haereses* 4.8.2)—and to Christians in general, following 1 Peter 2:9; Revelation 1:6; 5:10; 20:6.[4] Christians constituted "the true high-priestly race of God" (Justin, *Dialogue with Trypho* 116.3; see also Irenaeus, *Adversus haereses* 4.8.3; 5.34.3), whose principal sacrifice was the oblation of their lives but also included the offering of worship, both eucharistic and noneucharistic (e.g., *Didache* 14.1; Justin, *Dialogue with Trypho* 117.1ff.; Irenaeus, *Adversus haereses* 4.17.5–6).

This imagery was continued in the centuries that followed. Tertullian was insistent that laypeople were priests (*De oratione* 28), and in his Montanist period even thought that they might offer the Eucharist as well as baptize in the absence of an ordained minister (*De exhortatione castitatis* 7.3). Similarly, the baptismal anointing of a Christian was interpreted by some in a priestly sense (*Didascalia* 3.12; Tertullian, *De baptismo* 7), and the eucharistic prayer in the *Apostolic Tradition* speaks of Christians as having been made worthy to stand before God and minister/serve as priests.[5] Moreover, both widowhood (Tertullian, *Ad uxorem* 1.7) and martyrdom (Cyprian, *Epistula* 76.3) could also be described as special forms of priestly consecration.

---

[4] See above, p. 15.

[5] *Apostolic Tradition* 4.11. There has been a debate over whether the missing Greek original of the text had the verb *hierateuein*, "to exercise the priesthood," or *leitourgein*, "to minister," although both have connotations of service in the sanctuary in this context. See Paul F. Bradshaw, Maxwell E. Johnson, and L. Edward Phillips, *The Apostolic Tradition: A Commentary*, Hermeneia (Minneapolis: Fortress Press, 2002), 48.

Alongside this, however, began to develop a different usage, the seeds of which can already be seen at the end of the first century: *Didache* 13.3 compares Christian prophets to high priests when speaking of the offering of first fruits; and as we have seen, *1 Clement* cites the example of the assignment of different cultic roles to different ministers in the Old Testament Law as an argument against Christians transgressing the appointed limits of their respective ranks (40–41), and also uses the cultic expression "offered the gifts" in relation to bishops rather than the Christian community as a whole (44.4). These passages, however, are unique within Christian literature of the first two centuries, and in any case do not go as far as explicitly saying that Christian ministers *are* priests. It is not until the third century that sacerdotal terminology starts to be used regularly and in a more literal manner to refer to the ordained.

Tertullian uses sacerdotal language in this way somewhat hesitantly. He applies the term chief or high priest (*summus sacerdos*) to the bishop only once in his writings, and then in a context that suggests it may perhaps have been a metaphor occasioned by the particular argument rather than a regular term for the office: "Of giving [baptism], the chief-priest (if he may be so called), the bishop, has the chief right, then presbyters and deacons, yet not without the authority of the bishop" (*De baptismo* 17.1). And he uses the word priest (*sacerdos*) with reference to the bishop only twice, both instances belonging to his Montanist period (*De exhortatione castitatis* 11.2; *De pudicitia* 21.17).[6] Although on one occasion he does say that presbyters belong to the *ordo sacerdotalis* (*De exhortatione castitatis* 7), the other passages where he might seem to call them *sacerdotes* are all ambiguous (e.g., *De pudicitia* 20.7). Similarly, the *Didascalia*, while acknowledging that Christ is the true high priest, at the same time calls bishops "high priests," and describes deacons, presbyters, widows, and orphans as the equivalent of Levites (2.26.1–4). However, this is a passage that concerns the offering of tithes, and thus the comparison seems to be intended more to justify their financial support than to ascribe cultic status to them, as also seems to be the

---

[6] See further Maurice Bévenot, "Tertullian's Thoughts about the Christian Priesthood," in *Corona Gratiarum*, vol. 1 (Bruges: Nijhoff, 1975), 125–37, here at 128–29.

case in *Didache* 13.3 mentioned above. The same appears to be true when the later Syrian church order, the *Testamentum Domini*, called widows, readers, and subdeacons "priests" (1.23).

Cyprian also uses the precedent of the Levites receiving tithes from the other tribes (Num 18) to justify clergy being financially supported by the laity and so refraining from work themselves (*Epistula* 1.1), and he regularly calls the bishop *sacerdos*, reserving *summus sacerdos* for Christ alone (e.g., *Epistula* 63.14). He understood presbyters to share in the priesthood exercised by the bishop (e.g., *Epistula* 61.3.1), but scholars have disputed whether or not he regarded them as priests in their own right, independent of the priesthood of the bishop (see, e.g., *Epistulae* 40.1.2; 67.4.3). Indeed, some have maintained that presbyters were not called priests unequivocally until the fifth century, although the evidence does not seem to support that position. In Alexandria, Origen consistently described bishops as priests (e.g., *De oratione* 28; *Homiliae in Leviticum* 6.3), and certainly saw presbyters as also exercising a priesthood, albeit of an inferior kind to that of the bishop (*Homiliae in Exodum* 11.6; *Homiliae in Leviticum* 6.6). This concept was probably inspired by 2 Kings 23:4, which mentions both the high priest and "priests of the second order," and is one that recurs in later writings, including the classic Roman ordination prayer for presbyters, which equates them with the "men of a lesser order and secondary dignity" (*sequentis ordinis viros et secundae dignitatis*) chosen by God as assistants to the high priests in the Old Testament. Origen also explicitly compared the deacon to the Levite (*Homiliae in Josue* 2.1), and later Jerome spoke of bishops, presbyters, and deacons as being the equivalent of Aaron, his sons, and the Levites in the Old Testament (*Epistulae* 52.7; 146.2). Such typology subsequently became common, although a few ancient writers spoke instead of the diaconate as constituting a third order *within* the priesthood, the earliest extant instance of this view being Optatus of Milevis in the fourth century (*Adversus Donatistas* 1.13). This latter concept was taken up in later Eastern thought, but not in the West, which continued to use the image of the Levite to describe the diaconate and excluded deacons from the priesthood.

Regardless of whether presbyters were already designated as priests or not, we should abandon the romantic image that after the emergence of the monepiscopate, bishops were the only normal presidents at the Eucharist, with the presbyters forming a circle around them and only presiding on their own in exceptional circumstances. While such a picture may have been possible in places where the number of Christians was quite small and they could all gather in one place, it would have been totally impractical in a large city prior to the construction of huge basilicas in the late fourth century, and equally out of the question where the bishop's diocese extended far into the country. In these situations, presbyters would have had to be the regular eucharistic presidents, even if the extant literature does not give that practice much prominence,[7] and so it would only have been a matter of time before sacerdotal terminology began to be applied to them as well as to the bishop.

These two third-century developments—the sharp distinction drawn between clergy and laity and the idea of the ordained ministry as exercising a priesthood on behalf of the laity—gradually weakened the older view in which the ordained were understood as those who presided *within* a priestly people. We can see the beginnings of this in Tertullian, where the expression "offer [the Eucharist]" refers to the action of the president and not the whole community (e.g., *De virginibus velandis* 9.2), and it is developed in Cyprian, who speaks of the *sacerdos* (i.e., the bishop), not the whole people, acting "in the place of Christ" (*in vice Christi*) at the Eucharist: "For if Jesus Christ, our Lord and God, is himself the high priest of God the Father and first offered himself as a sacrifice to the Father, and commanded this to be done in his remembrance, then that priest truly functions in the place of Christ who imitates what Christ did and then offers a true and full sacrifice in the church to God the Father, if he thus proceeds to offer according to what he sees Christ himself to have offered."[8] Although thereafter some liturgical texts themselves might still carry the more ancient image of the common priesthood in which all Christians partici-

---

[7] For evidence of presbyters presiding alone in North Africa, see Cyprian, *Epistulae* 5.2; 15.1; 16.4; 34.1; and for the same in Rome, see Paul F. Bradshaw, "What Do We *Really* Know about the Earliest Roman Liturgy?," forthcoming in *SP* 53 (2013).

[8] *Epistula* 63.14. On the meaning of this, see further John D. Laurance, *Priest as Type of Christ: The Leader of the Eucharist in Salvation History according to Cyprian of Carthage* (New York: Lang, 1984).

pated, both theological discourse and ecclesiastical practice instead came to view ordination rather than baptism as the decisive point of entry into the priestly life.

This change of perspective is often interpreted as being largely the result of social pressures on the church, because in the ancient world a religion needed a priesthood. But this explanation does not seem sufficient to account for it. At the period when sacerdotal language first emerged, Christian apologists were still insisting that Christianity was not a religion like others in the ancient world. Moreover, Judaism, which survived the loss of the Temple by viewing synagogue worship as a surrogate for the cult, did not find it necessary to take this step at all. It is perhaps more likely, therefore, that what caused Christianity to begin to regard its ministers as priests was the increasing importance that came to be attached to authoritative leadership in the church's struggle against heresy and schism. In this situation the sense of the unity of the whole Christian community became less significant than the part played by the ordained ministers within it, and so, in turn, the pattern of Old Testament sacrificial worship gradually came to be seen as fulfilled in a more literal fashion in the persons of those ministers rather than in a more spiritual way by the body as a whole.

It is vitally important to recognize, however, that while the source of the image of priesthood for Christianity may be the cultic practices of the Old Testament, the concept of the sacerdotal office in the early church went far beyond merely the offering of sacrifice. Praxis shaped theory, and not the other way around. Thus, priestly service was not simply focused on the Eucharist but also included the celebration of other sacramental rites, and even more significantly was understood to extend to both preaching and teaching. So, for example, John Chrysostom in his homily on the day of his presbyteral ordination proclaimed that he had been placed among the priests and that the word was his sacrifice.[9]

---

[9] John Chrysostom, *Sermo cum presbyter fuit ordinatus* (PG 48:694, 699); see also p. 97 below for one of the Byzantine ordination prayers for a presbyter, which incorporates the phrase "exercise the sacred ministry (*hierourgein*) of the word."

We have seen that widows were singled out as particular objects of charity within the early Christian communities, but there are signs that they and other women once exercised a more active ministerial role in some places. We know that even at the end of the second century female prophets still took a prominent liturgical part in some Christian groups that were more on fringe, especially the Montanist movement, but it is still a matter of dispute whether women ever presided at worship in more mainstream traditions.[10] Yet the existence of prohibitions against them doing so would seem to suggest that at least there was fear that they might. So, for example, Tertullian denies women the right to teach or baptize, which some were apparently claiming on the basis of a spurious work attributed to the Apostle Paul in which the virgin Thecla did both those things;[11] and the *Apostolic Church Order*, a work usually regarded as having been written in the early fourth century but strongly argued by Alistair Stewart-Sykes as having been composed in the early third century out of even older source material, opposes any liturgical activities by women, especially presiding at the Eucharist.[12] Similarly, the *Apostolic Tradition* insists that widows should not be "ordained" but appointed "by the word only." Its extended and emphatic denial of ordination to them suggests that their status within the community from which this arose was leading some to view them in that way: "Hands shall not be laid on her, because she does not offer up the offering or the liturgy. But ordination is for the clergy for the sake of the liturgies, and the widow

---

[10] See, for example, Anne Jensen, *God's Self-Confident Daughters: Early Christianity and the Liberation of Women* (Louisville: Westminster John Knox Press, 1996), 182–86; Christine Trevett, "Spiritual Authority and the 'Heretical' Woman: Firmilian's Word to the Church in Carthage," in *Portraits of Authority: Religious Power in Early Christianity, Byzantium and the Christian Orient*, ed. J. W. Drijvers and J. W. Watt (Leiden: Brill, 1999), 45–62.

[11] *Acts of Paul and Thecla* 34, 41; Tertullian, *De baptismo* 17. See also *De virginibus velandis* 9.2, a work written while he was a Montanist, where he denies women the right to perform any liturgical functions, including teaching, baptizing, and offering the Eucharist.

[12] Alistair Stewart-Sykes, *The Apostolic Church Order: The Greek Text with Introduction, Translation and Annotation*, Early Christian Studies 10 (Strathfield, NSW: St. Pauls Publications, 2006), esp. 49ff.

is appointed only for the sake of the prayer, and this belongs to everyone."[13]

In the *Didascalia*, widows were encouraged to engage in intercession (3.5.2) but were specifically forbidden to teach (3.6.1–2), and all women were prohibited from baptizing: "For if it were lawful to be baptized by a woman, our Lord and Teacher would himself have been baptized by Mary his mother" (3.9). This curtailment of the ministry of women and the demand for widows to be under firm episcopal control that runs through the work suggests that the activities of widows in particular had posed a challenge and threat to the authority of the bishop.[14] On the other hand, the *Didascalia* introduces the office of female deacon in such an abrupt manner that it looks like a later interpolation into the text that had once allowed women in general to perform the prebaptismal anointing of female candidates because "it is not right that a woman should be seen by a man."[15] It does not use the term deaconess (in Greek, *diakonissa*), which did not come into currency until the fourth century, but the female form of the word for a deacon.

MINOR ORDERS

By the middle of the third century we encounter the existence of a number of other ministries exercised by men, those which would later be called "minor orders" to distinguish them from the offices of bishop, presbyters, and deacons. All our evidence for these comes from the West at this period. A letter written in 251 by Cornelius, Bishop of Rome, lists as existing in the city, in addition to the one bishop, forty-six presbyters, seven deacons, seven subdeacons, forty-two acolytes, and fifty-two exorcists, plus readers and doorkeepers.[16] Cyprian in North Africa at the same time makes

---

[13] Bradshaw, Johnson, and Phillips, *Apostolic Tradition* 10, Sahidic text. See also 71–73.

[14] See Charlotte Methuen, "Widows, Bishops and the Struggle for Authority in the *Didascalia Apostolorum*," *JEH* 46 (1995): 197–213; Alistair Stewart-Sykes, *The Didascalia Apostolorum: An English Version with Introduction and Annotation* (Turnhout: Brepols, 2009), 63–64.

[15] *Didascalia* 3.12. See Paul F. Bradshaw, "Women and Baptism in the *Didascalia Apostolorum*," *Journal of Early Christian Studies* 20 (2012): 641–45.

[16] Eusebius, *Historia ecclesiastica* 6.43.11.

frequent mention of the same minor orders (except doorkeepers) in his correspondence and implies that the bishop made appointments to them on his own authority. We have no information from Cyprian as to what ritual, if any, accompanied their appointment, but the *Apostolic Tradition*, which knows of both readers and sub-deacons but no other minor orders, directs that the bishop should appoint the former by presenting him with the book from which he was to read, but just name the latter (*Apostolic Tradition* 11, 13).

That there were just seven deacons at Rome (with seven sub-deacons to assist them) is a clear indication that the diaconate was understood here to be derived from the Stephen and his companions in Acts 6. This was a view shared by Cyprian (*Epistula* 3.3) and held almost universally thereafter.[17] We find the same pattern of seven deacons repeated in other churches at a later date, although not everywhere. Is it possible that the subdiaconate emerged to assist the deacons because while the limit was apostolically mandated, it was insufficient to cope with the large numbers of those in need of diaconal ministry?[18] Cornelius' letter states that the church in Rome was responsible for taking care of over fifteen hundred widows and other persons in distress.

We have already seen "a reader" mentioned by Justin Martyr, but that may only have meant "someone who reads" rather than a formally appointed official. Tertullian certainly implies that the office existed by the end of the second century, as he criticizes the Gnostics because among them individuals moved indiscriminately from one ministry to another: "today one is a deacon, who tomorrow will be a reader" (*De praescriptione haereticorum* 41). It is likely that this was the oldest of these minor orders—it is the only one mentioned in the *Apostolic Church Order*—and it would have been especially necessary where the bishop was illiterate, which was not unknown.[19] The fourth-century *Canons of Hippolytus* states

[17] Chrysostom was one of the few to reject this derivation: *Homilia in Acta Apostolorum* 14 (*PG* 60:116).

[18] It is worth noting that the *Didascalia* directs that there are to be as many deacons as are needed (2.34), the additional reference to subdeacons here apparently being an interpolation: see Stewart-Sykes, *The Didascalia apostolorum*, 157, n. 44.

[19] See Stewart-Sykes, *The Apostolic Church Order*, 60–61.

that a reader "is to have the virtues of the deacon."[20] Acolytes
are so named from the Greek *akolouthos*, a follower or attendant.
Although we have evidence from later sources as to their having
minor liturgical functions, there is no information from this earlier
time as to what the purpose of their appointment might have been.
Cyprian shows them as accompanying subdeacons as messengers
(e.g., *Epistulae* 45, 77, 78, 79).

ORDINATION IN THE THIRD CENTURY

Tertullian furnishes us with only the vaguest of indications about
the appointment of those he calls *seniores* who preside: they obtain
their position not through money but through repute (*Apologeticum*
39.5; see also *De praescriptione haereticorum* 41.6–7). We learn a little
bit more about ordination procedure at Rome in the early third
century from the account given by Eusebius of the extraordinary
election of Fabian as bishop there in 236:

> When all the brethren had assembled to select by vote him who
> should succeed to the episcopate of the church, several renowned
> and honorable men were in the minds of many, but Fabian, al-
> though present, was in the mind of none. But they relate that
> suddenly a dove flying down lighted on his head, resembling
> the descent of the Holy Spirit on the Savior in the form of a dove.
> Thereupon all the people, as if moved by one Divine Spirit, with all
> eagerness and unanimity cried out that he was worthy, and with-
> out delay they took him and placed him upon the episcopal seat.[21]

Although divine intervention such as this was obviously not a
normal part of the process, it is reasonable to assume that the other
elements mentioned were. The whole community participated
in the election, several candidates were considered, and eventually one was declared worthy and finally placed on the bishop's
seat. On the other hand, we should not assume that this account
included the totality of what constituted an ordination. It is obviously in abbreviated form, mentioning only aspects relevant to the
story, and so does not mention, for instance, prayer with the laying

[20] *Canons of Hippolytus* 7.
[21] Eusebius, *Historia ecclesiastica* 6.29.3–4; English translation from NPNF
2:275.

on of hands. Eusebius provides a little more detail about the ordination of presbyters at Rome in a letter written by Pope Cornelius about the appointment of Novatian as a presbyter there. Here it is said that his ordination had been opposed by all the clergy and many of the laity on the grounds that anyone who had received only clinical baptism was not allowed to enter the clergy, but the bishop, Fabian, had asked them to consent to him ordaining just this one.[22] It appears, therefore, that though a bishop might nominate candidates for ordination, the consent of clergy and laity was also required here.

From the writings of Cyprian we glean a little more information about the process of ordination both in North Africa and at Rome in the middle of the century, even if we do not know much about what happened elsewhere. Although he saw each bishop as sovereign within his own diocese, he understood bishops collectively to form a "college," and he was the first Christian writer unequivocally to designate them as the successors of the apostles (*Epistulae* 3.3; 66.4). He was also insistent that candidates were appointed to the episcopate by "the judgment of God"—that is, it was a divine act and not just a human one[23]—which was made manifest through the "testimony of the clergy" and "the suffrage of the people," and with the consent of other bishops of the province, who either were present or sent letters of approval (see *Epistulae* 43.1; 55.8; 59.5–6; 68.2). We also learn that candidates for the episcopate might be drawn from those who had served in other ministries, as he affirms that Cornelius was not made Bishop of Rome suddenly but was "promoted through all the ecclesiastical offices" (*Epistula* 55.8).[24]

---

[22] Ibid. 6.43.17. Canon 12 of the Council of Neocaesarea in 315 also prohibits those who had received clinical baptism—i.e., when ill and therefore without the full process of initiation—from being ordained as presbyters because their confession of faith was not voluntary but made through fear of death, although it does allow exceptions if the candidate showed subsequent zeal and faith or if there was a shortage of alternatives.

[23] See further Roger Gryson, "Les élections ecclésiastiques au IIIe siècle," *Revue d'histoire ecclésiastique* 68 (1973): 353–404, here at 377–78.

[24] On Cyprian and the ordination of bishops, see further Takeo Osawa, *Das Bischofseinsetzungsverfahren bei Cyprian* (Frankfurt: Peter Lang, 1983); Alexander W. H. Evers, "*Post populi suffragium:* Cyprian of Carthage and the Vote of

In a letter to the church in Spain, Cyprian describes the above practices as being of "divine tradition and apostolic observance" and as being maintained in "nearly all the provinces," having previously cited as scriptural warrants that ordained ministers should be chosen in the presence of the people, Numbers 20:25-27, where Eleazar is appointed "before all the congregation," Acts 1:15, where the replacement for Judas is chosen "in the midst of the disciples," and Acts 6:2, where the apostles ordain "deacons" in the presence of all (*Epistula* 67.4–5). The need for absent bishops to send letters means that either a period of time had to elapse between the local community's initial choice and its final confirmation or that the bishops just subsequently ratified an appointment that had already been made.[25] It also suggests that the purpose of the presence of other bishops was not as the transmitters of sacramental grace but as witnesses to the regularity of the proceedings and as expressions of their approval. Nonetheless, once they were there, it would have been inevitable that they would not have remained for long as passive spectators of a presbyterally conducted rite but would have arranged for one of their number to take over the central act of prayer and the imposition of hands, as we find in later rites.

We should note that Cyprian acknowledges that the involvement of other bishops was observed only in "nearly all the provinces" in his day, and there is some evidence to suggest that in Alexandria the older custom of presbyters presiding at the ordination of their new bishop persisted at least until the middle of the third century, if not later,[26] and the same may well also have been the case elsewhere. Indeed, the fact that the Council of Nicaea in 325 found it necessary to legislate for the participation of other bishops suggests that it was not even accepted everywhere by the early fourth century.[27]

---

the People in Episcopal Elections," in *Cyprian of Carthage: Studies in His Life, Language and Thought*, ed. Henk Bakker, Paul van Geest, and Hans van Loon (Leuven: Peeters, 2010), 165–80.

[25] Gryson, "Les élections ecclésiastiques au IIIe siècle," 385, n. 1, favors the latter interpretation.

[26] See Albano Vilela, *La condition collégiale des prêtres au IIIe siècle* (Paris: Beauchesne, 1971), 173–79, and the works cited in n. 5 there.

[27] See C. W. Griggs, *Early Egyptian Christianity: From Its Origins to 451 C.E.* (Leiden: Brill, 1990), 132–33.

Canon 4. It is by all means proper that a bishop should be appointed by all the bishops in the province; but should this be difficult, either on account of urgent necessity or because of distance, three at least should meet together,[28] and the suffrages of the absent [bishops] also being given and communicated in writing, then the ordination should take place. But in every province the ratification of what is done should be left to the Metropolitan.

Canon 6. Let the ancient customs in Egypt, Libya and Pentapolis prevail, that the Bishop of Alexandria have jurisdiction in all these, since the like is customary for the Bishop of Rome also. Likewise in Antioch and the other provinces, let the Churches retain their privileges. And this is to be universally understood, that if any one be made bishop without the consent of the Metropolitan, the great Synod has declared that such a man ought not to be a bishop. If, however, two or three bishops shall from natural love of contradiction, oppose the common suffrage of the rest, it being reasonable and in accordance with the ecclesiastical law, then let the choice of the majority prevail.[29]

Similar prescriptions are repeated in the fourth-century *Apostolic Constitutions* and in the canons of other Councils.[30] There might be a clue to the origin of this practice in the *Apostolic Church Order*, where, in situations in which there exist less than twelve potential candidates for the position of bishop within a community, a neighboring church is to be asked to send three men to examine those candidates, although obviously in this case not being themselves bishops.[31] A minimum of two or three witnesses to determine a case was a longstanding biblical tradition (see, e.g., Deut 17:6; 19:15; Matt 18:16; 2 Cor 13:1; 1 Tim 5:19).

---

[28] Canon 20 of the Council of Arles, the first interprovincial council in the West, held in 314, had desired the presence of seven bishops in addition to the one presiding, but if this was not possible, then a minimum of three would suffice, thus upholding the validity of the ordination of Caecilian as Bishop of Carthage with only three bishops present against Donatist objections.

[29] English translation from NPNF (Series 2) 14:11, 15.

[30] *Apostolic Constitutions* 3.20.1; 8.27; 47.1; Council of Antioch (341), Canon 19.

[31] *Apostolic Church Order* 16, in Stewart-Sykes, *The Apostolic Church Order*, 108–9.

As far as presbyters and deacons were concerned, Cyprian's normal practice was to consult the clergy and people before making a new appointment, but in exceptional circumstances he dispensed with this. In this way he ordained Numidicus the confessor as a presbyter to help replace those who had lapsed under persecution (*Epistula* 40); and he ordained two other confessors, Aurelius and Celerinus, as readers because "divine approval" had already preceded their appointment, and he intended both of them to become presbyters eventually. In the case of Aurelius he adds that it was done "by me and my colleagues who were then present," presumably meaning some clergy of the diocese. We learn from what he says that it was readers here and not deacons who were entrusted with the reading of the gospel (*Epistulae* 38; 39). He also speaks of making a certain Saturus a reader and the confessor Optatus a subdeacon, the former having already been entrusted with the task of reading on Easter Day and the latter having already been appointed as one of the readers for the presbyters who instructed the catechumens (*Epistula* 29).[32]

Cyprian's willingness to dispense with the advice of the clergy and people may not simply be occasioned by these particular situations of necessity, however, but may be connected to a broader change in his attitude toward his presbyters. Although originally having regarded them as his counselors whom he consulted on a range of matters, he came instead to treat them more firmly as his inferiors after he had to resist attempts by some of them to act independently of him in permitting the reconciliation of those who had lapsed under persecution.[33] This view of presbyters as the bishop's subordinates increasingly became the norm everywhere thereafter. On the other hand, the situation in North Africa was complicated by the existences of bodies of lay *seniores*, "elders," in the churches. Unknown anywhere else, they continued to be an integral part of both the Donatist and the Catholic churches in North Africa in the fourth and fifth centuries and seem to have constituted an advisory council to the bishop in administrative and

[32] On the translation of this text, see Gryson, "Les élections ecclésiastiques au IIIe siècle," 362, n. 2.

[33] See Vilela, *La condition collégiale des prêtres au IIIe siècle*, 288–303.

disciplinary matters. Because they were unique to this region, it has been concluded that they arose out of the particular forms of leadership that were traditional in African culture.[34]

ORDAINED MINISTRIES IN THE FOURTH CENTURY

The relationship between the orders of bishop, presbyter, and deacon, and the relative functions to be exercised by each, continued to be a matter of contention in the fourth century. Canon 15 of the Council of Arles (314) observed that deacons "in many places offer [the Eucharist]," and ordered that to stop. Canon 18 directed that deacons "of the city" (probably meaning Rome) were not to presume too much for themselves and ought to do nothing important without a presbyter's knowledge. Canon 18 of the Council of Nicaea refused to allow them to give communion to presbyters, because it was not permitted that those "who have no right to offer should give the Body of Christ to those who do offer." They were not to receive communion before the bishop did, as certain deacons were doing. They were to "remain within their own bounds, knowing that they are the ministers of the bishop and the inferiors of the presbyters." They were to receive communion after the presbyters from the hand of the bishop or a presbyter, and they were not to sit among the presbyters. Canon 20 of the Council of Laodicea (ca. 363) even denied them the right to sit in the presence of a presbyter unless directed to do so by the presbyter. Jerome observed this also to have been the custom at Rome but added that "although bad habits have by degrees so far crept in that I have seen a deacon, in the absence of the bishop, seat himself among the presbyters and at social gatherings give his blessing to them."[35]

It seems to have been this increase in power and prestige of deacons, resulting in a challenge to the status of presbyters, which was partly responsible for a reaction among some fourth-century

---

[34] See W. H. C. Frend, "The *seniores laici* and the Origins of the Church in North Africa," *JTS* 12 (1961): 280–84; Brent D. Shaw, "The Elders of Christian Africa," in *Mélanges offerts en hommage au Révérend Père Étienne Gareau* (Quebec: Éditions de l'Université d'Ottawa, 1982), 207–26; Alistair Stewart-Sykes, "Ordination Rites and Patronage Systems in Third-Century Africa," *Vigiliae Christianae* 56 (2002), 115–30.

[35] Jerome, *Epistula* 146.2; English translation from NPNF (Series 2) 6:289.

theologians, who stressed the ways in which bishops and presbyters were equal and consequently possessed a shared superiority to deacons. To this may be added their difficulty in finding a clear distinction between presbyters and bishops in New Testament texts. Thus Chrysostom, commenting on 1 Timothy 3:8-10 and noting that the writer had gone directly from speaking about bishops to deacons (apparently having passed over the presbyterate), explained that "the reason of this omission was that between presbyters and bishops there was no great difference. Both had undertaken the office of teachers and presidents in the church, and what he has said concerning bishops is applicable to presbyters. For they are only superior in having the power of ordination, and seem to have no other advantage over presbyters."[36]

Jerome adopted a similar point of view: "I am told that someone has been mad enough to put deacons before presbyters, that is, before bishops. For when the Apostle clearly teaches that presbyters are the same as bishops, must not a mere server of tables and of widows be insane to set himself up arrogantly over men through whose prayers the body and blood of Christ are confected?" After citing Philippians 1:1, Acts 20:28, Titus 1:5-7, 1 Timothy 4:14, 1 Peter 5:1-2, 2 John 1, and 3 John 1 in support of his case, Jerome continues: "When subsequently one presbyter was chosen to preside over the rest, this was done to remedy schism and to prevent each individual from rending the church of Christ by drawing it to himself. . . . For what function, excepting ordination, belongs to a bishop that does not also belong to a presbyter? . . . All alike are successors of the apostles."[37] Jerome's contemporary, the anonymous theologian known as Ambrosiaster, also argued that bishops and presbyters shared the same priesthood and that the bishop was the first among presbyters.[38]

[36] John Chrysostom, *In epistulam I ad Timotheum* 11.1; English translation from NPNF 13:441.

[37] Jerome, *Epistula* 146.1; English translation from NPNF (Series 2) 6:288–89.

[38] Ambrosiaster, *Commentaria*, on 1 Timothy 3:10. See further David N. Power, *Ministers of Christ and his Church* (London: Chapman, 1969), 78–81; Roger E. Reynolds, "Patristic 'Presbyterianism' in the Early Medieval Theology of Sacred Orders," *Mediaeval Studies* 45 (1983): 311–42, here at 313–16.

But there were also tensions between episcopal and presbyteral authority. This is particularly evident in fourth-century Rome, with efforts by the bishop to require churches within the city walls presided over by presbyters to use bread already consecrated at the papal mass and to insist on all who were baptized there receiving the post-baptismal laying on of hands and anointing from the bishop and not from presbyters.[39] The lack of a narrowly hierarchical understanding of the three offices also seems to persist to some extent in later practice, where a candidate for the episcopate might be elevated directly from the diaconate, without the presbyterate being viewed as a necessary intervening step.[40]

Election of a bishop by the people continued in the West in the fourth century,[41] but in the churches of the East it gradually gave way to election by his fellow bishops alone. So, for example, although Canon 18 of the Council of Ancyra in 314 had preserved the right of the people to reject an episcopal candidate of whom they did not approve, Canon 12 of the Council of Laodicea some fifty years later directed that bishops were to be appointed by the judgment of the metropolitans and neighboring bishops, and Canon 13 stated that their election was not to be committed to the people.[42] There are also clear signs that the whole process was beginning to be subject to corruption in the new environment in which bishops were now prominent figures in society. Chrysostom complained that different parties supported different candidates for unworthy reasons, such as belonging to an illustrious family or being wealthy, concluding that "many ordinations nowadays do not proceed from the grace of God but from human ambition" (*De sacerdotio* 3.15; 4.1); and Gregory Nazianzen, after describing an incident at Caesarea in which threats of violence were used in an attempt to secure the ordination to the episcopate of a particular candidate,

[39] See Bradshaw, "What Do We *Really* Know about the Earliest Roman Liturgy?"

[40] See below, p. 136.

[41] See Peter Norton, *Episcopal Elections 250–600: Hierarchy and Popular Will in Late Antiquity* (Oxford: Oxford University Press, 2007).

[42] Interestingly, the ordination prayer for a presbyter in the *Apostolic Constitutions* states that he has been elected, but "by the vote and judgment of the whole clergy" rather than by the people.

similarly observed: "I am almost inclined to believe that the civil government is more orderly than ours in which the divine grace is proclaimed." He went on to commend the election of Athanasius as Bishop of Alexandria in 328 for having taken place "by the vote of the whole people, not in the evil fashion which has since prevailed, nor by means of bloodshed and oppression" (*Oratio* 15.33–35; 21.8).

CONCLUSION

Although our sources of information for this period are rather limited, we can see that by the end of the fourth century, most of the characteristics of the ordained ministry with which we are familiar in later centuries were then emerging, even if as yet the relationship between the different orders and their distinctive functions were not yet finally settled. However, development does not seem to have taken place at the same pace everywhere, and so, for example, while Rome and North Africa seem to have established a full complement of minor orders before the middle of the century, that does not seem to have been the case in some other parts of the world.

Chapter 4

Early Ordination Rites

Our knowledge of the details of early ordination practice is even more limited than our knowledge of the form of the ordained ministry at this period because of the paucity of sources at our disposal. Besides the *Apostolic Tradition* and its derivatives (which may not always reflect actual practice), the only liturgical text for ordination older than the seventh century is the *Euchologion* of Sarapion of Thmuis, compiled in Egypt in the middle of the fourth century, and that contains only the prayers to be used and not any rubrics that might have informed us of the context and ritual structure into which they were to be fitted.[1]

THE *APOSTOLIC TRADITION*

As indicated in an earlier chapter, the *Apostolic Tradition* seems to be made up of a number of layers from different periods of time between the second and the fourth century and from different parts of the world. It is therefore quite difficult to use it as reliable historical evidence for the practice of ordination at any particular date and in any particular place. On the other hand, it may be possible to separate those strata to a certain extent in order to chart some trends in the evolution of ordination against the other evidence we have reviewed in the preceding chapter. The task is not made easy, however, by the fact that, apart from a few fragments, the original Greek text is not extant and has to be deduced, insofar as that is possible, from the translations and versions that exist in various ancient languages.[2] It also needs to be remembered that this is not

---

[1] Text, translation, and commentary in Maxwell E. Johnson, *The Prayers of Sarapion of Thmuis: A Literary, Liturgical, and Theological Analysis*, Orientalia Christiana Analecta 249 (Rome: Pontificio Istituto Orientale, 1995).

[2] On these, see Paul F. Bradshaw, Maxwell E. Johnson, and L. Edward Phillips, *The Apostolic Tradition: A Commentary*, Hermeneia (Minneapolis: Fortress Press, 2002), 6–11.

a liturgical text as such, a book that was actually used in the celebration of rites, but a collection of instructions and some prayers, which may not have ever been followed verbatim in any ancient Christian congregation.

The Rite for a Bishop

This section confronts us with two distinct difficulties in accepting the extant text as its oldest form. First, the various linguistic versions differ markedly with regard to their mention of the participation of other bishops in the whole procedure. While both the Latin text and the version in *Apostolic Constitutions* 8 include "those bishops who are present" in the list of those who are to assemble for the ordination, the Sahidic, Arabic, and Ethiopic versions have "deacons" instead, and insert a somewhat clumsy reference to bishops in the next sentence: "all the bishops who have laid their hands on him shall give consent." On the other hand, the *Canons of Hippolytus* does not refer to the presence of bishops at all until the final sentence of the instructions, when it suddenly and rather oddly says: "they choose one of the bishops and presbyters; he lays his hand . . ."[3] Gregory Dix thought that this was a sign of what he called "theoretical presbyterianism" on the part of the redactor of the *Canons of Hippolytus*,[4] but in the light of the variations in the other versions, it seems more likely that Edward Ratcliff was correct when he claimed that "discernible between the lines of the several versions of *Apostolic Tradition* there are signs which can be taken as indicating that, in its original form, the direction instructed the presbyters to conduct the proceedings."[5]

We may therefore propose that the first part of the directions in *Apostolic Tradition* 2.1–4 originally looked something like this:

[3] *Apostolic Tradition* 2. See Bradshaw, Johnson, and Phillips, *The Apostolic Tradition: A Commentary*, 24–25.

[4] Gregory Dix, *The Treatise on the Apostolic Tradition of St Hippolytus* (London: SPCK, 1937), lxxviii–lxxix.

[5] E. C. Ratcliff, "Apostolic Tradition: Questions concerning the Appointment of the Bishop," *SP* 8 (1966): 266–70, here at 269 = idem , *Liturgical Studies*, ed. A. H. Couratin and D. H. Tripp (London: SPCK, 1976), 156–60.

> Let him be ordained bishop who has been chosen by all the people, and when he has been named and accepted, let all the people assemble together with the presbytery on the Lord's day. When all give consent, let the presbytery lay hands on him, and let all keep silence, praying in the heart for the descent of the Spirit.

This is our first explicit reference to ordinations taking place on a Sunday, but it does not seem to have been a universal practice. Alistair Stewart-Sykes has pointed out that in the fictitious *Life of Polycarp*, his ordination as bishop is said to have taken place on the Sabbath, and that the same practice appears to underlie the directions for a bishop's ordination in the fourth-century *Apostolic Constitutions*, as the enthronement of the new bishop there is to take place early in the morning, followed by the celebration of the Eucharist, after the recitation of the ordination prayer on the previous day (presumably Saturday).[6] This difference of day may well be related to differing practices with regard to Saturday fasting. Later evidence indicates that ordinations, like baptisms, were usually preceded by a period of preparatory fasting, and so are likely to have taken place on Sundays in those regions where Saturdays were days on which fasting was permitted and on Saturdays in those regions where it was not.

If the reconstruction above is what the earliest form was like, then the various references to the involvement of other bishops would have been supplied later by the individual redactors of the versions in order to bring the text into line with what had by their day become the standard contemporary practice. As we have seen, the oldest reference to the involvement of other bishops appears in the letters of Cyprian and even he does not claim that it was universal at the time, so there is nothing intrinsically improbable in locating the original form of these directions somewhere in the first half of the third century.

The second reason not to accept the extant text as the oldest form is that the rite looks as if it is a composite one, formed by the

---

[6] Alistair Stewart-Sykes, *The Life of Polycarp*, Early Christian Studies 4 (Sydney: St Pauls Publications, 2002), 61–64. Although usually regarded as a fourth-century work, Stewart-Sykes argues that it should be assigned to the third century.

combination of two originally distinct elements, the above section and then what follows it in *Apostolic Tradition* 2.5. This is suggested particularly by an apparent double imposition of hands and by the rather strange use of the conjunction *ex quibus*, "from whom," in the Latin version at what seems to be the point at which the two texts are joined: "from whom let one of the bishops present, being asked by all, laying [his] hand on him who is being ordained bishop, pray, saying . . ."[7] In the first of the two rites the presbyters originally laid hands together on the candidate and all prayed in silence for the descent of the Holy Spirit; in the second—and very probably later—rite, it was one of the bishops (or was it one of the presbyters?) who acted on behalf of the others, laying hands alone on the candidate and saying an ordination prayer. It thus reveals two quite different ways of conducting an ordination. The former has otherwise disappeared almost without trace in later traditions, where communal prayer occurs only as a preliminary to an ordination prayer proper, and a collective imposition of hands appears only in texts derived from the *Apostolic Tradition* itself.[8]

In addition, the ordination prayer is so very different from the majority of later ordination prayers that it seems unlikely to have been typical of those of the pre-fourth-century period. (Indeed, Eric Segelberg attempted to discern an original text beneath what he regarded as later strata, but his reconstruction is not convincing.[9]) We are fortunate in that this is one of the rare places in the document where a Greek text had been preserved that seems close to the form of the original.

> God and Father of our Lord Jesus Christ, the Father of mercies and God of all comfort, dwelling on high and looking on that which is lowly, knowing all things before their creation, you who gave [the] rules of [the] church through the word of your grace, who foreordained from the beginning a righteous race from Abraham, appointing rulers and priests, and not leaving your sanctuary

---

[7] See further Bradshaw, Johnson, and Phillips, *Apostolic Tradition: A Commentary*, 24–29.

[8] See *ORACEW*, 30–32, 44–46.

[9] Eric Segelberg, "The Ordination Prayers in Hippolytus," *SP* 13 (1975): 397–408.

without a ministry, who from the beginning of the world was pleased to be glorified in those whom you chose; and now pour forth the power that is from you, of the spirit of leadership that you gave to your beloved servant Jesus Christ, which he gave to your holy apostles, who established the church in [every] place [as] your sanctuary, to the unceasing glory and praise of your name.

Knower of the heart, Father, bestow on this your servant, whom you have chosen for the episcopate to feed your holy flock and to serve as high priest for you blamelessly, ministering night and day; unceasingly to propitiate your countenance, and to offer to you the gifts of your holy church; and by the high-priestly spirit to have authority to forgive sins according to your command, to assign lots[10] according to your bidding, to loose every bond according to the authority that you gave to the apostles, to please you in gentleness and a pure heart, offering to you a sweet-smelling savor; through your servant Jesus Christ our Lord, through whom [be] glory, power, honor to you, with the Holy Spirit, now and always and to the ages of ages. Amen.[11]

The recalling of God's activity among the people of the old covenant and especially his raising up of both rulers and priests is not merely incidental: it witnesses to a belief in the fundamental continuity of God's work throughout history, the promise of the new covenant in the old and the fulfillment of the old covenant in the new. The mention of both rulers and priests is an indication of the dual character of the office to which the bishop was seen as succeeding, and this is confirmed by the second half of the prayer, where, on the one hand, it is the power of the spirit of leadership that God is asked to pour forth so that the bishop may shepherd his people, and on the other hand, it is also said to be in order that he may serve as high priest.

Not only does the prayer use this latter expression rather than the more common "priest" to designate the bishop and speak of

---

[10] On this expression, see above, p. 40.

[11] *Apostolic Tradition* 3. This translation follows the Greek text preserved in the *Epitome of Apostolic Constitutions* 8, amending it only where the scholarly consensus believes one of the other versions has retained a more authentic reading. For these textual matters and for the source of the scriptural allusions in the text, see Bradshaw, Johnson, and Phillips, *Apostolic Tradition: A Commentary*, 30–33.

him as possessing authority "through the high-priestly spirit," but its overall strongly sacerdotal character and its detailed listing of the powers of the episcopate is unlike most ancient ordination prayers for a bishop. While it is true that most of these prayers do have some reference to the priestly character of the episcopal office, in nearly every case this is peripheral to the main imagery of the prayer, and so appears to be a later addition. Only the classic Roman ordination prayer has as its central theme the priestly character of the episcopate, and even this does not enumerate the individual functions belonging to the order, as that in the *Apostolic Tradition* does, but concentrates instead on the inner qualities requisite in a true bishop as the spiritual counterpart of the Old Testament high priest. Similarly, no other extant prayer from ancient times lists in its primary stratum the powers and functions of the episcopate in the way that this one does. In other prayers, the fundamental images are generally those of shepherd and teacher, with either the precise liturgical and pastoral functions associated with the office left largely unspecified (as, for example, in the case of the Byzantine rite) or with their being added in what are obviously secondary strata in the prayer originating in later centuries (as in the East and West Syrian rites).[12]

In contrast to this, nowhere in this prayer is there any explicit reference to prophetic or teaching functions to be exercised by the new bishop, suggesting that such a ministry was not seen as fundamental to the episcopal office in the tradition in which the prayer arose. Finally, while it contains a clear affirmation that the choice of the candidate was seen as the work of God ("whom you have chosen for the episcopate") and not just that of the congregation, the bishop's office is not directly equated with that of the apostles: it is merely the same spirit of leadership which they received that is being sought for the ordinand. Moreover, the prayer implies that the bestowal of the Holy Spirit was effected by a fresh outpouring at each ordination in response to the prayer of the church and not by its transmission from ordainer to ordinand, as in later thought.

---

[12] See below, pp. 94–96.

The Rite for a Presbyter

This rite also raises questions. The direction that the presbyters as well as the bishop are to lay their hands on the ordinand is unparalleled in ancient ordination rites, except for those directly dependent on this text. The Latin version reads: "And when a presbyter is ordained, let the bishop lay [his] hand on his head, the presbyters also touching [him], and let him say according to those things that have been said above, as we have said above about the bishop, praying and saying . . . ."[13] Does it therefore contain the remnant of a very old tradition, one that may antedate the existence of a distinct episcopate when presbyters collectively laid hands on a new member of their order? And did the emergence of the episcopal office lead to the need to include in *Apostolic Tradition* 8.6–8 the explanation that the presbyters' touching did not mean that they were doing what the bishop did? "But on a presbyter let the presbyters also lay on hands on account of the common and like spirit of the clergy. For the presbyter has the power of this alone, that he may receive, but he does not have the power to give. For this reason he does not ordain the clergy, but at the ordination of a presbyter he seals while the bishop ordains."[14] And was it the possibility of misinterpretation that caused the practice subsequently to disappear from virtually all other ecclesiastical traditions? Or was it merely a local custom that did not survive later standardization, or even merely the invention of the compiler?

There is a further puzzling feature about these directions, in that they seem to suggest that the same prayer should be used for a presbyter as for a bishop, but then immediately provide the text of a quite different prayer. This has produced a variety of explanations by scholars, among them that it meant that the first part of the prayer for a bishop should be used, but when the petitions pertaining to the episcopate were reached, this one should be substituted, a suggestion strongly rejected by others as requiring too much

---

[13] *Apostolic Tradition* 7.1. See further Bradshaw, Johnson, and Phillips, *Apostolic Tradition: A Commentary*, 56–57.

[14] Latin version. See further Bradshaw, Johnson, and Phillips, *Apostolic Tradition: A Commentary*, 60–61.

subtlety of thought in the readers. No one view has won general approval.[15]

Several scholars have claimed to see a strongly Jewish background to the prayer for a presbyter. Thus, Gregory Dix was of the opinion that its substance might go back to the earliest Jewish-Christian synagogues governed by a college of presbyters, or even to pre-Christian Jewish practice,[16] and a similar view was put forward by Albano Vilela.[17] Pierre-Marie Gy, however, was more cautious, admitting that "one could suspect some rabbinic background, especially in connection with the typology of the seventy elders and Moses," but adding the warning that "for the ordination of rabbis, as for the berakah, one should not give excessive value to rather late texts."[18] This caution seems very wise in the light of Lawrence Hoffman's conclusions about rabbinic ordination at this early period referred to in the first chapter.[19]

However, this prayer certainly has a more primitive feel to it than the prayer for the bishop, especially as the text has only the briefest reference to Christ at the beginning and end and a total absence of any clear New Testament allusions. Its central focus is on the typology of the seventy elders appointed by Moses to govern (Num 11:16f.) and on the presbyterate's corporate role in governing the Christian community. There is no clear indication of the existence of a distinct episcopal order, and no hint of a sacerdotal understanding of the presbyterate here, although elsewhere the directions about appointing a deacon deny that the deacon is ordained to the priesthood (8.2), implying that presbyters are—a statement apparently belonging to a different stratum of the document.

---

[15] See further ibid., 55.

[16] Gregory Dix, "The Ministry in the Early Church," in *The Apostolic Ministry*, ed. Kenneth E. Kirk (London: Hodder & Stoughton, 1946), 183–303, here at 218.

[17] Albano Vilela, *La condition collégiale des prêtres au IIIe siècle* (Paris: Beauchesne, 1971), 354.

[18] Pierre-Marie Gy, "Ancient Ordination Prayers," *SL* 13 (1979): 70–93, here at 82. See also Georg Kretschmar, "Die Ordination im frühen Christentum," *Freiburger Zeitschrift für Philosophie und Theologie* 22 (1975): 46–55.

[19] See above, p.7.

God and Father of our Lord Jesus Christ, look upon this your servant and impart the spirit of grace and of counsel of the presbyterate that he may help and govern your people with a pure heart, just as you looked upon the people of your choice and commanded Moses that he should choose presbyters whom you filled with your Spirit that you gave to your servant. And now, Lord, grant to be preserved unfailingly in us the spirit of your grace and make [us] worthy, that believing in you we may minister in simplicity of heart, praising you through your servant, Christ Jesus, through whom to you [be] glory and power, Father and Son with the Holy Spirit, in the holy church, both now and to the ages of ages. Amen. [20]

Allen Brent has argued that because of this different vision of the role of the ordained ministry from the more sacerdotal picture of the episcopate, both prayers cannot have been "part of an original single rite of the Roman community,"[21] and Alistair Stewart-Sykes has taken Brent's line of argument further still and claimed, improbably, that the prayer for the bishop is the older of the two and that for the presbyter a third-century interpolation, but from within the same school as that in which the bishop's prayer arose.[22] It seems on the contrary to have stemmed from a community where bishops were unknown that was led by a corporate presbyterate, and is probably much older than the prayers for a bishop and a deacon.

Apostolic Tradition 9.1–2 contains an unusual provision for those who had confessed the faith under persecution and been imprisoned: they consequently have the "honor of the presbyterate" and do not need to receive the imposition of hands for it. While some scholars claim that it was only the "honor" of the presbyterate that they received and not its active ministry, others disagree, and Brent has argued that, even though this provision is apparently not

---

[20] *Apostolic Tradition* 7.2–5. This translation follows the Latin version. For textual variants, see Bradshaw, Johnson, and Phillips, *Apostolic Tradition: A Commentary*, 55–58.

[21] *Hippolytus and the Roman Church in the Third Century: Communities in tension before the Emergence of a Monarch-Bishop*, Supplements to Vigiliae Christianae 31 (Leiden: Brill, 1995), 305; see also 465–91.

[22] Alistair Stewart-Sykes, "The Integrity of the Hippolytean Ordination Rites," *Augustinianum* 39 (1999): 106–16.

otherwise evidenced elsewhere, it can be detected behind Cyprian's opposition to presbyters reconciling those who had lapsed under persecution.[23]

The Rite for a Deacon

The directions concerning the appointment of a deacon (*Apostolic Tradition* 8) are surprisingly lengthy and exhibit a somewhat confused air, suggesting that they have undergone a series of amendments over time. They are insistent that the bishop alone lays his hand on a deacon and that the deacon has no part in the priesthood or in the counsel of the clergy, in contrast to the presbyters. This implies that all these things had been matters of contention as the relationship between presbyters and deacons had been gradually worked out. It is said that a candidate for the diaconate is to be "chosen according to those things that have been said above," but in fact nothing had been said about how presbyters were to be chosen, so this can only refer to the appointment of the bishop, where election by the community was prescribed. If this is what is intended, it contrasts with both the *Didascalia* and the letters of Cyprian, which state that the bishop appointed deacons, although Cyprian did usually consult the clergy and people before acting, and remnants of a popular approbation can also be seen in a number of later ordination rites.[24]

The ordination prayer itself appears to combine the typology of the *diakonia* of Christ, found from Ignatius of Antioch onward, with that of the Old Testament Levite (although the word itself is not used) occurring in Origen and other later writings, whose duty is to serve the "high priest." This suggests that this prayer belongs to the same stratum of material as the ordination prayer for the bishop, although as the Latin version is incomplete here, its reconstruction has to be rather tentative:

> God, who created all things and ordered [them] by [your] word,
> Father of our Lord Jesus Christ, whom you sent to serve your will
> and manifest to us your desire, give the spirit of grace and caring to

[23] Allen Brent, "Cyprian and the Question of *Ordinatio per Confessionem*," *SP* 36 (2001): 323–37.

[24] See below, pp. 84–86, 109, 119–20.

this your servant, whom you have chosen to serve for your church and to offer in your holy of holies that which is offered to you by your high priest to the glory of your name, so that ministering without blame and with a pure conscience, he may be worthy of this office and glorify you . . .

THE *CANONS OF HIPPOLYTUS*

Thought to have been compiled in Greek in Egypt in the early fourth century but preserved only in an Arabic translation of a missing Coptic intermediary, this work is a fairly radical reworking of the *Apostolic Tradition* with significant additions. As suggested above, however, it may well preserve traces of an older form of that work in its directions about the ordination of a bishop. Its version of the bishop's ordination prayer is also interesting, as it excises all the high priestly language from the prayer in the *Apostolic Tradition*.[25] It is tempting to wonder if once again it has retained a more primitive text, but a close comparison of the two suggests that this is unlikely, and that it is the compiler of the *Canons of Hippolytus* who has been responsible for deleting an aspect of the episcopal office that was foreign to his local tradition.

In the case of the ordination of a presbyter, apparently confused by the seemingly contradictory instructions in this regard in the *Apostolic Tradition*, the *Canons of Hippolytus* simply directs that

one is to do for him everything that one does for the bishop, except the sitting on the seat. One is to pray over him all the prayer of the bishop, except only the name of the bishop. The presbyter is equal to the bishop in everything except the seat and ordination, because to him is not given the power to ordain.[26]

We have already encountered a reference to seating as part of the ordination of a bishop in Eusebius' account of the ordination of Fabian at Rome;[27] it is also mentioned in other early works[28] and is a standard feature of later rites of East and West, which is hardly

[25] See *ORACEW*, 110.

[26] Ibid., 111.

[27] See above, p. 49.

[28] *Vita Polycarpi* 23; *Apostolic Constitutions* 8:5; Synesius, *Epistula* 67. See further E. Stommel, "Die bischöfliche Kathedra im christlichen Altertum," *Münchener Theologische Zeitschrift* 3 (1952): 17–32. Stewart-Sykes, *The Life of*

surprising as the bishop's chair was an important symbol of his presidential role in the community. In the West it developed into a separate rite of enthroning. The minimizing of the distinction between bishops and presbyters is echoed in other fourth-century writings.[29]

In the case of a deacon, the directions extend his service from the bishop alone to the presbyters as well and spell out more clearly his responsibility toward the sick and needy, but the prayer itself does not mention any of these aspects. Entirely independent of the prayer in the *Apostolic Tradition*, it refers to "Stephen and his companions" as the model for the diaconate rather than the servanthood of Christ, and asks that the ordinand may be filled "with power and wisdom like Stephen" (Acts 6:8, 10). There is no explicit reference to any liturgical functions of the diaconate. It refers simply to the quality of the minister's life, asking that he may triumph over all the powers of the devil, be without sin, set an example to others, and "save a multitude in the holy church."[30]

THE *APOSTOLIC CONSTITUTIONS*

This church order is usually thought to have been composed in or around Antioch in the second half of the fourth century. The principal source for its ordination rites is the *Apostolic Tradition*, but it has made significant alterations to this that reflect either what was current practice in the region where it was composed or alternatively what the compiler desired to see introduced there.

The Imposition of the Gospel Book

One of the most notable features of the rite for a bishop is the direction that deacons are to hold the book of the gospels open over the head of the ordinand at exactly the point where one would have expected there to be a laying on of hands, which is not mentioned. This raises the possibility that the imposition of the gospel book is not meant merely to supplement the laying on of hands but to replace it. The ceremony is mentioned in other fourth-century sources,

---

Polycarp, 50–55, suggests the installation of Jewish rabbis as the source of the custom.

[29] See above, p. 55.

[30] See *ORACEW*, 111.

which interpret it in different ways. Palladius (*Dialogus historicus* 16) alludes to it only briefly, but Severian of Gabala in Syria explains it as a symbol of the descent of the Holy Spirit on the candidate. He believed that the appearance of the Holy Spirit in the form of tongues of fire on the apostles at Pentecost was the sign of their ordination, and that "the custom remains even to the present: because the descent of the Holy Spirit is invisible, the Gospel is placed on the head of him who is to be ordained high priest; and when this is done, one must not see anything other than a tongue of fire resting on his head—a tongue, because of preaching, a tongue of fire, because of the saying, 'I have come to cast fire on the earth.'"[31]

There is also a reference to the practice in a homily attributed to Chrysostom. Here it is interpreted as being a symbol of the submission of the bishop to the law of God, and the equivalent in the New Covenant of the high priestly crown of Aaron: "In the ordinations of priests [i.e., bishops] the Gospel of Christ is placed on the head so that the ordinand may learn that he receives the true crown of the Gospel, and so that he may learn that even if he is the head of all, yet he acts under these laws, ruling over all and ruled by the law, judging all and being judged by the Word. . . . The fact that the high priest has the Gospel is a sign that he is under authority."[32] As with many of the homilies included among Chrysostom's works, its authenticity has been questioned, and it has on other grounds been ascribed to Severian of Gabala by several scholars. However, the fact that the interpretation given to the ceremony here differs from that in the work of Severian cited earlier may cast some doubt on this attribution.

Pseudo-Dionysius, writing in the fifth or sixth century, is the first to mention explicitly that the ordination included the imposition of the hand as well as the imposition of the book, which he describes simply as "the Scriptures," rather than the Gospels. He believed that the book was laid on the bishop because it symbolized "all the sacred words and works" given to him, which he transmitted proportionally to others.[33]

---

[31] PG 125:533. See Joseph Lécuyer, "Note sur la liturgie du sacre des évêques," *Ephemerides Liturgicae* 62 (1952): 369–72.

[32] *De legislatore* (PG 56:404).

[33] Pseudo-Dionysius, *De ecclesiastica hierarchia* 5.3.7.

But what was the original meaning of this ceremony? The diversity of the interpretations given to it implies that its earlier purpose had been forgotten. Edward Ratcliff conjectured that it may possibly have been the vestige of an ancient practice of attempting to discern the divine choice of candidate by reference to the passage at which the book fell open, a version of the casting of lots used at the appointment of Matthias (Acts 1:26),[34] but this seems very unlikely as in every case the ceremony is firmly associated with prayer for the ordinand rather than with the remains of the electoral process in the rite. Its real origin, therefore, still remains a mystery. The evidence suggests that the custom was originally peculiar to Syria, and the fact that its meaning was in doubt by the end of the fourth century implies that it was no recent innovation there but already of some antiquity. It is conceivable that it may have been adopted when a separate episcopal office first emerged from a corporate presbyterate, and it was thought inappropriate for presbyters to lay hands on a bishop as they had presumably done up until then when ordaining new presbyters. Alternatively, the ceremony may have been introduced when neighboring bishops began to attend those episcopal ordinations and challenge the right of the local presbyterate to conduct the proceedings. Rather than deciding whether presbyters or bishops should perform the imposition of hands on the ordinand, the dilemma may perhaps have been resolved by the adoption instead of the imposition of the book of the gospels by deacons, the Gospel of Christ symbolizing the action of Christ himself ordaining a new member of the apostolic college.

If this conjecture is correct, then only later would the imposition of the book have become a supplement to the imposition of the hand, as the Syrian tradition accommodated itself to ordination practice elsewhere. It is therefore possible that in the case both of the *Apostolic Constitutions* and also of papal ordination at Rome,[35] the absence of any explicit reference to an imposition of the hand really does mean that the gesture was not used. On the other hand,

[34] Ratcliff, "Apostolic Tradition," 268 = *Liturgical Studies*, 158. See the criticism by Octavian Bârlea, *Die Weihe der Bischöfe, Presbyter und Diakone in vornicänischer Zeit* (Munich: Societas Academica Dacoromana, 1969), 179, n. 89.
[35] See below, p. 118.

not too much significance can be given to the absence of any direct reference to the imposition of hands in the latter case, as the early Roman *ordines* do not always mention it in the case of the conferral of all the other orders, where presumably it was in fact employed.

The Ordination Prayer for a Bishop

As is the case with all its euchology, the *Apostolic Constitutions* expands considerably the text of the prayer from the *Apostolic Tradition*. In addition to piling up attributes of God the Father, this version gives a more prominent place to Christ: it was through his incarnate mission that structures of the church were established, it is through his mediation that God is now asked to pour forth the power of the Spirit, and it was through him that the Eucharist the new bishop will offer was instituted. Additional references are also made to the Spirit: the structures of the church were established "by the witness of the Paraclete," and among the gifts sought for the new bishop is "the fellowship of the Holy Spirit." Perhaps not surprisingly, the Old Testament typology, too, is expanded, with the priestly theme being given some precedence over that of leadership. Although acknowledgment is made here that Samuel was both priest and prophet, this latter image is not taken up in the rest of the prayer, which adheres closely to the list of episcopal functions enumerated in the *Apostolic Tradition*, merely adding that the bishop is to "gather the number of those being saved" and making a more explicit reference to the celebration of the Eucharist. In this process it defines the "sweet-smelling savor" more narrowly than in the *Apostolic Tradition*, as referring to this liturgical act rather than to the offering of the bishop's whole life. Finally, we may note that the episcopal college itself is also given greater prominence in the prayer: the "bishops present" are closely associated with the apostles, and they are also designated as the agents through whom God is asked to pour forth his Spirit on the ordinand.[36]

The Ordination Prayer for a Presbyter

This prayer also is, not surprisingly, considerably expanded from its source in the *Apostolic Tradition*. It strengthens the christological

[36] See *ORACEW*, 113–14.

dimension somewhat with an opening reference to God's activity through Christ in both creation and preservation, and it then asks for the increase of the church and of the number of those who preside in it—thus maintaining the concept of the presbyterate as the collegial leadership of the church found in the *Apostolic Tradition*. To this vision, however, the prayer adds references to a ministry of the word and of healing to be exercised by the new presbyter ("labor in word and deed"; "filled with works of healing and the word of teaching, he may in meekness instruct your people"), and employs the sacerdotal term *hierourgias*, "holy services," to denote these presbyteral functions. These additions, as we shall see later, reflect the role that is assigned to the presbyterate in other Eastern ordination prayers. It is also worth noting that the *Apostolic Constitutions* does not follow its primary source, the *Apostolic Tradition*, here and prescribe a laying on of hands by bishop and presbyters but directs that the bishop alone is to do so, the presbytery and deacons merely standing around.[37]

The Ordination Prayer for a Deacon

This prayer has hardly any resemblance to that in the *Apostolic Tradition*. It rejects the servanthood of Christ as the model for the diaconate and instead refers to Stephen as the first deacon, describing him as "the protomartyr and imitator of the sufferings of your Christ," and asking for the same gift of the Holy Spirit and power that he received (Acts 6:8, 10). It goes on to speak in general terms of the exercise of a sacred ministry, and of eventual promotion to a higher order.[38]

Deaconesses and Minor Orders

This is the oldest source to include a rite for the institution of deaconesses, placed immediately after that for deacons and closely resembling it, consisting of a prayer invoking the Holy Spirit accompanied by the imposition of the bishop's hand. It is followed by similar prayers with imposition of hands for both subdeacon and reader, again the first time such a ritual is known to have been

[37] Ibid., 114–15.
[38] Ibid., 115.

prescribed for those offices. However, it should be noted that the word *ordination* appears neither at the beginning of the instruction concerning deaconesses nor that for readers, whereas it does in the cases of the deacon and subdeacon. This may be intended to indicate a subtle distinction in status between the various offices: the deacon is ordained in the presence of the presbytery and deacons; the deaconess is instituted in the presence of the presbytery, deacons and deaconesses; the subdeacon is ordained, but not in public; the reader is instituted, but not in public.[39] In the light of this, the disagreement between Roger Gryson and Aimé Georges Martimort as to whether deaconesses were here thought of as receiving a sacramental ordination and as being part of the clergy may not only be anachronistic but also oversimplistic: the categorization of the liturgical ministries of the early church cannot be reduced to a simple division between clergy and laity.[40]

Is this partial assimilation of these rites to those for bishops, presbyters and deacons, however, simply the product of the imagination of the compiler or does it have some real foundation in the ecclesiastical tradition from which the *Apostolic Constitutions* came? This question obviously cannot be answered with total certainty, but that fact the later Eastern rites also do the same suggests that this trend was already evident in fourth-century Syria. The alternative possibility—that the provisions of those rites were directly influenced by the contents of the *Apostolic Constitutions*—seems unlikely.[41]

The prayer for a deaconess offers three biblical precedents to justify the office—women in the Old Testament who were endowed with prophetic spirit; the birth of Christ from a woman; and the somewhat shadowy female figures who are said to have ministered at the entrance of the tent of the testimony in Exodus 38:8 and 1 Samuel 2:22 (adding the gratuitous assumption that they also continued to exercise this ministry in the later temple). Images

[39] Ibid., 116.

[40] Roger Gryson, *The Ministry of Women in the Early Church* (Collegeville, MN: Liturgical Press, 1976), 62–63, 115–20; Aimé Georges Martimort, *Deaconesses: An Historical Study* (San Francisco: Ignatius Press, 1986), 75, n. 66.

[41] Although it is suggested in the case of the deaconess by Martimort, *Deaconesses*, 75.

similar to the first two of these also occur at the beginning of a prayer for a deaconess in the Byzantine rite, albeit in the reverse order, which suggests that they may already have been traditional in the euchology of fourth-century Syria. The third, on the other hand, is not otherwise found in prayers for deaconesses, and may therefore be an attempt by the compiler to find a biblical foundation for what was apparently the principal function of deaconesses in his situation, the supervision of the admission and seating of women in the liturgical assembly, mentioned elsewhere in his work.[42] There is no mention here of the functions of visiting women in their homes and anointing female baptismal candidates that had been assigned to female deacons in the *Didascalia* and are reproduced from that source earlier in the *Apostolic Constitutions* (3.16.1–4).

The fact that women endowed with the spirit of prophecy are mentioned may seem to suggest that deaconesses, too, had some sort of prophetic or teaching ministry, but this need not necessarily follow. The prayer for a reader also asks for the gift of the prophetic spirit and even compares the reader's role to that of Ezra! But there is no other evidence that would support the notion that readers did have so important a standing in Christian worship at this period. Thus, both cases may owe more to the compiler's enthusiasm to find some Old Testament typology for the office than be a reflection of the true status of the order in the church.

Finally, the prayer contains a hint that the liturgical ministry of women may not have been too readily accepted in the milieu in which it was composed: the inclusion of a petition to cleanse the candidate from all filthiness of flesh and spirit, echoing 2 Corinthians 7:1, seems to imply the existence of some doubt as to whether they were sufficiently holy for such a task, especially as the quotation has no special reference to women in its original context. Such a view would hardly be surprising in the light of common attitudes toward the ritual impurity of women in the early church.

Following the model of other ordination prayers, the prayers for both subdeacon and reader employ Old Testament typology to define the offices being bestowed. The prayer for a subdeacon looks

---

[42] *Apostolic Constitutions* 2.57.10; 2.58.4–6; 8.28.6. See also Ps.-Ignatius, *Ad Antiochenses* 12.2.

to the gatekeepers of the tent of the testimony, who are ranked immediately below priests and Levites in 1 Chronicles 9, and focuses on the responsibility for the liturgical vessels as his principal function. As we have already noted, the prayer for a reader asks for the bestowal of the spirit of prophecy on the candidate.

TESTAMENTUM DOMINI

Another derivative of the *Apostolic Tradition*, thought to have been composed in Greek in the fifth century but now surviving only in Syriac, Ethiopic, and Arabic translations,[43] its version of the prayer for a bishop is even more expanded. Once again, in addition to an increase in the attributes of God the Father, Christ is given a prominent place in the early part of the prayer, this time through references to his salvific mission and the illumination he brought to the church. The Holy Spirit too features strongly, being invoked on the ordinand three times in the course of the prayer. On the other hand, the Old Testament typology is not as extensive as in the *Apostolic Constitutions*, the figure of Enoch alone being added to that of Abraham. The reason for this choice is to be found in a major new theme the author has woven into the prayer—the correlation between heavenly and earthly sanctuaries—because Enoch was said to have been assumed into heaven (Gen 5:21-24; Heb 11:5). The pattern for the ministry of the church is not now primarily that of the Old Testament but the unseen ministry above. In contrast to the prayer in the *Apostolic Constitutions*, the episcopal college is not mentioned and the apostolate receives only a brief reference. What is sought for the bishop in the prayer is chiefly the gift of the personal qualities requisite for the effective exercise of his priestly and princely office rather than the power to perform specific functions. In this there is an emphasis on an intercessory role on behalf of his people, and some hint of a teaching ministry, which is made more explicit in a preceding preparatory prayer.[44]

---

[43] See Michael Kohlbacher, "Wessen Kirche ordnete das Testamentum Domini Nostri Jesu Christi?," in *Zu Geschichte, Theologie, Liturgie und Gegenwartslage der syirchen Kirchen*, ed. Martin Tamcke and Andreas Heinz (Münster: LIT Verlag, 2000), 55–137.

[44] See *ORACEW*, 117–18.

Its prayer for a presbyter is also expanded, amplifying both the description of the Spirit being invoked on the ordinand and also the qualities that are expected of him. On the other hand, these developments do not really offer any clearer picture of the nature and function of the office being conferred. The presbyter is expected to display such virtues as "holiness" and "cheerfulness and patience," and to offer praise day and night and bear the cross of Christ, but it is not obvious in what way his role was thought to differ from that of any other Christian, especially as the Spirit that is sought for him is said to be that which was given to the disciples of Jesus "and to all those who through them truly believed in you." "Help and govern" do remain from the original version, but as at other points in his work the author of the *Testamentum Domini* is capable of maintaining fidelity to his source even when it differs from the practice known to have been current in his own locality, not too much can be built on this expression. The fact that the prayer twice asks for wisdom for the ordinand may be a hint of a teaching ministry, and there is the interesting petition that he may be worthy "to shepherd your people," which is normally used in reference to the episcopate rather than the presbyterate. Its appearance here may imply that the presbyter was now seen as sharing to some extent in a ministry formerly exercised by the bishop. Perhaps surprisingly in a prayer of this date, there is a complete absence of sacerdotal language, even though in the directions concerning ordination "priest" is generally used in place of "presbyter."[45]

The prayer for a deacon is expanded partly by the addition of further appellatives of God and Christ, and partly by extending the petitions for the ordinand. Although the spirit of caring is no longer mentioned, God is asked to make him love orphans and widows and to give him the qualities of diligence, serenity, strength, and power. If this corresponds in any way with the realities of the historical situation and is not merely a flight of fantasy by the compiler, it suggests that concern for the needy had here become a major feature of the deacon's office, even if it were not so in the world in which the *Apostolic Tradition* originated.[46]

[45] Ibid., 119.
[46] Ibid., 120.

With regard to the ministry of women, this church order paints a rather curious picture. The order of widows is retained from the *Apostolic Tradition*, and appears to be accorded considerable importance. Thus, for example, during the eucharistic oblation the widows are directed to stand behind the presbyters, on the left side, opposite the deacons on the right, and they are to receive communion after the deacons, and before the subdeacons and readers (1.23.1). The form of institution of a widow also has some features in common with the higher orders: the same Syriac word is used to denote the process as is employed for those orders, and it takes place after she has been "chosen" and involves a prayer, but of a very general nature that includes no biblical typology or petitions for grace and power to fulfill any specific ministerial functions.[47] Elsewhere in the document widows are assigned duties that are very similar to those of the female deacons in the *Didascalia* (1.40.2; 2.8.12). Yet this cannot simply be dismissed as a case of the substitution of the nomenclature of its literary source, since the *Testamentum* also mentions the existence of deaconesses. They are accorded a role greatly subordinate to that of the widows, who apparently are to supervise them. Nothing at all is said about their appointment, and they are directed to receive communion with the laity and not with the other ministerial orders, as the widows were (1.23.14). They were to remain near the door of the church (1.19.7), which might seem to imply that their principal duty was to supervise the arrival and seating of women in the liturgical assembly, but elsewhere it is said that a deacon controlled the entrance of both men and women, and that the deacons—assisted by readers and subdeacons—kept order among women in the church (1.36.1–4; 2.19.1). The only function that the deaconesses are described as performing is the taking of communion to any pregnant women unable to attend the Easter Eucharist (2.20.7). They are thus something of an enigma.

Appointment to the minor orders is described somewhat differently from that of widows: although the same word is used in the rite for a subdeacon as for widows, a different term is employed for the reader, and neither of them is said to have been "chosen," nor

---

[47] Ibid., 120–21.

does a form of prayer seem to have been prescribed for them. The reader is simply given the book of readings accompanied by an exhortation or charge from the bishop. It is said that the bishop is to pray over the subdeacon, but the text which follows is a similar exhortation or charge. In both cases, the exhortation expects the recipients will eventually be promoted to a higher rank.[48]

THE PRAYERS OF SARAPION

By comparison with all these prayers, the prayer for a bishop in the *Euchologion* of Sarapion is extremely simple. It differs, however, not merely in its form but in its theological ideas. In contrast to the prayer in the *Apostolic Tradition* but in line with the modifications we have observed in its later derivatives, this prayer begins not with Old Testament typology but with God's sending of Christ to the world, and it continues with references to his sending of the apostles and his ordination of bishops. In this way it not only emphasizes that ordination is the action of God but sets the episcopal office in line of succession to the apostolate, a concept that also recurs later in the prayer, when God is asked to make this ordinand "a holy bishop of the succession of the holy apostles." When this theme is coupled with the fact that God is here addressed as the "God of truth," and is asked to bestow the same Spirit as was bestowed on his "own/genuine" servants, prophets, and patriarchs, it suggests an origin in a community troubled by heresy and hence saw the bishop primarily as the guardian of true apostolic tradition, a development we have not previously encountered in ordination euchology. There is also a complete absence of Old Testament cultic imagery, as was the case in the *Canons of Hippolytus*, which is similarly thought to have originated in Egypt, nor is there any reference to the liturgical dimension of the office, the images used all being of teaching/leadership—prophets, patriarchs, shepherd.[49]

The prayer for a presbyter describes that office as "a steward of your people and an ambassador of your divine oracles," to reconcile the people to God. It also asks for the spirit of truth, for wisdom, for knowledge (twice), and for right faith. All this

---

[48] Ibid., 121.
[49] Ibid., 122–23.

suggests that, unlike the *Apostolic Tradition*, it was composed in a situation where the primary, if not exclusive, focus was on a teaching ministry, and there was no sense of the presbyterate acting as a collegial governing body.[50] According to the fifth-century church historian Socrates,[51] preaching by presbyters at Alexandria was prohibited after the time of Arius (ca. 250 – ca. 336), for fear of the spread of further heresies, and hence this prayer must have originated before that step was taken, or alternatively the situation must have been different at Thmuis or wherever it was composed.

It is true that the ministry of reconciliation may have been understood to involve more than the preaching of the good news, but this is not made explicit, and although the prayer does contain the same allusion to the appointment of elders by Moses as mentioned in the *Apostolic Tradition*, it is employed in a very different way. God is not asked to make the ordinand a presbyter like those whom Moses appointed to govern the people but to give him a share of the spirit of Christ just as God once gave a share of the spirit of Moses to others. Thus the parallel is drawn not between the two offices but between God's action in sharing the Spirit both then and now; and the emphasis does not fall on the ordinand's reception of the spirit of the corporate presbyterate (indeed the word presbyter does not appear anywhere in the prayer at all) but on his individual participation in the spirit of Christ. The presence of this typology does not necessarily mean that it must have been copied directly from the *Apostolic Tradition*, especially as there is no sign of any awareness of that document elsewhere in the collection of prayers, and it is quite possible that the author has reworked what was a common image for the presbyterate in early times.[52]

The prayer for a deacon to some extent combines the diaconal models of Christ and of Stephen and his companions encountered in the other early prayers. It sets the institution of the diaconate within the context of God's sending of Christ, and refers unequivocally to "the seven deacons," who, it says, were chosen "through

---

[50] Ibid., 122.

[51] Socrates, *Historia ecclesiastica* 5.22; see also Sozomen, *Historia ecclesiastica* 7.19.

[52] It also occurs in the fourth ordination prayer of the Melkite rite; see below, p. 98.

your only-begotten." It is no more explicit than the other texts, however, with regard to the nature of the office to which the deacon is ordained: all that is sought for him is the "spirit of knowledge and discernment," so that he may serve in his *leitourgia* "in the midst of the holy people."[53]

Although the *Euchologion* of Sarapion does mention the existence of subdeacons, readers, and interpreters, it does not include any prayers for use at their appointment, which suggests that such had not yet developed in that tradition. The ministry of women is not mentioned.

CONCLUSION

The limited evidence for this period leaves us with unanswered questions, among them: Was the silent prayer and corporate laying on of hands, apparently underlying the rite for a bishop in the *Apostolic Tradition*, something that was once widely practiced and eventually superseded, or just the custom of one local tradition? Why was the ordination prayer that eventually accompanied it so sacerdotal in character when the earliest forms of the other, presumably later, prayers of the East and West were not, except for that in the Roman rite, which did not enumerate episcopal functions in detail as that in the *Apostolic Tradition* did? What else besides prayer by the bishop constituted the rites for the ordination of presbyters and deacons? In the end, these contemporary sources will not suffice to gain a clearer picture of the earliest ordination practices; we need to turn to the later texts of East and West in order to penetrate beneath them and unearth the older traditions out of which they have evolved.

[53] See *ORACEW*, 122.

Chapter 5

Ordination Rites in the Churches of the East

There are eight main ancient families of ordination rites within the churches of the East: those of Alexandria (the Coptic rite, also used by the Ethiopian Orthodox Church), Armenia, Constantinople (the Byzantine rite), East Syria (the Assyrian Church of the East and the Chaldean Church), Georgia, Lebanon (the Maronite rite), and two traditions from West Syria (the Syrian Orthodox Church, often previously called the Jacobite rite, and the Melkite Church). Like all the other liturgies of the various Eastern churches, the ordination rites of the different traditions have undergone some development and expansion in the course of their history, and because the oldest manuscripts date only from the eighth century onward—and in some traditions are very much later than that[1]—some effort is required to uncover their earlier forms. The older manuscripts tend to provide only for bishops, presbyters, deacons, subdeacons, and readers, although some of them lack a rite for a bishop (probably because it was not regularly needed in each diocese but only by the patriarch), and some also include forms for deaconesses and *chorepiscopoi* (rural bishops). Later pontificals often add rites for appointment to other offices, among them cantors, archdeacons, abbots and abbesses, metropolitans, and patriarchs.[2]

Despite the superficial diversity of the various traditions, they display many similarities of structure and sometimes of text as well. Some of these resemblances are the consequence of the later

[1] For details of the available sources, see *ORACEW*, 5–14. The eighth-century Byzantine manuscript Barberini 336 is now available in a critical edition, *L'eucologio Barberini gr. 336*, ed. Stefano Parenti and Elena Velkovska (Rome: CLV, 1995; 2nd ed., 2000).

[2] For a study of the Coptic rite for a patriarch, see Emmanuel Lanne, "Dans la tradition alexandrine l'ordination du patriarche," in *Ordination et Ministères: Conférences Saint Serge, XLIIe Semaine d'études liturgiques*, ed. Achille Triacca and Alessandro Pistoia (Rome: CLV, 1996), 139–55.

influence of one tradition on another, and especially the spread of West Syrian and/or Byzantine features to other churches, which can sometimes be detected by the fact that they duplicate the equivalent indigenous liturgical units. Nevertheless, behind all this can be seen a common ritual pattern from which they all appear to derive, a pattern that is shared to a great extent by the earliest Western sources, too. This widespread convergence inspires confidence that the pattern is ancient and may be traced back to at least the end of the fourth century if not before. The rites for a bishop, a presbyter, and a deacon all once consisted of:

- proclamation of the result of the election, and acclamation of assent by the people
- a bidding, inviting the people to pray for the ordinand
- prayer by the people for the ordinand
- the sign of the cross made on the forehead of the ordinand
- a substantial prayer said by the presiding bishop while laying his hand on the ordinand
- the exchange of a ritual kiss
- the celebration of the Eucharist

In the case of the ordination of a bishop may be added the imposition of the gospel book prior to the imposition of the hand and his solemn seating at the conclusion of the rite, about which we have spoken in the previous chapter. This basic pattern subsequently became obscured by the addition of further elements to the rites, and especially by the tendency to acquire additional ordination prayers and in some cases to associate the imposition of the hand with the proclamation and bidding rather than the prayer (see further below).

PROCLAMATION OF THE RESULT OF THE ELECTION AND ACCLAMATION OF ASSENT BY THE PEOPLE

The important place accorded to the election of a candidate for ordination in early Christianity should not be understood as pointing to some notion of the ideal of democracy, nor, at least at first, to the principle that a congregation had the right to choose its own ministers. Nor was it seen as in any way opposed to the divine calling of a minister, but on the contrary it was understood as the means by which God's choice of a person for a particular ecclesiastical office was discerned and made manifest. As both patristic writings and the prayers in the rites themselves make clear, it was always considered that it was God who chose and ordained the ministers through the action of the church. There was thus no dichotomy between actions "from below" and "from above." The church's discernment of God's choice might on occasion even override an individual's own lack of a sense of vocation, and it contrasts with more modern views of the primacy of the "interior call." Once the divine choice had been revealed in this way, then the church might proceed to pray that God would bestow on the one whom he had appointed the requisite qualities for the effective discharge of the office.

As time went by, however, as we have noted in the first chapter, the ritual of prayer and the imposition of the hand came to be thought of as the *real* act of ordination, the means by which the office itself was bestowed on the candidate, with election merely as a dispensable preliminary to it. However, a distinction in terminology still tended to be retained between the ordination of bishops, presbyters, and deacons on the one hand and admission to the minor orders on the other, when they, too, adopted the imposition of hands, *cheirotonia* being used for the former but *epithesis* for the latter.

Moreover, in spite of the decline of the electoral process, vestiges of the former arrangement can still be detected among the preliminaries of the later ordination rites of the Eastern churches (and, as we shall see in the next chapter, in the West, too). It appears that originally at the election of a bishop the people had cried out, *Axios*, "Worthy!" because the fifth-century ecclesiastical historian Philostorgius recounts that, when the Arian Demophilos was appointed as Bishop of Constantinople in 370, many of the people shouted *Anaxios*, "Unworthy!" instead of *Axios*.[3] The oldest manuscript of the Armenian rite for the ordination of deacons and presbyters (ninth/tenth century) preserves a memory of this same procedure for them, too. The rite begins with an announcement of the choice of the candidate, made by a deacon in the case of an

---

[3] Philostorgius, *Historia ecclesiastica* 9.10 (PG 65.576C).

ordination to the diaconate and by a presbyter in the case of an ordination to the presbyterate.

> They call N. from being a clerk to the diaconate of the Lord/from the office of deacon to that of priest, to the service of holy Church, to its ministration, in accordance with the testimony of himself and of the congregation: he is worthy.[4]

The final statement was doubtless originally intended to be a question, to which a congregational response was expected, as it still is the version in another manuscript probably dating from no later than the thirteenth century:

> Divine and heavenly grace that always fulfills the needs of the holy ministry of the apostolic Church. They call N. from the diaconate to the priesthood for the ministration of the holy Church. According to the testimony of himself and of the congregation, is he worthy?" *And the congregation say three times*: "He is worthy."[5]

Some such formulary was apparently already known to Pseudo-Dionysius in the late fifth/early sixth century, as he refers to an *anarresis*, "proclamation," in his description of the rite of ordination: "The bishop makes the proclamation of the ordinations and the ordinands, the mystery signifying that the consecrator, beloved by God, is the interpreter of the divine choice. He does not lead the ordinand to ordination by his own grace, but he is moved by God for all the consecrations."[6] Other allusions to "the divine grace" in connection with ordination imply that it may have been in use at least in Antioch before the end of the fourth century.[7]

Although the Armenian tradition does not preserve a rite for a bishop in the earliest manuscript, the later episcopal rite also

---

[4] *ORACEW*, 128–29.

[5] British Museum Add. 19.548; in F. C. Conybeare, *Rituale Armenorum* (Oxford: Clarendon Press, 1905), 237.

[6] Pseudo-Dionysius, *De ecclesiastica hierarchia* 5.3.5 (PG 3:512).

[7] See John Chrysostom, *Sermo cum presbyter fuit ordinatus* 4 (PG 48:700); the reference to his ordination in Theodoret, *Historia ecclesiastica* 5.27.1; and Chrysostom, *De sacerdotio* 4.1 and Gregory Nazianzen, *Oratio* 15.35, both quoted above, pp. 56–57.

retains the same triple congregational response,[8] and this acclamation of assent occurs in other Eastern traditions as well, but now moved to the end of the whole act of ordination, presumably once the people's role in the election itself had disappeared. The earliest example of this switch is in the rite for a bishop in the fifth-century *Testamentum Domini*.[9]

THE BIDDING

In the early Armenian rite the formula provided for the announcement of the results of the election were then repeated in a variant form by the bishop, but omitting the words "he is worthy" at the end and instead linked to an invitation to pray for the candidate: "I lay hands upon him. Do you all offer up your prayers that he be worthy to serve in the rank of the diaconate before God and the holy altar/in the rank of priesthood without blemish before the Lord all the days of his life." A similar combined proclamation/bidding formulary exists in one form or another in all later Eastern rites for bishops, presbyters, and deacons, and in some cases is extended to the minor orders as well.[10] This combination presumably occurred as the result of the displacement of the congregational acclamation of assent to the end of the rite.

Bernard Botte argued that its most primitive version was that in the eighth-century Byzantine rite, where it is said to be read from a scroll. Its wording is identical in the conferral of all three offices apart from the name of the particular order:

> The divine grace, which always heals that which is inform and supplies that what is lacking, appoints the presbyter N., beloved by God, as bishop. Let us pray therefore that the grace of the Holy Spirit may come upon him.[11]

---

[8] Heinrich Denzinger, *Ritus Orientalium*, vol. 2 (Würzburg: Stahel, 1863 = Graz: Akademische Druk- und Verlagsanstalt, 1961), 361.

[9] See *ORACEW*, 118.

[10] It occurs in relation to the subdeacon in the Coptic and Syrian Orthodox rites, and both the reader and the subdeacon in the East Syrian and Melkite rites: see *ORACEW*, 141, 146–57, 176, 201–3.

[11] *ORACEW*, 133–36.

Botte thus overlooked the probability that it had previously existed as two independent liturgical units and even went on to make the implausible claim that it was intended to be the sacramental form of ordination itself! He admitted that it was pronounced by a deacon in the later Coptic and Syrian Orthodox rites, and so could not have that function there, and was also in a preliminary position in the Byzantine rites for the presbyterate and diaconate in the eighth-century Barberini manuscript. But he judged that the Byzantine rite for the episcopate, together with the East Syrian and Maronite rites, had retained the true primitive usage in which the proclamation was made by the presiding bishop during the imposition of the hand. Its apparent relegation to a less central position in the other rites he believed to have been the result of the introduction of secondary elements—a second imposition of the hand in the Syrian Orthodox rite and the ordination prayers themselves in the Byzantine tradition: these tended to push the formulary into the shade.[12]

Most other scholars have rightly rejected Botte's theory. Pierre-Marie Gy pointed out that Pseudo-Dionysius made a clear distinction between the proclamation, which was common to all three orders, and the invocations (*epikleses*), which were proper to each of them and through which the consecrations were effected. Gy suggested that the formulary grew rather than declined in importance in the course of the centuries as the ordination prayers came to be recited in a low voice for reasons of reverence: the second Byzantine prayer was already recited in this way while the litany was still being said in the eighth-century Barberini manuscript, and later the first prayer too would be performed in a similar manner.[13]

Not only was Botte applying to the rites a completely Western and anachronistic sacramental theology, but he failed to see that

[12] Bernard Botte, "La formule d'ordination 'La grâce divine' dans les rites orientaux," *L'orient syrien* 2 (1957), 285–96.

[13] Pierre-Marie Gy, "Ancient Ordination Prayers," *SL* 13 (1979): 75. See also Emmanuel Lanne, "Les ordinations dans le rite copte: leurs relations avec les Constitutions Apostoliques et la Tradition de saint Hippolyte," *L'orient syrien* 5 (1960): 81–106, here at 82–83; Jean Tchékan, "Elements d'introduction à l'étude de la liturgie byzantine des ordinations," *Compagnie de Saint-Sulpice: Bulletin du Comité des Études* 10 (1968): 190–208, here at 201.

the formulary was simply a bidding to which the imposition of the hand had in some traditions later become attached from its proper association with the ordination prayer. Moreover, he was mistaken about the East Syrian rite, as the formulary there is recited *before* the imposition of the hand, as it is also in the eleventh-century Grottaferrata manuscript of the Byzantine rite at the ordination of a bishop as well as in the rites for the presbyterate and diaconate. In that manuscript the version for a bishop contains an opening phrase that strengthens its association with the electoral process: "By the vote and approval of the most divinely-beloved bishops and the most holy presbyters and deacons . . . "[14] It seems highly improbable that this variation could have been a late addition, especially as the election had, in practice, been restricted to the episcopal college alone for many centuries. It is therefore likely that this is a survival from the more ancient tradition, which had already undergone some modification in the Barberini manuscript.

Although Botte was right that the Byzantine version eventually came to be adopted in one form or another by all other Eastern rites, it is clear that prior to this, various traditions had their own equivalents of it. Thus, while the Coptic rites seem to have inherited the Byzantine formulary through the West Syrian tradition, the rite for a bishop there has an extensive proclamation/bidding of its own. The Georgian rite similarly has a rather lengthy formulary of the same kind, pronounced by a deacon, which was used, with appropriate modifications, in appointment to all three orders. This may have originated in the Jerusalem tradition, and has no doubt undergone some expansion and elaboration in the course of its history. It is followed by another formulary, said by the bishop, which has some resemblance to the Byzantine one: "The grace of God heals the sick, satisfies them that are in need: hands are laid on this our child."[15]

This combination of proclamation and bidding created a sort of bridge between the two parts of the ordination process, announcing the result of the election and inviting the congregation to pray

---

[14] *L'Eucologio Constantinopolitano agli inizi del secolo XI*, ed. Miguel Arranz (Rome: Pontificia Università Gregoriana, 1996), 142.

[15] *ORACEW*, 149–50; 166–67.

for the ordinand. Its wording confirms that the exercise of human choice was thought of as manifesting the divine will, and that the ordination was seen as effected by the grace of the Holy Spirit acting in response to the prayer of the church.

PRAYER OF THE PEOPLE FOR THE ORDINAND

One would naturally expect that the prayer of the people, in one form or another, would follow the bidding, and this certainly seems to have been the original practice, but in the course of time the importance of prayer by the whole community in ordination seems to have been lost. In some cases another presidential prayer now intervenes, in others it has fallen out altogether or left only a trace of its former existence.

Thus, in the Barberini manuscript of Byzantine rites, the triple response, "Lord, have mercy," is explicitly mentioned as following the proclamation/bidding only in the case of the episcopate, but it may also have been practiced in the other rites that employ the same formulary (presbyters, deacons, and deaconesses), even though it is not specified in the rubrics. In every case, however, a litany with appropriate petitions for the ordinands appears, not directly after the bidding, but after the first of two ordination prayers has been said. This unusual arrangement suggests that the first ordination prayer is a later addition to the rites that destroyed the natural liturgical sequence and left the *Kyrie* response high and dry. Though such litanies were normally led by a deacon, in the rite for the episcopate a bishop fulfills this function, and in the rite for the presbyterate it is undertaken by a presbyter.[16]

In the early Armenian rite the litany similarly intervenes between the first and second ordination prayers for deacons and presbyters. This arrangement is very probably the result of Byzantine influence on the structure of the services, and not part of the indigenous tradition, and it does not persist in later manuscripts. In the East Syrian rites the ordination prayers follow directly after the biddings, while the Syrian Orthodox rites have only the response, "Lord, have mercy," following the proclamation/bidding, but no litany as such. The Coptic and Maronite rites are similar,

---

[16] Ibid., 133–35.

except that in the case of the episcopate in the former, a full litany with a special suffrage for the ordinand does still intervene after the bidding.[17]

In the ancient Georgian rite, the deacon who pronounces the bidding is directed to say three times, "Lord, have mercy and make him worthy." This was doubtless originally a congregational response, and may be a conflation of two responses that were earlier quite separate, an acclamation of assent to the candidate's worthiness in reply to the announcement of his election and the normal form of supplication. A litany occurs here in the text at the beginning of the whole collection of prayers, but with a rubric that directed it to be used at the ordination of bishops, presbyters, and deacons. Presumably it was intended to be said between the bidding and the ordination prayers. Finally, in the Melkite ritual a threefold "Lord, have mercy" follows the first bidding, and then comes the Byzantine proclamation/ bidding formulary and a litany, except in the rite for the diaconate where the litany comes in what was very probably its original position, prior to Byzantine influence, directly after the first bidding. Like that bidding, the litany is said by a presbyter at the ordination of a presbyter, and by the chief deacon at other ordinations.[18]

THE IMPOSITION OF THE GOSPEL BOOK AT THE ORDINATION OF A BISHOP

This ceremony, found in the *Apostolic Constitutions* and other fourth-century sources,[19] occurs in all later Eastern rites[20] but was performed by one or more of the bishops themselves rather than by deacons, as in the *Apostolic Constitutions*. However, as it was also deacons who performed it at Rome,[21] that seems to confirm that the

[17] Ibid., 129, 131, 143, 145, 150, 158, 160, 163, 178, 181, 183, 191, 194, 197.

[18] Ibid., 166, 206.

[19] See above, pp. 69–71.

[20] Scholars had traditionally thought that in the Coptic rite it was limited to the consecration of the patriarch alone, but see Heinzgerd Brakmann, "Zur Evangeliar-Auflegung bei der Ordination koptischer Bischöfe," in *Eulogēma: Studies in Honor of Robert Taft, SJ*, ed. Ephrem Carr et al., Studia Anselmiana 110 (Rome: Centro Studi S. Anselmo, 1993): 53–69, for a contrary view.

[21] See below, p. 118.

original custom had been as described in the *Apostolic Constitutions* and that Eastern practice had subsequently changed in order to increase episcopal involvement in the rite. In the Syrian Orthodox and Maronite rites, two bishops hold the book open over the head of the ordinand during the imposition of the hand. In the Byzantine rite it is performed by the archbishop, with the other bishops present also touching the book. Moreover, the open book is here laid on the head *and neck* of the ordinand and apparently understood as symbolizing "the yoke of the Gospel" that the new bishop received, since in later manuscripts of the rite this allusion is incorporated into the first ordination prayer.[22] In the East Syrian rite the archbishop is directed to place the book on the back of the ordinand in such a way that "it faces the one who is to read from it," and a gospel reading from it follows, after which the book is closed and left on the ordinand's back during the imposition of the hand and the prayers.[23] These modifications reinforce our earlier judgment that the real meaning of the ceremony had been lost, its form being deliberately altered in order to make it more intelligible.

THE SIGN OF THE CROSS

The earliest allusion to the use of the sign of the cross in ordination is found in the *Canons of Hippolytus*, where the prayer for a deacon contains the clause, "make him triumph over all the powers of the Devil by the sign of your cross with which you sign him."[24] Its existence at Antioch at the ordination of bishops in the fourth century is attested by John Chrysostom,[25] and the "cruciform seal" immediately after the imposition of the hand is mentioned by Pseudo-Dionysius as being common to all the major orders (*De ecclesiastica hierarchia* 5.2), with later Eastern rites confirming this to be the case, except that it normally precedes rather than follows the imposition of the hand. The use of the sign of the cross in early

---

[22] See *L'Eucologio Constantinopolitano*, ed. Arranz, 143. Although these rites do not specify whether the open book faced up or down, later practice has been that it faces down.

[23] *ORACEW*, 133, 163, 183, 198.

[24] Ibid., 111.

[25] John Chrysostom, *Adversus Judaeos et Gentiles* 9 (PG 48:826); *Homilia in Matthaeum* 54 (PG 58:537).

baptismal rituals may have provided the precedent for its adoption in Eastern ordination practice, especially as it is given a similar interpretation: the *Canons of Hippolytus* implies that it was seen as apotropaic, while Pseudo-Dionysius says that it signified "the cessation of all carnal desires and the imitation of the divine life."

THE IMPOSITION OF THE HAND

As indicated earlier, some Eastern rites display a tendency to associate the beginning of the imposition of the hand (usually specified as the right hand) with the first formula spoken by the presiding bishop, which may be called a prayer in the text even if it is not strictly speaking one, rather than with what appears to have been the original ordination prayer. This is the case in the early Armenian rites for deacons and presbyters, in the eighth-century Byzantine rite for a bishop (but not those for presbyters and deacons) and in the Maronite and Melkite rites, where the imposition of the hand begins at the proclamation/bidding formula.[26]

In every Eastern rite, however, it is the presiding bishop alone who lays his hand on the ordinand, and only in a few cases are there signs of obviously secondary attempts to associate others with him in this action. In the East Syrian rite for a bishop, the other bishops place their right hands on the ordinand's sides, and in the Coptic rite they lay their hands on the ordinand's arms and not on his head. In the Armenian rite for a presbyter, a rubric directs that after the ordinand kneels down, "the priests lay their hands upon his" [sic], leaving where the hands are to be placed unclear. A parallel rubric in the rite for the diaconate specifies that it is on "his hands."[27] Later manuscripts of the presbyteral rite, however, while exhibiting some further confusion over the rubric, seem to agree that it is the ordinand's shoulders on which the other priests are to lay a hand.[28] Both the Syrian Orthodox and Maronite rites display a unique feature in relation to the imposition of the hand for all three orders: the presiding bishop extends his hands over the consecrated bread and wine three times before proceeding to lay his right hand on the ordinand. This ceremony seems to have

[26] *ORACEW*, 128, 130, 133, 191, 194, 197, 206, 209.
[27] Ibid., 128, 130, 151, 163.
[28] See Conybeare, *Rituale Armenorum*, 236–37.

been introduced in order to express the idea that it was not the presiding bishop himself but Christ who ordained his ministers, and it
was his spiritual power that was bestowed on them.[29]

Although none of the patristic sources make any reference to
the posture to be adopted by ordinands during the ordination
prayer and imposition of the hand, Pseudo-Dionysius stated that
candidates for the episcopate and presbyterate were to kneel on
both knees, and a candidate for the diaconate on his right knee (*De
ecclesiastica hierarchia* 5.2) This is supported by the more extensive
rubrics found in some of the later texts, except for the Armenian,
which speaks instead of the left knee for a deacon.[30]

THE ORDINATION PRAYER

As indicated earlier, there is a common tendency in the Eastern
rites for ordination prayers to multiply, either by the addition what
may have been a local alternative to the principal prayer or by the
incorporation of prayers from foreign sources. Thus, the Byzantine
rite has two ordination prayers for each order, one immediately
after the bidding and the second, probably more original one, after
the litany.[31] The oldest Armenian rites have adopted the same pattern (doubtless from Byzantine influence) although the prayers are
different in content and the rite for presbyters has a third prayer
after the liturgy of the word. The East Syrian rites also have two
prayers, the first located even before the bidding itself and identical in every case except for the name of the office being conferred.
The Georgian rites have three prayers for each order, one of them
drawn from the *Testamentum Domini* and another with parallels to
the principal prayer in the East Syrian rite. In the Syrian Orthodox
tradition, several preparatory and supplementary prayers have
grown up before and after the principal ordination prayer. The
Coptic rites combine prayers from this source with material from
the *Apostolic Constitutions*. The Maronite rites each have a number
of prayers, suggesting a long process of accretion, some of them
analogous to prayers in the Syrian Orthodox tradition, others with

[29] *ORACEW*, 178, 181, 183, 191, 195, 197.

[30] Ibid., 128.

[31] For reasons to think that the first prayer is a later composition than the
second, see ibid., 51–52, 64–65.

resemblances to ones in the Melkite tradition, and others with no known parallel. One prayer in the rite for deacons is a version of a Byzantine one, and one in the rite for a bishop is derived from the *Apostolic Constitutions*. Something similar is true of the Melkite rite. Some prayers resemble Georgian texts (which has led to the suggestion that they both derive from Jerusalem[32]), others are similar to Byzantine prayers, others to those in the Maronite rites, and still others have no clear parallels.[33]

1. For a Bishop

In the case of prayers for a bishop, there is evidence of an even closer literary connection between the different rites. In five of the six traditions that have rites for the episcopate in their oldest manuscripts, there is a substantial amount of common material in one of their prayers. The following is the Byzantine version, the elements common to the other prayers being indicated by the use of italics:

> Lord our *God, who*, because human nature cannot sustain the essence of your divinity, by your dispensation *have established teachers* subject to the same passions as ourselves who approach your throne to offer you sacrifice and oblation for all your people;
> Lord, *make him* who has been made dispenser of the high-priestly grace *to be an imitator of you, the true shepherd, giving his life for your sheep, guide of the blind, light of those in darkness, corrector of the ignorant, lamp in the world, so that, after having formed* in this present life *the souls who have been entrusted to him, he may stand before your judgment-seat without shame and receive the great reward* which you have prepared for those who have striven for the preaching of your Gospel. For yours are mercy and salvation.[34]

Although part of this is an allusion to John 10:15 and a quotation from Romans 2:19-20, it is inconceivable that each tradition

---

[32] See further Heinzgerd Brakmann, "Die altkirchlichen Ordinationsgebete Jerusalems," *Jahrbuch für Antike und Christentum* 47 (2004): 108–27.

[33] See the table of relationships between the prayers in *ORACEW*, 243.

[34] *ORACEW*, 134. See the synopsis of the parallels in the prayers, ibid., 246–47, and further discussion of their origin, ibid., 50–55; also Frans van de Paverd, "Ein Gebet zur Bischofsweihe aus dem vorbyzantinischen Jerusalem," in *Eulogēma*, ed. Carr, 511–23, who argues for a Jerusalem origin for the common core.

would have lighted on the latter independently, especially as it is a very strange passage to choose for this purpose, because in its original context it had nothing to do with ordination or ministry but formed part of a critical passage directed toward the Jews. Although the Byzantine version is the shortest of the prayers containing the common material and so might be thought to have been the source of all the others, this is unlikely in its present form, as there are at least two peculiarities that suggest it, too, has undergone some modification: it is addressed, not to God the Father, but to Christ ("you, the true shepherd")[35] and its description of teachers as those "who approach your throne to offer sacrifice and oblation" is a strange mixture of images, and appears to be a secondary adaptation made in order to incorporate a cultic dimension rather than a part of the primary stratum of the prayer.

The presence of such similar euchological material in very diverse contexts suggests that the nucleus of this prayer is as old as some of the patristic sources and was in established use before the divisions that took place in the Eastern churches during the fifth century. It seems to have been ancient enough to have developed in at least two distinct forms prior to that time, with a Byzantine/Coptic trajectory on the one hand[36] and a Georgian/East Syrian (and perhaps Syrian Orthodox) version on the other. This second strand strengthened the christological dimension of the prayer (a development which we have already observed in the case of some of the patristic texts), introduced an explicit invocation of the Holy Spirit on the ordinand, and like the prayer in the *Canons of Hippolytus*, added a reference to the healing ministry of the bishop.

Thus, the two images of the episcopal office that seemingly constitute part of the original nucleus of the prayer are those of shepherd (as was true in the patristic sources, but here brought into

[35] The same is also true of the second prayer for a deacon. Gy, "Ancient Ordination Prayers," 82, suggested that this was part of a general Byzantine tendency to direct to Christ those prayers that came to be said in a low voice.

[36] Pierre-Marie Gy, "La théologie des prières anciennes pour l'ordination des évêques et des prêtres," *Revue des sciences philosophiques et théologiques* 58 (1974): 599–617, here at 604, considered that the description of God as unknowable at the beginning of the Byzantine version was characteristic of the theology of the Greek fathers at the end of the fourth century.

explicit association with Christ the true shepherd), and teacher/ guardian of the truth (a contrast with most of the patristic texts). Cultic/liturgical imagery seems to have had no place at all in the earliest stratum, but to have been gradually introduced at a later stage in the various traditions. In some cases a clumsy fusion of ideas took place, as with the teaching and priestly themes in the opening of the Byzantine prayer noted above, or the notion of the "perfect priest after the example of the true shepherd" in the Georgian version. In other cases, a simple addition was made, such as the insertion of "priests" after the Pauline "apostles, prophets, and teachers" in the East Syrian prayer. In the Syrian Orthodox prayer there was direct substitution, with, for example, "every priestly order" replacing "teachers," which resulted in an all but total obliteration of the earlier themes.

2. For a Presbyter

Although, as we have said, there has obviously been some borrowing from one source to another in the prayers for presbyters, no common nucleus seems to underlie the majority as it did in the case of the prayers for a bishop, but they appear to stem from several quite distinct euchological traditions, no doubt reflecting the considerable regional diversity in early ordination practice.

The second of the two prayers in the Byzantine rite seems to be the earlier. It also displays strong similarities to the first prayer in the Melkite rite and also to a longer prayer in the Syrian Orthodox rite, suggesting a common source for all three.[37] Unlike the equivalent prayers for a bishop and for a deacon, it does have an explicit petition for the gift of the Holy Spirit, but unlike the patristic texts, it does not define the presbyterate by means of biblical typology, probably because nothing could be found that was appropriate to the nature that the office was thought to have.

> O God, great in power and unsearchable in understanding, wonderful in your counsels beyond the sons of men, Lord, fill this man, whom you have willed to undertake the rank of the presbyterate, with the gift of your Holy Spirit so that he may be worthy to stand blamelessly at your altar, to proclaim the Gospel of your salvation, to exercise the sacred ministry of the word of your truth, to offer

[37] See *ORACEW*, 64–65, 134, 181, 209.

you gifts and spiritual sacrifices, and to renew your people by the baptism of regeneration; so that, being present at the second coming of our great God and Savior Jesus Christ your only Son, he may receive the reward of the good stewardship of his office in the abundance of your goodness. For blessed and glorified is your most honored and magnificent name.[38]

The presbyterate is not portrayed as a collegial governing body but instead the prayer employs strictly functional language. The use of the expression "exercise the sacred ministry (*hierourgein*) of the word," echoing Romans 15:16, "exercising the sacred ministry of the Gospel of God," strongly suggests that the priestly dimension of the office was seen as finding its fulfillment at least as much in the preaching of the word as in sacramental functions,[39] and this corresponds to what we know of the nature of the ordained ministry at Antioch in the fourth century, where presbyters took a prominent part in preaching but eucharistic presidency seems still to have been normally an episcopal prerogative.[40] The other versions of this prayer modify the references to proclaiming the Gospel and exercising the ministry of the word, because this later ceased to a function normally exercised by presbyters, and introduce the terms "priest" or "priesthood" instead, since these began to be used unequivocally to denote the presbyterate rather than the episcopate in the East in the fifth century.

The preaching of the word is also given the pride of place in a number of other Eastern ordination prayers. The first Georgian prayer, which parallels the second Melkite prayer, begins by

[38] Ibid., 135.

[39] See also above, pp. 43 and 73, for John Chrysostom's homily on the day of his presbyteral ordination, where he said that he had been placed among the priests and that the word was his sacrifice, and for the use of the noun *hierourgias*, "holy services," to denote presbyteral functions in the ordination prayer for presbyters in *Apostolic Constitutions*.

[40] See *Apostolic Constitutions* 2.57.9, and the evidence of John Chrysostom cited in Frans van de Paverd, *Zur Geschichte der Messliturgie in Antiocheia und Constantinopel gegen Ende des vierten Jahrhunderts*, Orientalia Christiana Analecta 187 (Rome: Pontificale Institutum Orientalium Studiorum, 1970), 131. According to the *Itinerarium Egeriae* (25.1; 26.1; 27.6–7; 42.1; 43.2, 3), the same seems to have been true at Jerusalem.

linking the earthly ministry to the ministry of heaven, much as was also done in the prayer for a bishop in the *Testamentum Domini*, but mentions only the function of true teaching in its petition for the ordinand. The same is true of the third Melkite prayer: while it refers in a general way to the discharging of services (*leitourgias*) on behalf of the church and to beseeching God's propitiation for all, the only function explicitly specified is the teaching of God's commandments. The third prayer in the Georgian rite, which occurs in a somewhat longer and apparently later form in the East Syrian rite, asks God to send the Holy Spirit on the ordinand that he may have "the word of teaching, for the opening of his mouth," before going on to mention the ministry of healing and the celebration of the Eucharist. The East Syrian version adds to this the administration of baptism. A similar list of functions also occurs in the fourth Melkite prayer—offering gifts and sacrifices, "utterance in the opening of his mouth," praying for the sick, the administration of baptism, and care of the needy.[41]

Two of the Armenian prayers for a presbyter, like the first Georgian/second Melkite prayer, also begin with a comparison of the heavenly and earthly ministries. The first of these goes on to speak of priests as being "shepherds and leaders" of the congregation, images that elsewhere are used of the episcopal rather than presbyteral order, before specifying the functions of "the word of preaching," the work of healing, the bestowal of the Spirit in baptism, and the celebration of the Eucharist. The second prayer merely asks for the bestowal of the sevenfold gifts of the Spirit so that the ordinand may teach and shepherd the people. The third Maronite prayer, which has some slight similarity to the first Georgian/second Melkite prayer, compares the heavenly and earthly ministries and refers to priestly, teaching, and governing/shepherding functions.[42]

3. For a Deacon

These prayers display both the same variation as to whether they use the typology of Stephen as was evidenced in the patristic prayers and also a similar tendency to reticence with regard to the

---

[41] See *ORACEW*, 160–61, 170–71, 210–12.
[42] Ibid., 130–32, 195.

actual functions of the diaconate. Where any details of the ministry are mentioned, they almost always relate to service at the altar rather than to any wider pastoral responsibility.

The first Byzantine prayer asks for the bestowal of the same grace that was given to Stephen, but has no explicit invocation of the Holy Spirit on the candidate. On the other hand, it does refer at the beginning to God in his *foreknowledge* sending down the Holy Spirit on those *destined* to be ministers: Is this perhaps a reflection of Acts 6:3 where the assembly are directed to choose men already "full of the Spirit" to be appointed to office? It gives little indication of the nature of the ministry for which the deacon is being ordained, except that it is related to the Eucharist. It speaks of "those destined . . . to serve at your immaculate mysteries," and cites 1 Timothy 3:9, "holding the mystery of faith in a pure conscience," which some commentators have thought may be intended here, though not in its original context, as a reference to the deacon's function of holding the chalice for the distribution of communion.[43] It ends with the quotation from 1 Timothy 3:13—"for those serving well will gain for themselves a good rank"—which we have already encountered in the deacon's prayer in the *Apostolic Tradition*, and here again the reference is not to ecclesiastical preferment but to the deacon's standing on the day of judgment.[44]

The second prayer, like the second prayer for a bishop, is addressed to Christ rather than to God the Father, but this appears to be a secondary development, as a Syrian Orthodox version of it begins in a completely different manner. The Byzantine form does not use the typology of Stephen, but in its extended introduction links the diaconate to Christ, not claiming that he directly instituted it as the *Euchologion* of Sarapion tried to do, but interpreting his saying in Matthew 20:27 ("whoever wishes to be first among you must be your servant [*doulos*]") as a prophetic word concerning it. The prayer then goes on to ask for the bestowal of appropriate gifts of the Holy Spirit, these being personal qualities rather than the powers to fulfill any specific function. It includes an insistent aside that ordination is indeed effected by the descent of the Spirit and not by

---

[43] See, for example, Martimort, *Deaconesses*, 156.
[44] *ORACEW*, 136.

the action of the bishop. This has the appearance of a later addition to the original text, though it is ancient enough to have also been included in the Syrian Orthodox version.[45] The inclusion of such a strongly defensive doctrinal statement in the prayer suggests that there was some controversy over the issue, and it may have been added in the late fourth century, since John Chrysostom makes a similar statement in one of his writings: "For this is ordination: the man's hand is imposed, but God does all and it is his hand that touches the ordinand's head when he is rightly ordained."[46]

The Syrian Orthodox version, also found in the Maronite rite, modifies the Byzantine prayer in several ways: it supplies an introduction that sets the ordination of the deacon within an ecclesial framework; it introduces a reference to Stephen, though without the designation "protomartyr"; and it expands the second half of the prayer with petitions for right judgment on the part of those responsible for choosing ordinands. Some of these petitions also occur in the preliminary prayer, "Lord God of hosts . . . ," used in all Syrian Orthodox ordinations from subdeacon upward.[47]

The first ordination prayer for a deacon in the Georgian rite (here described as for an archdeacon) parallels the second prayer in the Melkite rite. It defines the diaconate neither in relation to Christ, who is only mentioned briefly toward the end of the prayer, nor by the typology of Stephen, but simply as one of a list of diverse ministries bestowed by God on the church—teachers, deacons, presbyters, and ministers. This is an unusual combination of offices: it omits any explicit reference to bishops and does not follow a hierarchical order, nor is it an allusion to any New Testament listing. The Melkite tradition seems to have found it difficult to comprehend, and has tried to make some sense out of it by arranging the titles in pairs, altering "presbyters" to "priests" in the process. The prayer has no explicit epiclesis, which may be a sign of its an-

---

[45] But there strangely in the plural—"the imposition of the hands of us sinners." The same phrase also occurs in one of the Maronite ordination prayers.

[46] John Chrysostom, *Homilia in Acta Apostolorum* 14.3 (*PG* 60:116). He also implies in one of his baptismal homilies that the Antiochene baptismal formula was changed from the active to the passive form at this time in order to make a similar point.

[47] *ORACEW*, 178–79.

tiquity, but on the other hand, at least in its present form, it speaks of the ordinand's ultimate promotion to a higher rank, which does not seem to belong to the earliest concept of the office.[48]

The third Georgian prayer parallels the East Syrian ordination prayer, following the pattern of the rite for the presbyterate. This sets the creation of the diaconate in the context of the mission of Christ and of the apostles (the latter reference being expanded in the East Syrian prayer to prophets, apostles, priests, and teachers, apparently under the influence of Ephesians 4:11-12), and cites the example of Stephen and his companions. As in the first Georgian prayer, service at the altar is stated to be the principal function of the office, a point further strengthened in the East Syrian version by two additional references to the sacraments. There is, on the other hand, no mention of the ordinand's eventual promotion to a higher rank but merely the petition for a favorable verdict on the Day of Judgment.[49]

Of the remaining prayers of the Melkite rite, the first has the appearance of being a late composition, since extensive biblical quotation is not a characteristic of more ancient prayers, and it is very much built around Acts 6:5. However, as well as mentioning service of the altar, where it is the only prayer to refer explicitly to the diaconal function of giving communion to the people from the chalice, it also speaks of a ministry to widows and orphans—but has that been introduced simply because of the influence of Acts 6 rather than being a reflection of a genuine ministry of this kind? The position of the fourth prayer, after the bestowal of the symbols of office, suggests that it, too, is a late addition to the rite, even if it is not itself a late composition. It speaks simply of faithful service at the liturgy and of progress to a higher rank, though whether this is ecclesiastical or eschatological is not entirely clear.[50]

The first of the two Armenian prayers for the diaconate, like two of those in the rite for the presbyterate, uses the comparison of the heavenly and earthly ministries. It goes on to set the diaconal office within an ecclesial context and then prays for the gift of

[48] Ibid., 169, 207.
[49] Ibid., 158—59, 170.
[50] Ibid., 206–8.

appropriate personal qualities for the ordinand. Service at the altar is again designated as the principal function of the order, and the example of Stephen is invoked: he is here described not only as the first martyr and first deacon and minister of God's worship but also as an apostle! There is no explicit epiclesis, though it prays that the ordinand "filled with the Holy Spirit, may stand fast . . . " and eventually be worthy of promotion to the priesthood. The second prayer is much shorter, and does contain a petition for the gift of the Holy Spirit. Once again, ministry at the holy table is described as the chief function of the office, and the remainder of the prayer seeks God's protection for the new minister. Like the first Armenian prayer, those prayers in the Maronite rite which are without parallel in other traditions also employ the comparison of heavenly and earthly ministries.[51]

THE KISS

The only concluding symbolic ceremony mentioned in the *Apostolic Tradition* and its derivatives was the exchange of a kiss between the assembly and a new bishop, except for the *Apostolic Constitutions*, which included the seating of the new bishop and placed the kiss after that.[52] It does not appear to be merely the kiss of peace that would normally occur within the eucharistic rite, for what evidence there is from the ante-Nicene period suggests that the latter formed the conclusion of the prayers of the faithful rather than the beginning of the eucharistic action.[53] The ordination kiss seems instead to have been intended to express the acceptance by the community of their new relationship with the one ordained.

No indication is given by any of the patristic sources as to whether a similar kiss was also exchanged in the case of the presbyterate and diaconate, with the sole exception of the *Testamentum Domini*, which directs that both "priests and people" are to give the kiss of peace to a newly ordained presbyter.[54] On the other hand, it

[51] Ibid., 128–29, 192–93.

[52] Ibid., 108, 110, 114, 119.

[53] See Justin Martyr, *Apology* 1.65.2; Tertullian, *De oratione* 18; Michael Philip Penn, *Kissing Christians: Ritual and Community in the Late Ancient Church* (Philadelphia: University of Pennsylvania Press, 2005).

[54] *ORACEW*, 119.

is a consistent feature of later Eastern rites. Pseudo-Dionysius, for example, describes it as an element common to all the orders and interprets it as symbolizing "the sacred communion of like minds and their loving joy toward one another" (*De ecclesiastica hierarchia* 5.2). By then, however, the ritual had apparently been clericalized: the kiss was given to the newly ordained minister by the bishop and all the clergy, and no reference is made to the laity's involvement in the action.

Although no directions are given about the kiss in the ninth-century Armenian text, the closing prayer in each of the rites does make reference to its existence, and describes it as a welcome given by all. Later manuscripts of the rite for the presbyterate, however, while preserving the prayer in this form, direct that the salutation be done only by the bishop and the other priests. [55] In Byzantine practice there was a further development, and participation became restricted to those thought of as effecting the ordination: thus, only the bishops present kiss a newly ordained bishop, and only the presiding bishop kisses a new presbyter or deacon. No mention is made of a kiss in the case of a deaconess or subdeacon in this tradition, but it is recorded in the case of the reader, though here it is differently described, the word "peace" being used.[56] On the other hand, in other traditions the kiss is sometimes described as being given *by* the newly ordained deacon, presbyter, or bishop *to* the other ministers present.

OTHER CONCLUDING CEREMONIES

The only other concluding ceremonial actions in the eighth-century Byzantine rite for a bishop are the bestowal of the *omophorion*, the Eastern equivalent of the Western pallium as a symbol of episcopal office, and his seating in the episcopal chair, the one coming before the kiss and the other after. In the Byzantine rite for a presbyter, the bishop similarly vests the newly ordained with the robes of his office, gives him the kiss, and seats him with his fellow presbyters. The same is true in the case of a deacon, except that instead of his being seated with fellow deacons, he is given the fan

---

[55] See Conybeare, *Rituale Armenorum*, 242.
[56] *ORACEW*, 134, 136–37, 139.

with which to perform his duty of fanning the eucharistic elements on the altar, and after receiving communion himself, he is given the chalice and assists in giving communion to the people.[57] Similar ceremonies conclude the other Eastern rites, and a number of the later texts—the Coptic, East Syrian, Maronite, Melkite, and Syrian Orthodox—include a solemn declaration that the candidate has been duly ordained to the particular order, as well as adding some unique features. Thus, the East Syrian rite includes the presentation of the book of the Epistles to a new deacon, the book of Gospels to a new presbyter, and the pastoral staff to a new bishop. In the Syrian Orthodox rite, both deacon and presbyter receive a thurible, and a bishop the pastoral staff. In the Maronite rite a new presbyter performs several actions that symbolize the liturgical duties of his office—incensing, and carrying the gospel book and then the paten in procession, and a new deacon reads a passage from the Epistles as well as incensing, carrying the Epistle book in procession, and waving the chalice veil. In the Melkite rite a presbyter is given the gospel book and reads John 1:1-3, and is then given the consecrated bread and proclaims the invitation to communion, "Holy things for holy people." A deacon is likewise given the gospel book and reads the same passage before receiving the eucharistic vessels and the fan. The Byzantine rite itself also gives a distinctive function to the new presbyter in the eucharistic consecration that follows the ordination: he holds one of the pieces of bread in his hands throughout the prayer, bowing over the holy table. Like the Melkite custom, this is obviously intended to give symbolic expression to his new role as a participant in eucharistic presidency.[58]

THE CELEBRATION OF THE EUCHARIST

With the sole exception of the East Syrian tradition, which permits ordinations to take place at any time, Eastern rites consistently locate ordinations within a eucharistic celebration, although the Byzantine and Melkite traditions do allow the diaconate to be conferred during the Liturgy of the Presanctified instead, as the diaconal liturgical function can equally be exercised there. However,

[57] Ibid., 134, 136–37.
[58] For later developments of this ceremony, see Tchékan, "Elements d'introduction à l'étude de la liturgie byzantine des ordinations," 204–5.

there are differences with regard to the precise point within the Eucharist at which the ordination is to take place. In the Byzantine rite the ordination of a bishop is located at the very beginning of the Eucharist, and the new bishop is then expected to read the Gospel, preach, and offer the oblation; a presbyter is ordained immediately after the entrance of the gifts, so that he may then fulfill his new liturgical role by participating in the eucharistic action, and a deacon at the end of the eucharistic prayer, so that he may then fulfill the diaconal function of assisting in the distribution of the consecrated elements to the communicants. The same is true of the Coptic rite, except that a deacon is ordained at the same point in the rite as the presbyter.

In the Maronite and Syrian Orthodox traditions, on the other hand, ordination to all the orders is deferred until the eucharistic consecration has been completed, in order that the consecrated bread and wine may be used in conjunction with the imposition of the hand (see above). However, in the case of the Maronite tradition, the oldest manuscripts suggest that the ordinations once came at an earlier point in the liturgy.[59] In the Syrian Orthodox rite a new bishop is directed to receive communion and then assume the presidency of the rite for the remainder of the celebration.

[59] See P. E. Gemayel, *Avant-messe maronite: histoire et structure*, Orientalia Christiana Analecta 174 (Rome: Pontificale Institutum Orientalium Studiorum, 1965), 125–33.

Chapter 6

Ordination Rites in the Medieval West

ROME

The oldest-known text containing the classical Roman ordination prayers is the seventh-century Verona Sacramentary, often also called the Leonine Sacramentary. This has the prayers for bishops, deacons, and presbyters, in that order. Surviving portions of this incomplete manuscript do not contain any provisions for subdeacons or other lesser clerics.[1] The next evidence for these prayers occurs in several eighth-century liturgical books, where it is conflated with ordination material that had been used elsewhere in Western Europe, known as the Gallican rite—the Gelasian Sacramentary, the *Missale Francorum*, and various adaptations of the Gelasian, especially the sacramentaries of Angoulême and Gellone.[2] The several manuscripts of the Gregorian Sacramentary in the ninth century contain a purer Roman text.[3] A later section of this book has brief prayers for instituting a cleric, a deaconess, a "handmaid of God," and an abbot or abbess.

The manner of performing the rites is described in some of the *ordines Romani*, or ceremonial handbooks, of this period, which in some cases include the text of the ordination prayers as well.[4] The

[1] Text in *Sacramentarium Veronense*, ed. L. C. Mohlberg (Rome: Herder, 1956), 118–22, 138–39.

[2] Texts in *Liber sacramentorum Romanae Aeclesiae ordinis anni circuli*, ed. L. C. Mohlberg (Rome: Herder, 1960), 24–28, 120–22; *Missale Francorum*, ed. L. C. Mohlberg (Rome: Herder, 1957), 6–13; *Liber sacramentorum Engolismensis*, ed. Patrick Saint-Roch (Turnhout: Brepols, 1987), 313–25; *Liber sacramentorum Gellonensis*, ed. Antoine Dumas (Turnhout: Brepols, 1981), 381–95.

[3] Text in *Le sacramentaire grégorien*, ed. Jean Deshusses, vol. 1 (Fribourg: Editions universitaires, 1971; 2nd ed., 1979), 92–98.

[4] *Ordines XXXIV–XL*: text in *Les ordines romani du haut moyen âge*, ed. Michel Andrieu, vols. 3–4 (Louvain: Spicilegium Sacrum Lovaniense, 1951, 1956). The most detailed analysis of the Roman ordination rites is to be found in Bruno

oldest of these, *Ordo* XXXIV, apparently dates from the middle of the eighth century. Here, the rites begin with the appointment of acolytes and subdeacons, followed by deacons and presbyters, and finally that of a bishop—a sequence that reflects the understanding of the various offices as forming ascending ranks that had developed by this time.[5] No mention is made in this *ordo* of any liturgical ceremony in connection with the other minor orders that existed at Rome—exorcists, readers,[6] and doorkeepers—perhaps because they were not directly associated with ministerial functions at the altar as now were acolytes and subdeacons. Both these orders could be conferred just before the distribution of communion during any eucharistic celebration, and the rite was extremely simple. It consisted essentially of the delivery of an appropriate symbol of the office accompanied by a short blessing: the acolyte was given the linen bag to hold the consecrated bread at the Eucharist,[7] and the subdeacon received the chalice. This custom goes back at least as far as the sixth century, as it is also described by John the Deacon.[8]

On the basis of these and other sources it is possible to reconstruct the ordination practice at Rome with regard to deacons, presbyters, and bishops at the beginning of the Middle Ages. Letters written by Pope Leo I in the middle of the fifth century indicate that, while he was aware that other churches did not always adhere to the custom of Sunday ordination, it was nevertheless the

---

Kleinheyer, *Die Priesterweihe in römischen Ritus* (Trier: Paulinus Verlag, 1962); but see also Sharon L. McMillan, *Episcopal Ordination and Ecclesial Consensus* (Collegeville, MN: Liturgical Press, 2005) for a close study of portions of the rite for bishops from the eighth to the twentieth century.

[5] English translation in *ORACEW*, 218–21. On orders as ascending ranks, see below, p. 136.

[6] *Ordo* XXXV, originating in France ca. 1000 CE, describes a Roman rite for a reader, but it appears that by this time the office was usually conferred on adolescents whose parents wished them to embark on an ecclesiastical career rather than on those intended primarily to exercise the liturgical function. Its form is similar to that for the other minor orders in the earlier *ordo*, consisting of the testing of the boy's ability to read, followed by a simple blessing by the pope.

[7] See Andrieu, *Les ordines romani* 2:70–71; 3:546, n. 3.

[8] John the Deacon, *Epistula ad Senarium* 10 (*PL* 59:404–5).

practice at Rome.[9] He implies, however, that the ordinations there actually took place on Saturday evening, which was regarded as the beginning of Sunday, in order that the preparatory fasting required of both the ordainers and the ordinands (see Acts 13:3; 14:23) might not be unduly prolonged. From at least the time of Pope Gelasius I (482–96), if not sooner, the ordinations of presbyters and deacons were regularly performed at the Saturday vigil mass of one of the four Ember seasons (the December one being preferred), because these were already regular times of fasting for the Roman church.[10] Although bishops could be ordained at any time of the year, they, too, might be ordained at one of those seasons for the same reason or even at the end of the Lenten fast in the Easter vigil itself, following the baptismal rite![11] Within the eucharistic liturgy, all ordinations took place after the gradual psalm and before the reading of the gospel. Although the reason for this location is nowhere explained, it may have been chosen because the preceding epistle reading at the ordination of a deacon was 1 Timothy 3:8-14 on the qualities required of a deacon and at the ordination of a bishop 1 Timothy 3:1-7 on the qualities required of a bishop; the presbyteral rite perhaps was attracted to the same position because by then men were commonly ordained deacon and then directly presbyter on the same occasion.[12] The sole exception was that of the ordination of the pope himself, which was placed at the very beginning of the Eucharist,[13] presumably so that he might then preside over the whole rite.

---

[9] Leo, *Epistulae* 6.6; 9.1; 10.6 (*PL* 54:620, 625–26, 634).

[10] On the origin of the Ember seasons, see Thomas J. Talley, "The Origin of the Ember Days: An Inconclusive Postscript," in *Rituels: Mélanges offerts à Pierre-Marie Gy, OP*, ed. Paul de Clerck and Eric Palazzo (Paris: Cerf, 1990), 465–72.

[11] See the letter of Pope Pelagius I (555–60) to the Bishop of Grumentum (*PL* 161:472).

[12] The thirteenth-century Pontifical of William Durandus (see below, n. 54), however, has a note that "in some churches" presbyters are ordained after the gospel.

[13] See *Ordo* XL A: Andrieu, *Les ordines romani* 4:297. The prayers of the rite were divided between the bishops of Albano, Porto, and Ostia.

In the case of ordinations to the diaconate and presbyterate, the process itself began earlier in the week with the reading of a document known as a *breve advocationis* by a lector at the stational services on the Wednesday and Friday, and then again apparently by the Pope himself at the beginning of the ordination liturgy. This announced the names of the candidates, the order to which they had been appointed, and the church to which they were assigned; it also invited anyone with an objection to any of the men to declare it. Thus, here it was silence rather than a vocal acclamation that signified the assent of the congregation.

In the case of the episcopate, the candidate was elected in his own diocese before being sent to Rome for ordination by the pope, and hence there was apparently no expression of approval within the rite itself. However, the acclamation of assent, *Dignus*, "Worthy," seems to have been used in ancient times at the election of the bishop of Rome. We noted in chapter 3 that in the account of the appointment of Fabian in 236 CE, the people unanimously cried that he was worthy.[14] While Augustine gives the impression that in fifth-century North Africa a variety of words of acclamation of assent might be used,[15] at the same period Arnobius the Younger implies that in Rome *Dignus et justus*, "Worthy and just," had now become the standard form,[16] possibly as a result of assimilation to the response in the eucharistic dialogue. The same expression is attested for Gaul in the sixth century by Gregory of Tours.[17]

Except in the case of the diaconate, the candidates entered already wearing the robes of the order to which they had been nominated. This is probably a remnant from the older view of ordination as a twofold process: the election as the means by which the candidate was actually appointed to the office and prayers offered for his successful fulfillment of that into which he had already entered. All three rites shared the same basic structure:

A. A bidding inviting the congregation to pray for the ordinands, which indicated that the selection of the candidates was

---

[14] See above, p. 49.
[15] Augustine, *Epistula* 213.
[16] Arnobius the Younger, *Commentarius in Psalmum* 105 (PL 53:485C).
[17] Gregory of Tours, *Historia Francorum* 2.13 (PL 71:212A).

understood to have been God's act. In the case of the diaconate, its form varies somewhat from source to source, but in the Verona Sacramentary it reads:

> Let us pray, dearly beloved, to God, the almighty
> Father, that on these his servants, whom he deems
> worthy to call to the office of deacon, he may mercifully
> pour the benediction of his grace and favorably pre-
> serve the gifts of the consecration bestowed.[18]

The bidding in the case of presbyters seems to imply that what was being sought was an increase in the grace already received by the ordinand:

> Let us pray, dearly beloved, to God the Father almighty
> that upon these his servants, whom he has chosen for
> the office of presbyter, he may multiply heavenly gifts,
> with which what they have begun by his favor they
> may accomplish by his aid; through.[19]

At the ordination of a bishop, however, according to the *ordines*, the pope used a formulary similar to those of the Eastern churches, which announced the name of the elect and invited the congregation to pray for him.

> The clergy and people of the city of N., with the consent
> of the neighboring dioceses, have chosen N., the deacon
> or presbyter, to be consecrated bishop. Therefore let us
> pray for this man, that our God and Lord Jesus Christ
> will bestow on him the episcopal throne to rule over his
> church and all its people.[20]

Because the text of this formulary was not included in the sacramentaries, the later recensions of them provided a simple bidding instead, in order to bring the rite as it was known there into line with those for deacons and presbyters.

---

[18] *ORACEW*, 216. For variant forms, see *Ordo XXXIV.7* and the Gregorian Sacramentary.

[19] *ORACEW*, 217. See Kleinheyer, *Die Priesterweihe*, 59–60.

[20] *Ordo XXXIV.38*; *ORACEW*, 220–21.

B. A litany of intercession, with *Kyrie* response.
C. A collect concluding the prayers of the people. Like the bidding, the one in the rite for deacons underwent a number of changes. The Gelasian Sacramentary and the Sacramentary of Angoulême read:

> Lord God, mercifully hear our prayers, that you may favorably attend with your assistance the things that are to be carried out by our service, and may justify the more by your choice those whom we believe according to our judgment should be offered for the holy ministries about to be sought . . . [21]

In the case of the presbyterate, the collect is much more straightforward:

> Hear us, O God of our salvation, and pour forth the benediction of the Holy Spirit and the power of priestly grace on these your servants, that you may accompany with the unfailing richness of your bounty these whom we present before your merciful countenance to be consecrated . . . [22]

In the case of the episcopate, things are more complicated. In addition to providing appropriate prayer-forms for certain parts of the Eucharist at an episcopal ordination (the Collect, the Secret, and the *Hanc Igitur*), the Roman rite has the peculiar feature of including not just one but two collects prior to the ordination prayer, the reason for which is unknown. Although the first one varies in content in the different liturgical books, the second is consistent: "Be gracious, Lord, to

---

[21] In the Verona Sacramentary this prayer occurs as the collect of the mass and a different and more developed prayer is found in this position, one that Miquel Gros, "Les plus anciennes formules romaines de bénédiction des diacres," *Ecclesia Orans* 5 (1988): 45–52, judged was once the ordination prayer proper, with the current collect having been connected instead with the process of election. In the *Missale Francorum* the collect quoted above is changed to form the conclusion of the bidding and there is no collect at this point, and in the Gregorian Sacramentary a new and briefer collect fills the gap.

[22] ORACEW, 217–18.

our supplications, and with the horn of priestly grace inclined over these your servants pour out upon them the power of your benediction . . . "[23]

D. A substantial ordination prayer, accompanied by the laying on of the presiding bishop's hand.[24] The Roman prayers for all three offices are built around Old Testament cultic imagery. After setting the ordained ministry in a christological and ecclesiological context, the prayer for deacons defines the office by the typology of the Levites, who constituted the third order of ministry in the Old Testament, and asks God to bestow on the ordinands the sevenfold grace of the Holy Spirit, an allusion to Isaiah 11:2, doubtless occasioned by numerical association with the seven "deacons" of Acts 6, even though the latter are not explicitly mentioned in the prayer. The specific functions the deacons are to exercise are not further explained, and the rest of the prayer merely defines the personal qualities required of them and refers to their eventual promotion to "higher things."

> Assist us, we beseech you, almighty God, giver of honors, distributor of orders, and bestower of offices; who, abiding in yourself, make all things new, and order everything by your Word, Power, and Wisdom, Jesus Christ, your Son our Lord—by everlasting providence you prepare and apportion to each particular time what is appropriate—whose body, your Church, you permit to grow and spread, diversified by a variety of heavenly graces and knit together in the distinction of its members, united through the wondrous law of the whole structure for the increase of your temple, establishing the service of sacred office in three ranks of ministers to do duty in your name, the sons of Levi having been chosen first, that by remaining in faithful vigilance over the mystical workings of your house, they might obtain by a perpetual apportionment an inheritance of everlasting blessing.

[23] Ibid., 215.
[24] Although this ritual gesture is not explicitly mentioned in the oldest *ordo* (XXXIV), it does appear in the other *ordines*.

Look favorably also on these your servants, we beseech you, Lord, whom we humbly dedicate to serve in your sanctuaries in the office of deacon. And although indeed being men we are ignorant of divine thought and highest reason, we judge their life as best we can; but things unknown to us do not slip by you, Lord, things hidden do not escape you. You are the witness of sins, you are the discerner of minds, you are able truly to bring heavenly judgment on them or else grant to the unworthy what we ask. Send upon them, Lord, we beseech you, the Holy Spirit, by whom, faithfully accomplishing the work of ministry, they may be strengthened with the gift of your sevenfold grace. May the pattern of every virtue abound in them: discreet authority, unfailing modesty, purity of innocence, and the observance of spiritual discipline. May your commandments be reflected in their conduct, so that by the example of their chastity they may win the imitation of the holy people, and displaying the testimony of a good conscience, may persevere strong and stable in Christ, and by fitting advancements from a lower rank may be worthy through your grace to take up higher things . . .[25]

The prayer for presbyters begins by citing a series of biblical examples in which God instituted subordinate ministries to assist the principal figures in his service: "men of a lesser order and secondary dignity" in relation to the high priests, the seventy elders in relation to Moses (Num 11:16-25), the two sons of Aaron in relation to their father, and finally from the New Testament, teachers in relation to the apostles. It then goes on to ask God to also grant to the ordinands "the office of second dignity," so that they may be assistants to the ordaining bishop, and ends with the petition already encountered in Eastern prayers, that they may ultimately render a good account of their stewardship and obtain their due reward.

Holy Lord, almighty Father, everlasting God, bestower of all the honors and of all the worthy ranks which do you service, you through whom all things make progress,

25 *ORACEW*, 216–17.

through whom everything is made strong, by the ever-extended increase to the benefit of rational nature by a succession arranged in due order; whence the priestly ranks and the offices of the Levites arose and were inaugurated with mystical symbols; so that when you set up high priests to rule over your people, you chose men of a lesser order and secondary dignity to be their companions and to help them in their labor. Likewise in the desert you did spread out the spirit of Moses through the minds of seventy wise men, so that he, using them as helpers among the people, governed with ease countless multitudes. Likewise also you imparted to Eleazar and Ithamar, the sons of Aaron, the richness of their father's plenty, so that the benefit of priests might be sufficient for the salutary sacrifices and the rites of a more frequent worship. And also by your providence, O Lord, to the apostles of your Son you added teachers of the faith as companions, and they filled the whole world with these secondary preachers.

Wherefore on our weakness also, we beseech you, O Lord, bestow these assistants, for we who are so much frailer need so many more. Grant, we beseech you, Father, the dignity of the presbyterate to these your servants. Renew in their inward parts the spirit of holiness. May they obtain and receive from you, O God, the office of second dignity, and by the example of their conduct may they commend a strict way of life. May they be virtuous colleagues of our order. May the pattern of all righteousness show forth in them, so that, rendering a good account of the stewardship entrusted to them, they may obtain the rewards of eternal blessedness . . .[26]

Three things are remarkable about this prayer. First, unlike the majority of other prayers we have studied so far, it is not an expression of the community's aspirations and desires for the ordinands' future ministry to them, spoken on their behalf by the bishop, but rather the articulation of the bishop's own view of their relationship to him, in spite of its being cast in the first person plural: they are to be "assistants to *our* weakness" and "virtuous colleagues of *our order*." Second, its principal focus

[26] Ibid., 218.

is quite obviously on the subordinate nature of the presbyteral role to that of the bishop, almost to the exclusion of all else, which seems to imply that it was composed in a situation in which there was some dispute as to the relationship between the two orders, such as we find in the late fourth century.[27] Third, while the typology of the seventy elders and the teaching function of the presbyterate have already been prominent in other rites we have studied, the dominant use here of cultic imagery to define the presbyteral order is something new, but it is in line with the other prayers of the Roman tradition.

In marked contrast to Eastern prayers, the prayer for bishops is also centered primarily around Old Testament cultic imagery, specifically that of the two ceremonies that constituted the ordination of the high priest—the vesting and anointing. The episcopate, however, is not portrayed as the direct descendant of this office but rather as its spiritual counterpart. After a brief allusion to heavenly worship, Moses appears not as a pattern for the leadership role of the bishop but as the communicator of the divine injunctions concerning liturgical vestments, and Aaron as the type of the high priest who wore the priestly robe. This vestment is understood as symbolic of the adornment of mind and spirit required of a Christian bishop, and God is asked to bestow on the ordinands the personal qualities that correspond to the richness of that outward dress and, in addition, to sanctify them with a spiritual unction corresponding to the oil that was poured on the head of Aaron and flowed over all his body.[28] There is no christological reference anywhere in the prayer, the Holy Spirit receives only a relatively incidental mention, and the only explicit designation

[27] See further Bernard Botte, "Secundi meriti munus," *Questions liturgiques et paroissiales* 21 (1936): 84–88; and on the theology of the prayer as a whole, David N. Power, *Ministers of Christ and His Church* (London: Chapman, 1969), 58–70; Puglisi 1:116–24.

[28] Pierre-Marie Gy, "Ancient Ordination Prayers," *SL* 13 (1979): 86, suggested that, in the light of a homily of Leo the Great (*Sermo* 48.1) and of patristic exegesis in general, this last image was understood allegorically as expressing the benefit which flowed from episcopal ordination over the whole body of the church. On the theology of the prayer as a whole, see Puglisi 1:107–15.

of a specific episcopal function is the petition that God would grant the ordinands a chair (*cathedra*) to rule the church.

> God of all the honors, God of all the worthy ranks, which serve to your glory in hallowed orders; God who in private familiar converse with Moses your servant also made a decree, among the other patterns of heavenly worship, concerning the disposition of priestly vesture; and commanded that Aaron your chosen one should wear a mystical robe during the sacred rites, so that the posterity to come might have an understanding of the meaning of the patterns of the former things, lest the knowledge of your teaching be lost in any age; and as among the ancients the very outward sign of these symbols obtained reverence, also among us there might be a knowledge of them more certain than types and shadows. For the adornment of our mind is as the vesture of that earlier priesthood; and the dignity of robes no longer commends to us the pontifical glory, but the splendor of spirits, since even those very things, which then pleased fleshly vision, depended rather on these truths which in them were to be understood.

> And, therefore, to these your servants, whom you have chosen for the ministry of the high priesthood, we beseech you, O Lord, that you would bestow this grace; that whatsoever it was that those veils signified in radiance of gold, in sparkling of jewels, in variety of diverse workmanship, this may show forth in the conduct and deeds of these men. Complete the fullness of your mystery in your priests, and equipped with all the adornments of glory, hallow them with the dew of heavenly unction. May it flow down, O Lord, richly upon their head; may it run down below the mouth; may it go down to the uttermost parts of the whole body, so that the power of your Spirit may both fill them within and surround them without. May there abound in them constancy of faith, purity of love, sincerity of peace. Grant to them an episcopal throne to rule your Church and entire people. Be their strength; be their might; be their stay. Multiply upon them your blessing and grace, so that fitted by your aid always to obtain your mercy, they may by your grace be devoted to you . . .[29]

[29] *ORACEW*, 215–16.

E. The exchange of a kiss. Like the Eastern rites, the process is concluded with a kiss, and also like Eastern practice, the later pontificals vary as to whether it is to be given *to* the newly ordained *by* the bishop and other ministers or the other way around, but in no case is it also shared with the laypeople. The rite for the diaconate additionally involved a vesting in stole and dalmatic at this point. The celebration of the Eucharist then continued.

THE GALLICAN AND SPANISH (OR MOZARABIC) RITES

In other parts of the West, ordination rites developed in a different way from the Roman practice. The oldest evidence for Gaul is found in a document known as the *Statuta ecclesiae antiqua*, perhaps written by Gennadius of Marseilles ca. 490 CE. It contains a collection of brief directions for the ordination of bishops, presbyters, and deacons, and also provides for the appointment of subdeacons, acolytes, exorcists, readers, doorkeepers, psalmists or cantors, and nuns. Rather than being a faithful reflection of the actual customs of the region at the time of its composition, this collection seems to be more an imagined ideal influenced in part by the material in the *Apostolic Tradition* and other literary sources. Nonetheless, its contents succeeded in finding their way into later liturgical texts and so strongly influenced the form of all medieval ordination rites, including those of Rome itself. For a bishop it enjoins the imposition of the gospel book and a collective laying on of hands by all bishops present, for a presbyter the imposition of hands by the bishop together with the presbyters, and for a deacon the imposition of hands by the bishop alone.

> 90. When a bishop is ordained, let two bishops put the book of the Gospels on his head[30] and hold it, and while one says the blessing over him, let all the rest of the bishops who are present touch his head with their hands.
> 91. When a presbyter is ordained, as the bishop blesses him and holds his hand on his head, let all the presbyters who are present also hold their hands beside the hand of the bishop on his head.

[30] Some manuscripts read "neck."

92. When a deacon is ordained, let only the bishop who blesses him put his hand on his head, since he is consecrated not for the priesthood but for the ministry.[31]

Charles Munier argued that there is no evidence to support the commonly held view that the author derived the ceremony of the imposition of the gospel book from its use in papal ordination practice. Moreover, it seemed unlikely that he would have dared to extend to all bishops something reserved in the West to the bishop of Rome alone. Munier suggested, therefore, that the source was the *Apostolic Constitutions*.[32] In contrast to both this and Roman practice, but in line with other Eastern rites, however, bishops and not deacons hold the book. No mention is made of it being open; consequently, in later Western rites the ceremony was performed with the book closed, except in the case of papal ordination,[33] until the Pontifical of Durandus at the end of the thirteenth century[34] extended to the consecration of all bishops the direction that it was to be opened and laid on the neck and shoulders (*not* head) of the candidate—a practice almost certainly derived from the Byzantine rite. The rest of the above directions, and especially that concerning deacons, closely resemble those in the *Apostolic Tradition*, and thus introduce a collective imposition of hands in the case of bishops and presbyters that was apparently otherwise foreign to this tradition.

Institution to the other offices is effected by the delivery of an appropriate symbol of office (except in the case of the psalmist, who can be appointed merely by the command of a presbyter, without reference to the bishop). This was the common method of appointment to civil office in the culture of the time. Other early Gallican

---

[31] *ORACEW*, 222.

[32] Charles Munier, *Les Statuta ecclesiae antiqua* (Paris: Presses universitaires de France, 1960) 179–80. For the equivalent ceremony in the *Apostolic Constitutions* and Eastern rites, see above, pp. 69–71, 90–91.

[33] See *Ordines* XXXV.64; XL A.5: Andrieu, *Les ordines romani* 4:44, 297; and on papal ordinations in general, Klemens Richter, *Die Ordination des Bischofs von Rom: Eine Untersuchung zur Weiheliturgie*, Liturgiewissenschaftliche Quellen und Forschungen 60 (Münster: Aschendorff, 1976).

[34] See below, n. 54.

evidence reveals no trace of the existence of the offices of acolyte or psalmist in this region, apart from a single inscription concerning an acolyte at Lyons in 517 CE.[35] However, the later Gallican texts provide for the appointment of five minor orders—subdeacons, exorcists, readers, acolytes, and doorkeepers, though the order of precedence varies. A specific prayer is prescribed for each one, and in nearly all instances a preceding bidding as well. In the *Missale Francorum* a delivery of symbols of office is mentioned only in the case of the subdeacon. The other texts, however, incorporate in full the directions of the *Statuta ecclesiae antiqua* for all the orders.[36]

If ritual forms of appointment for the minor orders ever existed in the Spanish tradition—which is certainly questionable—they have been lost, for the only text to have been preserved is that for a subdeacon, although provision is also made for appointing various other ecclesiastical offices not otherwise part of the normal clerical hierarchy, such as a sacristan and an overseer of books and scribes. For the subdeacon, there is both a substantial ordination prayer, which includes an invocation of the Holy Spirit, and also an elaborate delivery of symbols of office.[37]

No purely Gallican text of ordination rites for bishops, presbyters, and deacons is extant, but material deriving from that tradition is found combined with the Roman prayers in the eighth-century *Missale Francorum* and to a slightly lesser extent in the Gelasian Sacramentary and the various recensions of it. The rites all appear to have begun with an allocution to the people, announcing the nomination of the candidate to the office and inviting them to indicate their acceptance of him by shouting, "He is worthy." Interestingly, while the form in the rite for the episcopate continues to imply that the people have an inherent right of election, that for the presbyterate tends to stress the role of counsel and consultation instead and that for the diaconate makes it clear that their

[35] See Munier, *Les Statuta ecclesiae antiqua*, 172.

[36] *ORACEW*, 223–25, 237–39.

[37] *ORACEW*, 231–32. See also Roger E. Reynolds "The Ordination Rite in Medieval Spain: Hispanic, Roman, and Hybrid," in *Santiago, Saint-Denis and Saint Peter: The Reception of the Roman Liturgy in León-Castile in 1080*, ed. Bernard F. Reilly (New York: Fordham University Press, 1985), 131–55.

involvement is not absolutely necessary.[38] The much later Spanish rites have no equivalent texts: presumably they had disappeared when the people's acclamation of assent ceased to be a reality in that tradition.

The allocation was followed by a bidding to pray for the candidates—an extensive solemn form in the case of the episcopate but much briefer forms for the presbyterate and diaconate, which also appear in the Spanish tradition[39]—and then an ordination prayer. What had originally intervened between these two elements is unclear: was it simply silent prayer or had there once been a litany there? There is no trace of a concluding collect, as was the case at Rome.

In the case of the rite for a bishop, no ordination prayer as such has survived, but there is an interpolation, seemingly of Gallican origin, within the Roman prayer. Although this has commonly been regarded as a remnant of the original Gallican formulary, Bruno Kleinheyer argued that another oration only found in some English pontificals is, in fact, the true prayer that once belonged to this collection of texts, a conclusion also endorsed by Paul de Clerck.[40] This occurs first in the so-called Leofric Missal, in a portion of the codex believed to have been written in Lotharingia early in the tenth century. In the latter part of the same century, at Corbie in northern France, it was copied in the Sacramentary of Ratold. Evidently it did not find subsequent favor on the Continent, but it recurs regularly in later English rites. It exhibits some striking parallelism of thought with the prayer in the *Apostolic Tradition*.

---

[38] *ORACEW*, 225, 226, 228. The allocution for a deacon is terminated as if it were a prayer, but originally it must have been intended that the people should cry out, "He is worthy," as in the case of the episcopate and presbyterate. On the contents of those other two texts, see Puglisi 1:130–31, 136.

[39] *ORACEW*, 225, 226–27, 228–29, 232, 234.

[40] Bruno Kleinheyer, "Studien zur nichtromisch-westlichen Ordinationsliturgie. Folge 2: Ein spätantik-altgallisches Ordinationsformular," *Archiv für Liturgiewissenschaft* 23 (1981) 313–66; Paul de Clerck, "La prière gallicane 'Pater sancte' de l'ordination épiscopale," in *Traditio et progressio. Studi liturgici in onore del Prof. Adrien Nocent, OSB*, ed. G. Farnedi, Studia Anselmiana 95 (Rome: Pontificio Ateneo S. Anselmo, 1988): 163–76. On the theology of the prayer as a whole, see Puglisi 1:145–48.

Holy Father, Almighty God, who through our Lord Jesus Christ have from the beginning formed all things and afterwards at the end of time, according to the promise which our patriarch Abraham had received, have also founded the Church with a congregation of holy people, having made decrees through which religion might be orderly ruled with laws given by you; grant that this your servant may be worthy in the services and all the functions faithfully performed, that he may be able to celebrate the mysteries of the sacraments instituted of old. By you may he be consecrated to the high priesthood to which he is elevated. May your blessing be upon him, though the hand be ours. Command, Lord, this man to feed your sheep, and grant that as a diligent shepherd he may be watchful in the care of the flock entrusted to him. May your Holy Spirit be with this man as a bestower of heavenly gifts, so that, as that chosen teacher of the gentiles taught, he may be in justice not wanting, in kindness strong, in hospitality rich; in exhortation may he give heed to readiness, in persecutions to faith, in love to patience, in truth to steadfastness; in heresies and all vices may he know hatred, in strifes may he know nothing; in judgments may he not show favor, and yet grant that he may be favorable. Finally, may he learn from you in abundance all the things which he should teach your people to their health. May he reckon priesthood itself to be a task, not a privilege. May increase of honor come to him, to the encouragement of his merits also, so that through these, just as with us now he is admitted to the priesthood, so with you hereafter he may be admitted to the kingdom . . .[41]

The Gallican texts as a whole describe the orders of ministry in significantly different ways from the Roman formularies. The Gallican allocution to the people at the ordination of a bishop uses the images of shepherd, teacher, and priest for the episcopal office, while the bidding uses the term "high priest" (thus suggesting perhaps that this formulary belongs to a different strand in the evolution of episcopal typology than the allocution to the people), and also stresses the role of ruler and leader, and the interpolation in the Roman prayer, which is almost entirely a pastiche of biblical quotations and allusions, mostly from the New Testament,[42] speaks

---

[41] *ORACEW*, 236.

[42] See Kleinheyer, "Studien zur nichtromisch-westlichen Ordinationsliturgie," 335–38; on the theology of the prayer as a whole, see Puglisi 1:142–45.

of the ministry of preaching, teaching, reconciliation, and the exercise of discipline:

> May their feet, by your aid, be beautiful for bringing good tidings of peace, for bringing your good tidings of good. Give them, Lord, a ministry of reconciliation in word and in deeds and in power of signs and of wonders. May their speech and preaching be not with enticing words of human wisdom, but in demonstration of the Spirit and of power. Grant to them, O Lord, that they may use the keys of the kingdom of heaven for upbuilding, not for destruction, and may not glory in the power which you bestow. Whatsoever they bind on earth, may it be bound also in heaven, and whatsoever they loose on earth, may it be loosed also in heaven. Whose sins they retain, may they be retained; and whose sins they forgive, do you forgive. Whoever blesses them, may he be blessed; and whoever curses them, may he be filled with curses. May they be faithful and wise servants, whom you, Lord, set over your household that they may give them food in due season, in order that they may show forth an entire perfect man. May they be unwearied in watchfulness; may they be fervent in spirit. May they hate pride, love truth, and never be so overcome by faintness or fear as to abandon it. May they not put light for darkness nor darkness for light; may they not say evil is good nor good evil. May they be debtors to the wise and to the unwise, and may they have fruit of the benefit of all.[43]

The prayer for a presbyter asks that the ordinand may be an "elder," and refers both to a teaching ministry and also to his consecration of the body and blood of Christ.

> Author of all sanctification, of whom is true consecration, full benediction: you, Lord, spread forth the hand of your blessing on this your servant N., whom we set apart with the honor of the presbyterate, so that he may show himself to be an elder by the dignity of his acts and the righteousness of his life, taught by these instructions which Paul presented to Titus and Timothy: that meditating on your law day and night, O almighty one, what he reads he may believe, what he believes he may teach, what he teaches he may practice. May he show in himself justice, loyalty, mercy, bravery; may he provide the example, may he demonstrate the exhortation, in order that he may keep the gift of your ministry pure and untainted; and with

[43] *ORACEW*, 229–30.

the consent of your people may he transform the body and blood of your Son by an untainted benediction; and in unbroken love may he reach to a perfect man, to the measure of the stature of the fullness of Christ, in the day of the justice of eternal judgment with a pure conscience, with full faith, full of the Holy Spirit . . .[44]

Neither this prayer nor the Spanish one has an explicit epiclesis on the ordinand, although the other formularies of the rite, which may be less ancient, do mention the gift of the Spirit, and the Spanish prayer similarly views presbyters as the successors of the Old Testament elders, whom it believes were constituted for a ministry in the temple rather than for community leadership. This is the only allusion to the sacramental ministry of the presbyterate, however, since the remainder of the prayer stresses instead the teaching ministry. Both themes recur in the declaration that concludes the rite. It should also be noted that this ordination prayer is addressed, not to God the Father, but to Christ; we have already observed a similar tendency in the Byzantine ordination prayers.[45]

The prayer for a deacon in the Gallican rite uses the typology of Stephen and his companions to define the office, although the bidding also makes reference to the "Levitical blessing." The apostles are spoken of as having acted under the direction of the Holy Spirit in appointing the Seven, but there is no direct invocation of the Holy Spirit on the ordinands themselves, nor is the order set within a christological or ecclesiological context, but there is simply an implicit parallel between the diaconate and the ministry of angels. Ministry at the altar is the only function to receive mention.

Holy Lord, bestower of faith, hope, grace, and increase, who pour forth your good will through all the elements by the ministries of angels constituted everywhere in heaven and earth, vouchsafe also to shed the light of your countenance especially on this your servant N., that enabled by your favor he may grow as a pure minister at the holy altars, and by [your] indulgence [being] more pure, he

[44] Ibid., 227. On the theology of the prayer, see further Power, *Ministers of Christ and His Church*, 73–77; Puglisi 1:138–41.

[45] *ORACEW*, 234. On this rite, see further Michael Carlin, "The Mozarabic Rite of Presbyteral Ordination: A Diachronic Study," *Ecclesia Orans* 18 (2001): 25–40.

may become worthy of the rank of those whom your apostles, at the direction of the Holy Spirit, chose in sevenfold number, with blessed Stephen as their chief and leader, and being equipped with all the virtues required for your service, may find favor; through our Lord Jesus Christ.[46]

The prayer that follows the bidding in the Spanish rite for deacons is to a large extent an adaptation of the Roman prayer. It omits nearly all of the opening of the Roman version, including the Levitical typology, but inserts a reference to the choosing of the Seven by the apostles to be what it describes as "messengers of peace and ministry." The prayer then goes on to define the office still further by use of the images of Joshua attending Moses and of the young Samuel ministering in the temple, thus retaining service at the altar as its principal focus. Although some of these clauses may be of Spanish origin, the prayer as a whole is not the indigenous ordination prayer of this tradition, which Harry Boone Porter suggested was the oration that now follows it. This shorter second prayer uses the typology of both Levi and Stephen, the latter providing a model for the deacon's obligation to teach the Catholic faith and overcome its enemies—a reflection of the long struggle with Arianism with which the Spanish church was greatly preoccupied.[47]

We have no details as to how the early Gallican rite might have ended, but the Spanish rite concluded with the handing over of the gospel book to the new deacon, accompanied by an exhortation that not only referred to his functions of reading the liturgical gospel and ministering at the altar but also stressed the subordination of his office to both the presbyter and the bishop. In contrast to the rite for the presbyterate in this tradition, however, the final rubric speaks of him kissing the bishop rather than of the bishop giving him a kiss. Was this also intended as an expression of his subservience to the bishop?

[46] *ORACEW*, 225–26.

[47] Ibid., 232–33. Harry Boone Porter, *The Ordination Prayers of the Ancient Western Churches*, ACC 49 (London: SPCK, 1967), 59–60. Gy, "Ancient Ordination Prayers," 70, inclined to the less probable view that it had been preserved instead within the rite for an archdeacon.

As was indicated at the beginning of this chapter, by the eighth century the native Gallican texts were no longer being used alone but in combination with the formularies from the Roman tradition, so that, in the case of the diaconate and presbyterate, the Roman bidding, collect, and ordination prayer were followed by the Gallican bidding and ordination prayer. In the case of the episcopate, the Roman material came to dominate rather more: the lengthy Gallican bidding rapidly disappeared (it is preserved only in the *Missale Francorum*, where it is described as a collect!) and, as has already been noted, while some later English pontificals have a complete ordination prayer, rites elsewhere only have a Gallican interpolation within the Roman prayer.

The relevant directions from the *Statuta ecclesiae antiqua* also came to be placed at the head of the collection of formularies for each order in some sacramentaries as a first step in the process of combining rubrics with texts, which would lead, in time, to the emergence of complete pontificals. This had two very significant consequences for later Western practice. First, the purely idiosyncratic proposals of its compiler about a collective imposition of hands on bishops and on presbyters, as well as the imposition of the gospel book on a new bishop, apparently adopted from the *Apostolic Tradition* and the *Apostolic Constitutions* respectively and otherwise unknown in the West (except for the imposition of the gospel book at the ordination of the Pope), came to be adopted as standard practice throughout the West.[48] Second, placing these directions before the text of what was to be spoken in each case seems to have been the cause of the later practice of actually performing the collective imposition of hands in silence at the ordination of bishops and presbyters prior to even the bidding being said,

---

[48] Its influence can already be seen in the tenth-century Gallicanized Roman *Ordo* XXXV, which explains that when the pope himself ordains presbyters, he alone lays on hands, but when other bishops do it, two or three presbyters share in the action. See also John Gibaut, "Amalarius of Metz and the Laying on of Hands in the Ordination of a Deacon," *Harvard Theological Review* 82 (1989), 233–40, for examples of Gallican rites that unusually modify the directions of the *Statuta ecclesiae antiqua* to include presbyters along with the bishop in the imposition of hands on a deacon.

let alone the ordination prayer recited, and thus separating the ritual action from the prayer that it had previously accompanied.

By this period, the Gallican tradition included the custom of anointing the hands of a new presbyter, and soon afterward those of a new bishop also. At first, a new bishop's hands were anointed only if he were being promoted directly from the diaconate; if he were already a presbyter, the anointing that had already been performed at his presbyteral ordination was not repeated.[49] Eventually, in order to distinguish the presbyteral and episcopal anointings, the oil of catechumens was used for the former and chrism for the latter. Furthermore, although the Roman prayer for a bishop had been intended to be understood in a mystical and metaphorical sense, in northern Europe the reference to "the dew of heavenly unction" was taken more literally and was thought to refer to a physical anointing. Hence, since Frankish kings were already being anointed at their coronation, the anointing of the head of a new bishop soon followed, the action being inserted into the very middle of the ordination prayer itself.[50] Some scholars believe the practice of anointing those being ordained to be much older, on the basis of a reference by Gildas, a poet in the last days of Roman Britain, to "a blessing by which the hands of priests and deacons are hallowed." Most, however, take this to be metaphorical rather than literal, and judge the custom to be a new development of the eighth century.[51] Moreover, as the vestments worn by the clergy during the liturgy had now lost their relationship to formal secular dress and had acquired a sacral character, their bestowal on the ordinand was also beginning to be a liturgical act.

Although the details of later ordination rites varied from place to place, this composite pattern crystallized into what has been called the "Romano-Germanic Pontifical of the tenth century," originating

[49] See Michel Andrieu, "L'onction des mains dans le sacre épiscopal," *Revue d'histoire ecclésiastique* 36 (1930): 343–47.

[50] First attested by Hincmar of Rheims in the middle of the ninth century: *Hincmari archiepiscopi Remensis epistula 29 ad Adventium episcopum Metensem* (PL 126:186–88).

[51] See the study by Gerald Ellard, *Ordination Anointings in the Western Church before 1000 A.D.* (Cambridge, MA: Mediaeval Academy of America, 1933).

in the Benedictine monastery of St. Alban at Mainz.[52] The order followed in this book became normal throughout western Christendom, displacing all other local rites. By the eleventh century it was also largely accepted in Rome itself, and was the immediate source of the Roman pontificals of the twelfth and thirteenth centuries,[53] which were widely disseminated in the West. These were eventually superseded by a revised version compiled by William Durandus, Bishop of Mende in the south of France at the end of the thirteenth century.[54]

The fusion of the two traditions, Gallican and Roman, into one composite rite and its subsequent elaboration in the course of the Middle Ages is illustrated by the selected examples of the main features in the accompanying table. Although the order of the manuscripts is chronological, it must be remembered that a particular rite does not necessarily represent the uniform custom of that time period. There was much experimentation and interchange of practice before standardization was achieved in the sixteenth century.

As can be seen, the litany no longer occurs in its original position in the rites for the diaconate and presbyterate, between the Roman bidding and collect, but near the beginning of the rite, so that it need be said only once for both orders. Similarly, in the rites for presbyters and bishops the imposition of hands no longer occurs in conjunction with the ordination prayers, but before any of the formularies are said. It was performed in silence in the older texts of these rites, but this verbal vacuum did not last and it was eventually accompanied by an imperative formula similar to those that by now were said at other actions in the rites.[55] On the other hand, in the rite for the diaconate in the thirteenth-century Roman pontifical and the Pontifical of Durandus, the bishop is explicitly directed to perform the imposition of hands in the middle of the Roman

---

[52] Critical edition in *Le Pontifical romano-germanique du dixième siècle* 1, ed. Cyrille Vogel and Reinhard Else, ST 226 (Vatican City: Biblioteca Apostolica Vaticana, 1963), 20–36, 200–26. For its textual history, see further McMillan, *Episcopal Ordination and Ecclesial Consensus*, 71–99.

[53] See *Le Pontifical romain au Moyen-Âge* 1–2, ed. Michel Andrieu, ST 86–87 (Vatican City: Biblioteca Apostolica Vaticana, 1938–41).

[54] Ibid., 3, ST 88.

[55] For details, see below, pp. 146–47.

ordination prayer just before the words "send the Holy Spirit," and this had probably been the practice in the earlier books as well, even though the rubric about the imposition of hands occurs there before any of the formularies are said.

The later texts also reveal a number of additions to the earlier pattern. Chief among these is the *traditio instrumentorum*—the ceremonial handing over to the newly ordained of objects that symbolized his new office, accompanied by an appropriate impera- tive formula expressing the powers belonging to the order. This custom was derived from the minor orders, where it was already the principal ritual action in the ordination process, and it was also practiced in the conferral of office in civil life. Thus, in addition to the robes of his office, the deacon receives the book of the gospels, the presbyter a paten with bread and a chalice filled with wine and water, and the bishop the pastoral staff, ring, and gospel book.[56] A second imposition of hands on presbyters toward the end of the ordination mass, accompanied by the formula *Accipe Spiritum Sanctum, quorum peccata . . .* (Christ's commission to the apostles in John 20:22-23), originated in certain French churches in the twelfth century and then spread widely through its incorporation into the Pontifical of Durandus. In the thirteenth century, a newly ordained bishop began to concelebrate the ordination mass with his epis- copal colleagues and newly ordained presbyters with the bishop, each one individually saying all the words and performing all the same gestures as the presiding bishop; and the rite for a bishop ended with his seating or enthronement, even when it was not in his own cathedral, marking the final stage in the medieval transi- tion from presiding at the ordination Eucharist in his own cathe- dral to being the recipient of the ministry of the ordaining bishop elsewhere.

[56] The giving of staff and ring to the bishop, symbols of the bestowal of authority in civil life, apparently first began in Spain in the seventh century: see the Fourth Council of Toledo, Canon 28 (633 CE); Isidore of Seville, *De ec- clesiasticis officiis* 2.5.12 (*PL* 83: 783–84); and further Pierre Salmon, *Étude sure les insignes du pontife dans le rit romain: histoire et liturgie* (Rome: Officium Libri Catholici, 1955).

The Evolution of the Composite Rite

	Gelasian Sacramentary	Missale Francorum	Sacramentary of Angoulême	Romano-Germanic Pontifical	Roman Pontifical (13th cent.)	Pontifical of Durandus
Deacon	Presentation		Presentation	Presentation	Presentation	Presentation
	Litany		Litany	Litany	Litany	Litany
		Gallican address	Imposition of hands	Imposition of hands		Admonition to ordinands
				Gallican bidding	Gallican bidding	Gallican bidding
				Blessing of stole		
	Roman bidding	Roman bidding/ collect	Roman bidding	Roman bidding	Roman bidding	Roman bidding
	Roman collect		Roman collect	Roman collect	Roman collect	Roman collect
	Roman ordination prayer	Roman ordination prayer	Roman ordination prayer	Roman ordination prayer	Roman ordination prayer	Roman ordination prayer
				Vesting with stole	Vesting with stole	Vesting with stole
						Vesting in dalmatic
	Gallican bidding	Gallican bidding	Gallican bidding	Giving of gospel book	Giving of gospel book	Giving of gospel book
	Gallican ordination prayer	Gallican ordination prayer	Gallican ordination prayer	Gallican ordination prayer	Gallican ordination prayer	Gallican ordination prayer
				Vesting in dalmatic	Vesting in dalmatic	Another prayer
				Kiss	Kiss	Kiss

129

The Evolution of the Composite Rite—Cont'd

Presbyter

Gelasian Sacramentary	Missale Francorum	Sacramentary of Angoulême	Romano-Germanic Pontifical	Roman Pontifical (13th cent.)	Pontifical of Durandus
			Presentation	Presentation	Presentation
			Gallican address		Gallican address
					Admonition to ordinands
		Imposition of hands	Imposition of hands	Imposition of hands	Imposition of hands
	Gallican address	Gallican address			
Roman bidding	Roman bidding	Roman bidding	Roman bidding	Roman bidding	Roman bidding
Roman collect	Roman collect	Roman collect	Roman collect	Roman collect	Roman collect
Roman ordination prayer	Roman ordination prayer	Roman ordination prayer	Roman ordination prayer	Roman ordination prayer	Roman ordination prayer
Gallican bidding	Gallican bidding	Gallican bidding	Vesting in stole and chasuble	Vesting in stole and chasuble	Vesting in stole and chasuble
Gallican ordination prayer	Gallican ordination prayer	Gallican ordination prayer	Gallican bidding	*Veni Creator Spiritus*	Gallican ordination prayer
		Vesting in chasuble	Gallican ordination prayer	Gallican ordination prayer	*Veni Creator Spiritus*
	Anointing of hands	Anointing of hands	Anointing of hands	Anointing of hands	Anointing of hands
			Giving of paten and chalice	Giving of paten and chalice	Giving of chalice and paten
					Second imposition of hands
			Blessing; Kiss	Blessing; Kiss	Kiss; Instruction; Blessing

Bishop

1	2	3	4	5	6
			First Roman collect		Presentation
			Examination	Examination	Examination
			Vesting	First Roman collect	Vesting
			Gallican address	Vesting	First Roman collect
		Imposition of gospel book	Short bidding	Short bidding	Short bidding
		Imposition of hands	Litany	Litany	Litany
	Gallican address	Gallican address	Imposition of gospel book	Imposition of gospel book	Imposition of gospel book
Short bidding	Gallican bidding	Short bidding	Imposition of hands	Imposition of hands	Imposition of hands
Two Roman collects	Two Roman collects	Two Roman collects	Two Roman collects	Second Roman collect	Second Roman collect
Composite ordination prayer	Composite ordination prayer	Composite ordination prayer	Composite ordination prayer with anointing of head	Composite ordination prayer with anointing of head	Composite ordination prayer with anointing of head and *Veni Sancte Spiritus*
		Anointing of hands	Anointing of hands	Anointing of hands	Anointing of hands
			Giving of pastoral staff	Giving of pastoral staff	Giving of pastoral staff
			Giving of ring	Giving of ring	Giving of ring
				Giving of gospel book	Giving of gospel book
			Kiss	Kiss	Kiss; Giving of miter and gloves

Chapter 7

The Theology of Ordination in the Middle Ages

By the early Middle Ages the nature of the ordained ministry had changed dramatically from the situation in the first few centuries of the church's history. Ordinands were no longer leading Christians whom the local community had chosen from among its number to exercise the ministry of leadership there, but rather men who had embarked on ecclesiastical careers, who had generally served some form of apprenticeship in the lower orders and had been chosen for advancement to higher office by ecclesiastical or civil superiors. Before the Middle Ages were over the understanding of the nature of ordination would undergo further significant changes.

NOMINATION AND ELECTION

The notion of election by the whole Christian community continued to be maintained in the West, although as time went by secular rulers played an increasingly influential part in the choice of candidates for the episcopate and the people were expected simply to consent to their nominations. The same was often true of the appointment of presbyters to individual churches, which had the double consequence of weakening the authority of the bishop over the presbyterate and of diminishing the sense of the presbyterate as a corporate body.[1] Secular influence on episcopal nominations in particular did not please the ecclesiastical authorities, who viewed it as outside interference in their realm of authority, and by the eleventh century, reforms were put in process to exclude the civil rulers and limit the electorate to the cathedral chapter of

---

[1] For some account of these developments, see for example Kenan B. Osborne, *Priesthood: A History of the Ordained Ministry in the Roman Catholic Church* (New York: Paulist Press, 1988), 169–78.

the diocese concerned.[2] Yet, whatever the theoretical rights of others, by the thirteenth century, bishops were de facto nominated by the pope, although it was only in the 1917 Code of Canon Law of the Roman Catholic Church that this nomination was officially reserved to the Holy See.

CELIBACY

In the patristic period it had been the expectation that those who had been unmarried when they were ordained should remain celibate thereafter and married clergy whose wife died should not remarry. Periodically, attempts were made to go further and mandate that married clergy should also live celibate lives, but with limited success. Thus, the Spanish Council of Elvira in 305 decreed that "bishops, priests, deacons, and all clerics engaged in the ministry are forbidden entirely to cohabit with their wives and to beget children: whoever shall do so will be deposed from the clerical office."[3] On the other hand, when a similar rule was proposed in the East at the Council of Nicaea, it was opposed by Paphnutius, the respected bishop of one of the cities in Upper Thebes and himself unmarried, and the Council simply left it to married clergy to exercise abstinence if they wished.[4]

Thereafter in Eastern Christianity a distinction began to be made between bishops and other clergy over this matter. The Emperor Justinian's Code of Civil Law in the sixth century forbade anyone who had children or even nephews to be consecrated as a bishop, and the Council of Trullo (692) in canons 12 and 13 also mandated that a bishop be celibate, and if married, should separate from his wife after his consecration. Presbyters, deacons, and subdeacons, on the other hand, continued to be forbidden to marry after ordina-

---

[2] On the conduct of elections, see canons 23–25 of the Fourth Lateran Council; and on lay investiture in general, Robert Benson, *The Bishop-Elect: A Study in Medieval Ecclesiastical Office* (Princeton: Princeton University Press, 1968); Uta-Renate Blumenthal, *The Investiture Controversy: Church and Monarchy from the Ninth to the Twelfth Century* (Philadelphia: University of Philadelphia Press, 1988).

[3] Canon 33; but it is possible that this particular canon may belong to a somewhat later council.

[4] Socrates, *Historia ecclesiastica* 1.11.

tion, but if they were already married beforehand were permitted to engage in sexual intercourse with their wives, except at times they were required to minister at the altar.

In the West, by contrast, several early popes decreed celibacy for all clergy, and various regional councils issued similar edicts. By the time of Pope Leo I (d. 461), in theory no bishop, presbyter, deacon, or subdeacon could be married, although in practice this was not firmly enforced, and it was not until the eleventh and twelfth centuries that the discipline began to be effectively established. Pope Gregory VII published an encyclical in 1074 dispensing the people from their obedience to bishops who allowed married priests and in the following year forbade married priests or those who had concubines from saying mass or performing other ecclesiastical functions; canon 3 of the First Lateran Council (1123) mandated celibacy for all clergy; and canons 6 and 7 of the Second Lateran Council (1139) reiterated this, depriving all married clergy of their offices and in addition declaring all marriages of clergy to be invalid.[5]

Along with the urging of celibacy went other developments that marked out clergy from laity. Two early elements of this, both found from the beginning of the fifth century, were the adoption of special clerical dress, even outside the liturgy, and of the tonsure. With regard to the former, it might be truer to say that the clergy simply failed to keep up with changing fashions and their dress became distinctive by default. The latter was originally a haircut that was characteristic of monks that then seems to have been required of clergy as well. It soon acquired a liturgical rite for its imposition.

THE *CURSUS HONORUM*

We have seen that as early as the writings of Cyprian individuals might advance from one ecclesiastical office to another and not always remain for the rest of their life in the order to which they had originally been admitted. This facilitated a period of testing and training in one office before undertaking a more demanding min-

---

[5] Reference to most of the relevant primary sources for the early history of celibacy can be found in Christian Cochini, *The Apostolic Origins of Priestly Celibacy* (San Francisco: Ignatius Press, 1990), even if his argumentation is not always to be accepted.

istry in another. But such a probationary period was not absolutely essential, and it was possible, if unusual, for someone to be ordained directly as a presbyter or a bishop without first having been admitted to any other office. Gradually, however, various councils tried to ensure at least some prior experience in one or more of the minor orders before someone was ordained to what came to be called the holy or sacred orders of deacon, presbyter, or bishop. Rather than being seen as quite different kinds of ministries, the various offices were arranged in what was regarded as an ascending series of steps up a single ladder, known as the *cursus honorum*, a term and concept borrowed from civil and military use, and it was increasingly expected that ordinands would experience each of these in succession as they progressed in their career. However, at first this was neither universal nor uniform: the precise sequence was not yet standardized, some steps in it could be omitted, and direct ordinations to one of the sacred orders could still happen. Furthermore, there are signs that as early as the fifth century the time spent in each order was sometimes being shortened so that, for example, someone could pass through each of the grades from reader to presbyter within a single year, and by the mid-sixth century there are instances of someone passing through them all in a single day.[6] Treading on each step, however briefly, was beginning to be valued more than spending time on each and gaining experience. It was not until the eleventh century, however, that a uniform sequence of orders became agreed and sequential ordination through every one of the grades became invariable, although occasional protests were made against conferring them all in one day.[7]

THE NUMBER OF ORDERS

Within the Western liturgical books the rites of ordination were not usually clearly segregated from rites of admission to a whole variety of other offices, such as, for example, librarians and arch-

---

[6] For examples, see Pope Gelasius I (d. 495), *Epistula* 14.2; Pope Pelagius I (d. 561), *Epistula* 5.

[7] For further details of this development, see John St H. Gibaut, *The Cursus Honorum: A Study of the Origins and Evolution of Sequential Ordination* (New York: Lang, 2000).

deacons. This obviously gave rise to the question as to how many of them were actually ecclesiastical orders as such, which became a subject of much debate during the Middle Ages. Although many theologians recognized that minor orders had not existed separately in New Testament times, some understood them to have been contained implicitly within the diaconate[8] and all regarded their eventual development as part of God's providence. But exactly how many were there? From the fifth through sixteenth centuries in both East and West there existed a large number of short texts known as "the Ordinals of Christ" that listed each of the ecclesiastical orders (accepted as such by their authors) linked to some event in the life of Christ in which he was thought to have exercised that particular ministry and thereby foreshadowed and sanctioned that office. For example, he was said to have been an exorcist when he cast out demons from Mary Magdalene.[9] These reveal considerable variation in the particular offices chosen for inclusion and in the relative ranking given to them. From the seventh century onward there is evident a natural tendency to opt for the sacred number of seven, which came to be said to correspond to the seven gifts of the Spirit, but some spoke of eight or even nine, including such offices as cantors and grave diggers among the clergy.[10]

Perhaps rather surprisingly, the acolyte tended to be a late addition to the list of dominically sanctioned orders (even though the office itself was very ancient), becoming standard only in the late eleventh and early twelfth centuries. Among those committed to maintaining the number seven this added to the pressure to treat presbyters and bishops as belonging to the same order, about which more will be said later in this chapter. Some theologians, including the influential figures of Hugh of St Victor (1096–1141)

---

[8] See, for example, Thomas Aquinas, *Summa Theologiae* IIIa, q. 37, a. 2, ad. 2.

[9] For further details, see Roger E. Reynolds, *The Ordinals of Christ from Their Origins to the Twelfth Century*, Beiträge zur Geschichte und Quellenkunde des Mittelalters 7 (New York: de Gruyter, 1978).

[10] See Roger E. Reynolds, "'At Sixes and Sevens'—and Eights and Nines: The Sacred Mathematics of Sacred Orders in the Early Middle Ages," *Speculum* 54 (1979): 669–84.

and Peter Lombard (ca. 1096–1161),[11] dealt with the multiplicity of ecclesiastical ranks by distinguishing between an order as such and a "degree" or "dignity" within an order (e.g., an archdeacon), and this became standard in later medieval theology.

There was further variation with regard to the status of subdeacons in the early Middle Ages, some regarding them as one of the minor orders, others as one of the sacred orders, especially as some conciliar decrees applied the obligation of celibacy equally to them. It was only toward the end of the twelfth century that the subdiaconate came to be definitively treated as one of the sacred orders,[12] but although the rite for appointment to the office did subsequently acquire some of the features of the other sacred orders, especially the use of the litany, it never incorporated an imposition of hands as had the equivalent rites in the East.

THE NECESSITY OF A "TITLE"

It was a fundamental principle of early Christianity that no one could be ordained to any ecclesiastical office without an attachment to a specific ministerial vacancy. For example, a man could not simply be a bishop; he had to be bishop of a particular diocese. A presbyter had to have a designated ministry to exercise in a particular Christian community. There was even reluctance at first to permit someone to move from ministry in one place to another. This attachment was later called a "title," and ordinations without a title, "absolute" ordinations, were prohibited. The Council of Chalcedon (451) in its sixth canon declared such ordinations to be null.

Absolute ordinations have continued to be prohibited in the East, and similarly in the West it remained necessary for many centuries to have a title to a particular church before one could be ordained. However, at the Third Lateran Council (1179), canon 5 revealed a new interpretation being applied to that term: if a bishop ordained someone without a title "from which he may draw the necessities of life," the bishop himself was to provide his financial support

---

[11] Hugh of St Victor, *De sacramentis* 2.3.5 (PL 176: 423); Peter Lombard, *Sententiae* 4.24.14–15.

[12] See the extensive study by Roger E. Reynolds, "The Subdiaconate as a Sacred and Superior Order," in idem, *Clerics in the Early Middle Ages: Hierarchy and Image* (Brookfield VT: Ashgate, 1999), iv.

unless the person concerned could support himself or rely on his family. Similarly, a few years later, in 1198, Pope Innocent III wrote in a letter to the Bishop of Zamora: "Although our predecessors have decided the ordinations of those who were to be promoted without a specific title, to the detriment of those being ordained, to be null and void, we, however, desiring to act with kindness, wish only that support be provided to the ordained by the ordainers or their successors, until they obtain ecclesiastical benefices through them, lest we seem to neglect with a stony face the cries of poor clerics which we believe enter the ears of the Lord of Hosts." Thus, the title was now understood merely as supplying a source of financial support and no longer a specific context for the exercise of ministry as an essential prerequisite for ordination. In the future, the ritual act of ordination alone, outside of any ecclesial context, would be deemed in the West sufficient for its validity.[13] This came about because of the adoption of the concept of an "indelible character."

INDELIBLE CHARACTER

Although right from the early days appointment to office had been expected to be permanent (see for instance *1 Clement*), this permanence was not understood to preclude the possibility of someone being deposed for good reason, nor for many centuries did it prevent some bishops from deciding that clergy who had joined heretical and schismatic sects needed reordination if they returned to the Catholic Church and even that ordinations carried out by bishops thought to have heretical views should be regarded as invalid. Moreover, the opposition frequently mounted to clergy being allowed to return to the lay life offers a sure sign that this was happening in practice.[14]

All this was set to change in the late twelfth century, however, as a result of the appropriation by theologians of the period of Augustine of Hippo's understanding of ordination, which had all but been ignored in the intervening centuries. Although in his

[13] For the earlier history, see further Cyrille Vogel, *Ordinations inconsistantes et charactère inamissable* (Turin: Bottega d'Erasmo, 1978), especially 133–162.
[14] See Vogel, "*Laïca communione contentus*: Le retour du presbytre au rang des laics," in idem, *Ordinations inconsistantes et charactère inamissable*, 1–67.

controversy with the Donatists Augustine had been primarily concerned about the question of the permanence of baptism in heretical and schismatic groups, he had also referred to ordination in this connection:

> For the sacrament of baptism is what the person possesses who is baptized; and the sacrament of conferring baptism is what he possesses who is ordained. And as the baptized person, if he depart from the unity of the Church, does not thereby lose the sacrament of baptism, so also he who is ordained, if he depart from the unity of the Church, does not lose the sacrament of conferring baptism. For neither sacrament may be wronged. If a sacrament necessarily becomes void in the case of the wicked, both must become void; if it remain valid with the wicked, this must be so with both. If, therefore, the baptism be acknowledged which he could not lose who severed himself from the unity of the Church, that baptism must also be acknowledged which was administered by one who by his secession had not lost the sacrament of conferring baptism. For as those who return to the Church, if they had been baptized before their secession, are not rebaptized, so those who return, having been ordained before their secession, are certainly not ordained again; but either they again exercise their former ministry, if the interests of the Church require it, or if they do not exercise it, at any rate they retain the sacrament of their ordination; and hence it is, that when hands are laid on them, to mark their reconciliation, they are not ranked with the laity.[15]

Elsewhere Augustine had used the expression *character dominicus* of the permanent effect of baptism (see *Epistula* 98.5), and the scholastic theologians extended this idea to ordination as well, arguing that it, too, conferred a "character" on the recipient. In the thirteenth century Thomas Aquinas defined the character bestowed through the sacraments as a "spiritual power" (*spiritualis potestas*) pertaining to the worship of God that was "indelible," outlasting even death. In the particular case of ordination that power related to the dispensing of the sacraments, was possessed by all the orders, including the minor ones, and so indelible that even if a priest were returned to the laity, the character of ordination still

---

[15] Augustine, *De baptismo contra Donatistas* 1.2; English translation from NPNF 4:412. See also his *Contra Epistulam Parmeniani* 2.13.28; *De bono conjugali* 24.32.

remained.[16] This view—that ordination imprinted an indelible character on the soul—was included by the Council of Florence in 1439 in its Decree for the Armenians.[17]

PRIESTHOOD AND EPISCOPATE

We saw in an earlier chapter that the idea of the ordained ministry as in some way constituting a priesthood seems to have first arisen in the third century, with the bishop being given the title of "priest" or of "high priest" and presbyters regarded as sharing in a lesser way in his priesthood. This persisted in later centuries, but gradually the term "priest" began to be applied unequivocally to presbyters, because they, rather than the bishop, were seen as the normal eucharistic presidents. Bishops came to be commonly described as the successors of Aaron as high priest, and presbyters as the successors of the sons of Aaron as priests. This priesthood was at first understood in a broader sense to include various ministerial activities. We saw in the patristic period how Chrysostom viewed his presbyteral priesthood as fulfilled in preaching, and something similar was also true of some Western theologians in the early Middle Ages. Rabanus Maurus (ca. 780–856), for example, included baptizing and preaching along with confecting Christ's body and blood as expressions of priesthood.[18]

However, the emergence from the ninth century onward of an increase in the frequency of eucharistic celebrations offered for particular needs or purposes—the "votive mass," usually without other people being present, a "private mass"[19]—affected the understanding of priesthood, not just in making the Eucharist even more central to the presbyter's life, but changing his role from that of president of a eucharistic community to that of an individual

---

[16] Thomas Aquinas, *Summa* III, q. 63, a. 1–2, 5; q. 50, a. 4, ad. 3; IIIa, q. 35, a. 2. See David N. Power, *Ministers of Christ and His Church* (London: Chapman, 1969), 121.

[17] Text in Heinrich Denzinger–Adolfus Schönmetzer, *Enchiridion Symbolorum*, 32nd ed. (Freiburg: Herder, 1963), no. 1313.

[18] Rabanus Maurus, *De clericorum institutione* 1.6 (*PL* 107:302); for other examples, see Power, *Ministers of Christ and His Church*, 101–3.

[19] See David N. Power, *The Eucharistic Mystery: Revitalizing the Tradition* (Dublin: Gill & Macmillan, 1992), 164–71, 226–30, 248–49.

personally empowered to act on behalf of the people. It was inevitable, therefore, that priesthood came in time to be seen by most theologians exclusively in terms of its principal power, which was shared equally by bishops and presbyters, that of offering the eucharistic sacrifice, the *potestas in corpus eucharisticum*, with its other functions receding into the background. On the other hand, some later medieval theologians did acknowledge the importance of the secondary power of remitting and retaining of sins in the sacrament of penance,[20] which although earlier had been exercised by bishops, in the course of the Middle Ages came to be the regular responsibility of presbyters. Thus, Aquinas believed that Christ gave the apostles the principal power of priesthood at the Last Supper and its secondary power in his appearance to them after the resurrection (*Summa* IIIa, q. 37, a. 5, ad 2).

We saw in the previous chapter how the medieval ordination rites increasingly gave liturgical expression to this narrower understanding of priesthood. In the eighth century the rite for presbyters, and later that for bishops, began to include the consecration of the ordinand's hands by an anointing with oil, in the tenth century the climax of the ordination of presbyters became the handing over of a paten and chalice containing bread and wine for the Eucharist, and from the twelfth century onward a second imposition of hands accompanied by the formula *Accipe Spiritum Sanctum, quorum remiseris peccata* . . . (Christ's commission to the apostles in John 20:22-23), began to be added in many pontificals at the end of the ordination mass in that rite, in order to give specific expression to the bestowal of the secondary power of the remission of sins. Indeed, in the Pontifical of Durandus the chasuble, which had been bestowed earlier in the rite, had only been resting on the new priest's shoulders until that point but was then unrolled completely so as to indicate the completion of the priestly powers, a ceremony that was continued in the later pontificals.

If, however, the fullness of the priesthood and its powers were shared by presbyters and bishops alike, how were the two offices

---

[20] Among them, Duns Scotus (ca. 1265–1308), *Commentaria in sententias* 4.24.1. See Roger E. Reynolds, "Patristic 'Presbyterianism' in the Early Medieval Theology of Sacred Orders," *Mediaeval Studies* 45 (1983), 311–42.

related to one another? This was a question not raised in the East where priesthood was not viewed so narrowly and the bishop was still understood as being the central priestly figure. In the West, by contrast, the high priesthood ascribed to the bishop began to be interpreted in the eleventh century more in terms of his being a "super-priest," having additionally the power of rule or government in the church, the *potestas in corpus mysticum*, and some concluded that bishops had not been distinct from priests in New Testament times.

Thus, although throughout the early Middle Ages some theologians had continued to maintain the opinion articulated by Jerome and Ambrosiaster in the West in the fourth century about the essential equality of presbyters and bishops, there was a wider revival of this belief from the eleventh century onward, resulting not only from the new exclusive emphasis on the sacrament of the altar but, as we have seen earlier, from a commonly held belief that there could be no more than seven orders. While most canon lawyers held the view that episcopacy was a distinct order from the presbyterate, most—though it needs to be noted not all—later medieval theologians concluded that it was only a *dignitas* or a degree within the same order, and hence tended to speak of bishops being "consecrated" rather than "ordained."[21] This was a trend also evidenced in later medieval pontificals themselves, and where significantly the rite for a bishop was often not located together with the rites for the other orders but rather with the coronation of kings and emperors.

Aquinas adopted a rather more subtle position. Although in one place he clearly denies that the episcopate is an order (*Summa* IIIa, q. 37. a. 2), elsewhere he qualifies that opinion:

> Order may be understood in two ways. In one way as a sacrament, and thus, as already stated, every order is directed to the sacrament

---

[21] See Augustine McDevitt, "The Episcopate as an Order and Sacrament on the Eve of the High Scholastic Period," *Franciscan Studies* 20 (1960): 96–148; Seamus Ryan, "Episcopal Consecration: The Legacy of the Schoolmen," *Irish Theological Quarterly* 33 (1966): 3–38; R. P. Stenger, "The Episcopacy as an Ordo according to the Medieval Canonists," *Mediaeval Studies* 29 (1967): 67–112; Power, *Ministers of Christ and His Church*, 103–5, 115–19.

of the Eucharist. Wherefore since the bishop has not a higher power
than the priest, in this respect the episcopate is not an order. In another way order may be considered as an office in relation to certain
sacred actions: and thus since in hierarchical actions a bishop has
in relation to the mystical body a higher power than the priest, the
episcopate is an order. (*Summa* IIIa, q. 40, a. 5)

In other words, in relation to what was seen as the principal power
of priesthood, consecrating the body of Christ, bishops and presbyters were equal, but in relation to its secondary power in relation
to certain actions, bishops were superior to presbyters (see *Summa*
IIIa, q. 40, a. 4). This secondary power, although indelible, was not
a character, however, "because a man is not thereby placed in direct relation to God but to Christ's mystical body" (*Summa* IIIa, q.
38, a. 2, ad. 2).[22]

The distinction between an order and a dignity or rank within
an order proved insufficiently precise for the canon lawyers of the
twelfth and thirteenth centuries, however, who instead began to
distinguish between the spiritual power resulting from ordination itself (*potestas ordinis*) and the power to exercise ecclesiastical
jurisdiction (*potestas jurisdictionis*), a distinction that in the long
run created more problems than it sought to solve. The former
was permanent because of the indelible character bestowed in ordination, but the latter could be delegated, withheld, restricted, or
withdrawn by competent ecclesiastical authority. The consequence
of this separation of the two aspects meant that a presbyter had
power to celebrate the Eucharist by virtue of his ordination but required a mandate from the bishop in order to exercise that power.
Similarly, it was possible for someone to be a titular bishop, possessing the power of orders without actual jurisdiction in the place
of which he was nominally the bishop. Moreover, it was thought
that the bishop could even permit some of his own functions (including ordaining and confirming) to be exercised by presbyters,

---

[22] See further George Dolan, *The Distinction between the Episcopate and the
Presbyterate according to the Thomistic Opinion* (Washington, DC: Catholic University of America Press, 1950). All quotations from Aquinas are from the
translation of the *Summa* made by the Fathers of the English Dominican Province, 2nd ed. (London: Burns, Oates and Washbourne, 1920–25).

and instances are known of popes delegating to abbots of religious communities (themselves only presbyters) the right to ordain members of the community to the sacred orders.[23] Thus, not only could there be order without jurisdiction, there could be jurisdiction without order. There was disagreement, however, as to whether the episcopal power of jurisdiction derived from papal appointment or directly from God.

THE MATTER AND FORM OF THE SACRAMENT OF ORDERS

Up to the twelfth century, the term *sacramentum* was used in a quite broad sense to include many different sacred signs and symbols, and ordination did not always figure in the lists of these compiled by theologians. From the twelfth century onward, however, Peter Lombard's enumeration of just seven sacraments became generally accepted. He included among them ordination, which he defined as "a certain sign/seal (*signaculum*), that is, something sacred, by which a spiritual power and office is conferred on the one ordained" (*Sententiae* 4.24.13). By *signaculum*, a term with Augustinian roots, he meant the outward action of ordination, with which Aquinas later concurred, but Aquinas went beyond Lombard in equating the spiritual power with the "character" that he believed was imprinted in ordination discussed above (*Summa* IIIa, q. 34, a. 2).

We saw in the previous chapter how in the course of the medieval period the rites of ordination became complex and their central features obscured by numerous secondary accretions. Under the influence of the feudal system of the contemporary world around, theological interpretation of ordination became focused on it being the conferral of specific powers on an individual and not on service to a particular ecclesial community, and so many of the secondary accretions followed the ritual pattern of feudal appointments, the handing over of objects that symbolized the new office accompanied by imperative formulas expressing bestowal of the related powers, known as the *traditio instrumentorum*, a process

---

[23] Texts in Denzinger–Schönmetzer, *Enchiridion Symbolorum*, nos. 1145, 1146, 1290, 1435. See also L. N. Crumb, "Presbyteral Ordination and the See of Rome," *Church Quarterly Review* 164 (1963): 19–31; Stenger, "The Episcopacy as an Ordo according to the Medieval Canonists," 103–9.

that had begun with the minor orders and then spread to them all. (Similarly, the promise of obedience to their superiors made by both priests and bishops in their ordination from the Romano-Germanic Pontifical onward seems to derive from feudal practice.[24])

Thus, deacons received the book of the gospels with the words, "Receive the power of reading the gospel in the church of God both for the living and for the departed" (a formula obviously influenced by the following one for presbyters); presbyters received the paten and chalice containing bread and wine respectively and accompanied by the words *Accipe potestatem offerre sacrificium Deo missasque celebrare tam pro vivis quam pro defunctis* ("Receive the power to offer sacrifice to God and to celebrate mass both for the living and for the departed"); and as noted above already, a second imposition of hands also tended to be introduced near the end of the rite, accompanied by the formula *Accipe Spiritum Sanctum, quorum remiseris peccata . . .* (Christ's commission to the apostles in John 20:22-23). Bishops received the pastoral staff, ring, and gospel book. At the delivery of the pastoral staff the words were: "Receive the staff of the pastoral office, and may you be dutifully firm in correcting faults, making judgment without anger, softening the souls of those who hear in fostering virtues, not abandoning the censure of severity in tranquility"; those at the delivery of the ring: "Receive the ring, a sign of sure faith, so that adorned with pure faith, you may keep inviolate the spouse of God, namely the holy church"; and at the delivery of the gospel book: "Receive the Gospel, and go, preach to the people entrusted to you, for God is able to increase his grace in you."

This development also affected the primary ritual gesture of the rites, the imposition of hands, which had previously been performed in silence. In the thirteenth-century Pontifical of Durandus, the words "Receive the Holy Spirit for strength and to resist the devil and his temptations" are added to the action in the rite for deacons, even though it is performed immediately prior to the petition "send the Holy Spirit" in the middle of the Roman ordination prayer. While in the case of the rite for presbyters the first

---

[24] For a detailed account, see Leon F. Strieder, *The Promise of Obedience: A Ritual History* (Collegeville, MN: Liturgical Press, 2001).

imposition of hands continued to be done in silence (although the second imposition of hands has the John 20:22-23 quotation, "Receive the Holy Spirit . . ."), in the rite for bishops the shorter formula, "Receive the Holy Spirit," was said by all the bishops as they laid hands on the candidate.

This complexity of ritual actions and imperative formulae caused confusion to theologians in their attempts to define what constituted the principal elements of the sacrament. Some believed that the essential ritual action and the words that effected the ordination—its *matter* and *form* in scholastic terminology—had been instituted by Christ himself, but others thought that the church had been left to determine what they should be. While some argued that the imposition of hands must be essential because it went back to apostolic times, many others took the view that the *traditio instrumentorum* and its accompanying formula were the indispensable elements because they more clearly signified the transmission of power, with the imposition of hands merely a preparatory act for this. With regard to ordination to the presbyterate, some understood there to be a twofold action, corresponding to the twofold power of priesthood—the delivery of the paten and chalice conveying the power to celebrate the Eucharist and the final imposition of hands (that had only recently been added to the rite!) conveying the power to forgive sins—while still others thought that the priestly anointing must constitute at least part of what was vital.[25]

Thus, with regard to the essential "form" of ordination in general, Aquinas asserted: "This sacrament consists chiefly in the power conferred. Now power is conferred by power, as like proceeds from like; and again power is made known by its use, since powers are manifested by their acts. Wherefore in the form of order the use of order is expressed by the act which is commanded; and the conferring of power is expressed by employing the imperative mood" (*Summa* IIIa, q. 34, a. 4). On ordination to the presbyterate in particular, he specified the giving of the chalice (presumably a shorthand expression for "chalice and paten," as that was the

---

[25] For a convenient summary in English of the diversity of views, see E. C. Messenger, *The Reformation, the Mass and the Priesthood* 1 (London: Longmans, Green & Co., 1936), 80–94; for more detailed references, *Dictionnaire de théologie catholique* 11:1322–30.

typical sequence rather than the earlier "paten and chalice") as forming the essential act, dismissing the prayers, imposition of hands, and anointing as simply preparation for it:

> The principal act of the priest's Order is to consecrate Christ's body. Now he receives the power to this effect at the handing of the chalice. Therefore the character is imprinted on him then. . . . The bishop in conferring orders does two things; for he prepares the candidates for the reception of orders, and delivers to them the power of order. He prepares them, both by instructing them in their respective offices and by doing something to them, so that they may be adapted to receive the power. This preparation consists of three things, namely blessing, imposition of hands, and anointing. By the blessing they are enlisted in the Divine service, wherefore the blessing is given to all. By the imposition of hands the fullness of grace is given, whereby they are qualified for exalted duties, wherefore only deacons and priests receive the imposition of hands, because they are competent to dispense the sacraments, although the latter as principal dispensers, the former as ministers. But by the anointing they are consecrated for the purpose of handling the sacrament, wherefore the anointing is done to the priests alone who touch the body of Christ with their own hands; even as a chalice is anointed because it holds the blood, and the paten because it holds the body.
>
> The conferring of power is effected by giving them something pertaining to their proper act. And since the principal act of a priest is to consecrate the body and blood of Christ, the priestly character is imprinted at the very giving of the chalice under the prescribed form of words. (*Summa* IIIa, q. 37, a. 5)

Aquinas added that the deacon received his power at the delivery of the gospel book and the subdeacon at the delivery of the empty chalice (*Summa* IIIa, q. 37, a. 5, ad. 5). His views were endorsed by the fifteenth-century Council of Florence in its Decree for the Armenians,[26] although as scholars have pointed out, that can only have been referring to the matter and form of the *Western* rites, because its authors were well aware these actions did not exist in Eastern rites. Even this did not put an end to the disagreement between theologians as to which of the ceremonies really did

---

[26] Text in Denzinger–Schönmetzer, *Enchiridion Symbolorum*, no. 1326.

constitute the sacramental matter and form of ordination, however, and the vigorous nature of that continuing debate can be glimpsed beneath the caustic comments of the Protestant reformer William Tyndale (ca. 1492–1536): "Last of all, one singular doubt they have: what maketh a priest; the anointing, or putting on of the hands, or what other ceremony, or what words? About which they brawl and scold, one ready to tear out another's throat. One saith this, and another that; but they cannot agree."[27]

CONCLUSION

In the course of the Middle Ages, and especially from the eleventh century onward, the understanding of ordination underwent a dramatic transformation. From being seen as essentially for ministry within a specific community, it came to be viewed as the bestowal particular powers on an individual for his own use. These powers were primarily concerned with the celebration of the Eucharist rather than being directed toward the pastoral leadership of the church. And because of this narrow focus on the Eucharist, priesthood became the dominant image and the presbyterate its central manifestation. Moreover, the recovery and development of the Augustinian concept of an indelible character imprinted in the act of ordination led to the view that, provided that the ritual act had been correctly performed, an ordination was considered valid even if other conditions (such as attachment to a specific church, election by the community, or the possession of a genuine mandate for ministry) were not met. All these constituted a major departure from earlier ways of thinking and acting and were to have a profound effect on the future understanding of the nature of ordination.

---

[27] William Tyndale, *The Obedience of a Christian Man* (1528), in *Doctrinal Treatises and Introductions to Different Portions of the Holy Scriptures, by William Tyndale, martyr 1536*, ed. Henry Walter, Parker Society 42 (Cambridge: Cambridge University Press, 1848), 258.

Chapter 8

Orders and Ministry in the Churches of the Reformation

The Reformation movements that emerged in Western Christianity in the late Middle Ages questioned the hitherto accepted views about the sacrament of order on the same grounds as they challenged much medieval teaching about sacraments in general. They also extended this critique to the inherited understanding of the ordained ministry both as constituting a mediatorial priesthood, the primary function of which was the celebration of the Eucharist, and as being hierarchically structured according to divine providence. None of these, the Reformers argued, had any basis in the New Testament as they read it, and it was the New Testament that for them constituted the ultimate criterion against which all practices were to be tested.

Their exegesis of Scripture did not, however, take place in a vacuum. They were also influenced by their own experience of the ordained ministry as it was practiced in the church of their time. Hence, for example, widespread hostility to episcopacy was not only the result of their being unable to discern a distinction between bishops and presbyters in the pages of the New Testament but also their direct encounter with what they saw as the princely and autocratic abuse of episcopal power in the bishops of their own day. Similarly, their frequent demands for the laity to play a significant part in the choice of their clergy sprang not only from observing that election by the people seemed to have been the common practice in apostolic times but also from their view that men were being ordained who lacked the qualities that they thought necessary for a minister.

In studying the theology and practice of the sixteenth-century Reformers, two important factors need to be kept in mind. The first is that their views often changed and developed in response to unfolding events, and so an apparent lack of consistency in different works by the same author may frequently be because time had elapsed between the composition of one and the emergence of a more mature theology in another, or because a different audience with different concerns is being addressed in one work over against another. The second factor is that they were sometimes compelled to compromise their principles and adopt practices inconsistent with their doctrines of church and ministry.

SOME FORERUNNERS

One of the earliest figures in the movement toward reformation, the Englishman John Wycliffe (ca. 1329–84), asserted that only two orders of ministry, priests and deacons, had existed in primitive Christianity. As we have seen, some other medieval scholars would not necessarily have disagreed with this exegesis of the New Testament, but they would not have shared Wycliffe's conclusion about the illegitimacy of the church developing other orders in the course of time. Wycliffe thought that it was through the sin of pride that such orders and gradations had been introduced, and he attacked in particular the wealth and use of power by prelates (*Trialogus* 4.13). Some two centuries later William Tyndale denied that Order was sacrament because there was "no promise coupled therewith." According to the New Testament, all Christians were priests, and the presbyter was "an officer to teach, and not to be a mediator between God and us." The elaborate medieval rites of ordination were unnecessary: "neither is there any other manner or ceremony at all required in making of our spiritual officers, than to choose an able person, and then to rehearse him his duty, and give him his charge, and so to put him in his room."[1]

MARTIN LUTHER

Similar views on ordination and priesthood were expressed by the leading sixteenth-century German Reformer, Martin Luther

---

[1] William Tyndale, *The Obedience of a Christian Man* (1528), in *Doctrinal Treatises and Introductions to Different Portions of the Holy Scriptures, by William Tyndale, Martyr 1536*, ed. Henry Walter, Parker Society 42 (Cambridge: Cambridge University Press, 1848), 255–56, 259.

(1483–1546), as these extracts on the subject from his work, *On the Babylonian Captivity of the Church*, published in 1520, reveal:[2]

Of this sacrament the Church of Christ knows nothing; it was invented by the church of the Pope. It not only has no promise of grace, anywhere declared, but not a word is said about it in the whole of the New Testament. Now it is ridiculous to set up as a sacrament of God that which can nowhere be proved to have been instituted by God. Not that I consider that a rite practised for so many ages is to be condemned; but I would not have human inventions established in sacred things, nor should it be allowed to bring in anything as divinely ordained, which has not been divinely ordained; lest we should be objects of ridicule to our adversaries. . . .

I grant therefore that orders may be a sort of church rite, like many others which have been introduced by the Fathers of the Church, such as the consecration of vessels, buildings, vestments, water, salt, candles, herbs, wine, and the like. In all these no one asserts that there is any sacrament, nor is there any promise in them. Thus the anointing of a man's hands, the shaving of his head, and other ceremonies of the kind, do not constitute a sacrament, since nothing is promised by these things, but they are merely employed to prepare men for certain offices, as in the case of vessels or instruments. . . .

Resting, however, on this very weak foundation, they have invented and attributed to this sacrament of theirs certain indelible characters, supposed to be impressed on those who receive orders. . . .

After this they bring in their very strongest argument, namely, that Christ said at the last supper: "Do this in remembrance of me." "Behold!" they say, "Christ ordained them as priests." . . . Let us reply to them that in these words Christ gives no promise, but only a command that this should be done in remembrance of Him. . . .

How if they were compelled to admit that we all, so many as have been baptized, are equally priests? We are so in fact, and it is only a ministry which has been entrusted to them, and that with our consent. They would then know that they have no right to exercise command over us, except so far as we voluntarily allow of it. Thus it is said: "Ye are a chosen generation, a royal priesthood, a holy nation." (1 Pet. ii. 9.) Thus all we who are Christians are priests; those whom

[2] English translation from *First Principles of the Reformation or The 95 Theses and the Three Primary Works of Dr. Martin Luther*, ed. Henry Wace and C. A. Buchheim (London: John Murray, 1883), 227–36.

we call priests are ministers chosen from among us to do all things in our name; and the priesthood is nothing else than a ministry. Thus Paul says: "Let a man so account of us as of the ministers of Christ, and stewards of the mysteries of God." (1 Cor. iv. 1.)

From this it follows that he who does not preach the word, being called to this very office by the Church, is in no way a priest, and that the sacrament of orders can be nothing else than a ceremony for choosing preachers in the Church. . . .

Let every man then who has learnt that he is a Christian recognise what he is, and be certain that we are all equally priests; that is, that we have the same power in the word, and in any sacrament whatever; although it is not lawful for any one to use this power, except with the consent of the community, or at the call of a superior. For that which belongs to all in common no individual can arrogate to himself, until he be called. And therefore the sacrament of orders, if it is anything, is nothing but a certain rite by which men are called to minister in the Church. Furthermore, the priesthood is properly nothing else than the ministry of the word—I mean the word of the gospel, not of the law. The diaconate is a ministry, not for reading the gospel or the epistle, as the practice is nowadays, but for distributing the wealth of the Church among the poor. . . .

As far then as we are taught from the Scriptures, since what we call the priesthood is a ministry, I do not see at all for what reason a man who has once been made priest cannot become a layman again, since he differs in no wise from a layman, except by his ministerial office.

What Luther said here implies that everyone had the power to function as a minister of the Word and sacraments, subject to their being authorized to do so, and that there was no particular vocation to ordained ministry given to certain individuals by God. He repeated this belief in some of his other writings. On the other hand, in other works he does appear to make a firmer distinction between those who are preachers and the laity, in which the office of preaching does not derive directly from the priesthood shared by all Christians. His ambiguity on this subject has led to serious disagreements among scholars within Lutheranism, with some attempting to harmonize the apparent contradictions in order to show that either the one or the other was his true position, and others admitting to the existence of some inconsistency in his views depending on the period of his life when they were expressed and the particular audience he was addressing, which seems the more likely answer.[3] What should be noted is that the later Lutheran Confessions certainly adopt a more positive view of ordination as the call of particular individuals to ministry, and the *Apology of the Augsburg Confession* (1531) was even willing to describe it as a sacrament.[4]

From his understanding of the New Testament, Luther judged that the process of appointment should include the election or "calling" of the candidate by a local church and his commendation to the ministry by prayer and the imposition of hands in a public assembly. Luther could see no evidence in the New Testament for the office of bishop distinct from that of the presbyter, and hence some Lutheran churches (e.g., Sweden) retained the historic succession of the episcopate, others (e.g., Denmark) retained the office of bishop or superintendent but without the historic succession, and others (e.g., Germany) abolished the office altogether. Where the episcopate was retained, it was not regarded as having any inherent power to ordain but received that authority from the church.

What is believed to have been the first evangelical ordination was performed by Luther in Wittenberg on May 14, 1525, when he ordained Georg Rörer as deacon, although no detailed record of the rite used has been preserved. A rite of ordination was drawn up in the 1526 church order of Homberg in Hesse, though never used, and it was not until after 1530 that the increasing scarcity of ministers already ordained by Catholic bishops created the need for regular ordinations and the composition of suitable rites. The earliest were those drawn up by Johannes Bugenhagen (1485–1558) in

---

[3] See, for example, Brian Gerrish, "Priesthood and Ministry in the Theology of Luther," *Church History* 34 (1965): 404–22; Lowell Green, "Change in Luther's Doctrine of Ministry," *Lutheran Quarterly* 18 (1966): 173–83; Robert H. Fischer, "Another Look at Luther's Doctrine of Ministry," *Lutheran Quarterly* 18 (1966): 260–71; T. G. Wilkens, "Ministry, Vocation and Ordination: Some Perspectives from Luther," *Lutheran Quarterly* 29 (1977): 66–81; Gert Haendler, *Luther on Ministerial Office and Congregational Function* (Philadelphia: Fortress Press, 1981).

[4] Article XIII. See *The Book of Concord: The Confessions of the Evangelical Lutheran Church*, ed. Theodore G. Tappert et al. (Philadelphia: Muhlenberg Press, 1959), 212.

the church orders for Hamburg (1529), Lübeck (1531), and Pomerania (1535). In 1535 Luther himself produced an ordination rite that became the basis for those in most later church orders, including Mecklenberg (1552), Lüneberg (1564 and 1575), Mansfield (1580), Hoya (1581), Henneberg (1582), and Lauenberg (1585). Its influence can also be seen in Bugenhagen's later rites for Denmark (1537), Schleswig-Holstein (1542), Braunschweig-Wolfenbüttel (1543), and Hildesheim (1544), as well as in Laurentius Petri's rites for Sweden (1571).[5]

Bugenhagen thought that ordinations ought to take place in the congregation that had called the person. Luther, though sympathetic to this idea, preferred a more centralized practice, at least as a temporary expedient, since he believed that something was needed to replace the ecclesiastical hierarchy in supervision and legitimation of the actions of local churches. Hence ordinands were to be sent by the authority of the secular ruler to be examined by appointed persons, usually the theological faculty of a university, and if found acceptable, ordained there. Because the ordination rites developed out of earlier forms devised for the ritual installation into parochial charges of those already ordained, and versions of them continued to be used for the local installation of those who were ordained in a central location, some theological ambiguity between ordination and installation resulted in early Lutheranism.

Early Lutheran ordination rites varied considerably in their details, but were always held within a congregational celebration of the Eucharist, and typical features were the following:

---

[5] More extensive study of these rites and their theology in Puglisi 2:3–69; Ralph F. Smith, *Luther, Ministry, and Ordination Rites in the Early Reformation Church* (New York: Lang, 1996); Bryan D. Spinks, "Luther's Other Major Liturgical Reforms: 2, The Ordination of Ministers of the Word," *Liturgical Review* 9 (1979): 20–32. For later practice and theology, see Ralph Quere, "The Spirit and the Gifts Are Ours: Imparting or Imploring the Spirit in Ordination Rites?," *Lutheran Quarterly* 27 (1975): 327–46, here at 333–41, and for the Nordic countries, *Rites of Ordination and Commitment in the Churches of the Nordic Countries: Theology and Terminology*, ed. Hans Raun Iversen (Copenhagen: Museum Tusculanum Press, 2006), 75–263, 433–71.

1. prayer by the people for the ordinand, usually introduced by a bidding and often concluded with a collect and incorporating a hymn, either *Veni Sancte Spiritus* in Luther's rite and its various derivatives (which had been used in Durandus' Pontifical at the consecration of a bishop and as an alternative to *Veni Creator Spiritus* at the ordination of priests in the season of Pentecost) or Luther's own hymn, "Now let us pray to the Holy Spirit," in some other rites (the first stanza of which was a German sacred folk song existing since the early Middle Ages);

2. appropriate biblical readings[6] and an address by the presiding minister on the qualities and duties required of a minister, followed by one or more questions to the ordinand; and

3. imposition of hands by all the ministers present, in Luther's rite accompanied by the Lord's Prayer and (optionally) an ordination prayer invoking the Holy Spirit on the ordinand; in some other rites the prayer preceded the laying on of hands and another prayer or a declaratory formula accompanied the action and might be followed by a further prayer invoking the Holy Spirit and by the Lord's Prayer.

The rites generally concluded with the words of 1 Peter 5:2-4, used as a charge to the newly ordained, and another hymn, "Now let us pray to the Holy Spirit," in Luther's rite and its derivatives and *Te Deum laudamus* in others, the latter having already been used as a concluding hymn in Durandus' rite for the ordination of bishops. The appointment of a bishop or superintendent was similar, often using the same prayers, but was a little more elaborate. The ordination prayer used by Luther himself was as follows:

> Merciful God, heavenly Father, thou hast said to us through the mouth of thy dear Son our Lord Jesus Christ: "The harvest truly is plenteous, but the laborers are few. Pray ye therefore the Lord of the harvest, that he will send forth laborers into his harvest" [Matt 9:37-38]. Upon this thy divine command, we pray heartily that thou wouldst grant thy Holy Spirit richly to these thy servants, to

---

[6] In Luther's rite and its derivatives, 1 Tim 3:1-7 and Acts 20:28-31, thus affirming the identity of bishops and presbyters in New Testament times; other rites included Matt 28:18-20 or John 20:21-23, Titus 1:5-9; and 2 Tim 3:14–4:5.

us, and to all those who are called to serve thy Word so that the company of us who publish the good tidings may be great, and that we may stand faithful and firm against the devil, the world, and the flesh, to the end that thy name may be hallowed, thy kingdom grow, and thy will be done. Be also pleased at length to check and stop the detestable abomination of the pope, Mohammed, and other sects which blaspheme thy name, hinder thy kingdom, and oppose thy will. Graciously hear this our prayer, since thou hast so commanded, taught, and promised, even as we believe and trust through thy dear Son Jesus Christ our Lord, who liveth and reigneth with thee and the Holy Ghost, world without end. Amen.[7]

JOHN CALVIN AND THE REFORMED TRADITION

John Calvin (1509–64) belongs to a second generation of Reformers. While sharing many of the views of his predecessors, his exegesis of New Testament texts set out in his magnum opus, *The Institutes of Christian Religion*, led him to somewhat different conclusions about a pattern of ministry that would be in accord with Scripture. He claimed that the first three categories of ministers mentioned in Ephesians 4:11—apostles, prophets and evangelists—had been intended only as temporary offices to secure the foundation of the church, though they might again be raised up in extraordinary situations, but the other two, pastors and teachers, were meant to be the regular offices of the church,[8] together with two others, elders and deacons. Although he believed that in the Bible the terms *bishops*, *presbyters*, and *pastors* were used synonymously, he interpreted Romans 12:8 and 1 Corinthians 12:28 as referring to the existence of "seniors selected from the people to unite with the bishops in pronouncing censures and exercising discipline" (IV.3.8). Similarly, he believed that Romans 12:8 spoke of the existence of two classes of deacons concerned with the poor: one administered alms and the other took care of the poor and sick

[7] *Luther's Works 53: Liturgy and Hymns*, ed. Ulrich S. Leupold (Philadelphia: Fortress Press, 1965), 122–26.

[8] Jean Calvin, *Institutes of the Christian Religion* IV.3.4–5. All references to this work and extracts quoted here are from the English translation by Henry Beveridge in 1599. See also J. L. Ainslie, *The Doctrines of Ministerial Order in the Reformed Churches of the Sixteenth and Seventeenth Centuries* (Edinburgh: T & T Clark, 1940).

(IV.3.9).[9] In Reformed practice, however, the office of teacher eventually tended to be absorbed into that of the pastor.

The two principal parts of the pastor's office were "to preach the Gospel and administer the sacraments" (IV.3.8), and no one ought to assume this office without being duly called to it, by which Calvin meant "the external and formal call which relates to the public order of the Church, while I say nothing of that secret call of which every minister is conscious before God" (IV.3.10–11). According to his reading of the New Testament, this call required "the consent and approbation of the people," but with other pastors presiding over the election to ensure its regularity (IV.3.15). As for an ordination rite,

> it is certain that when the apostles appointed anyone to the ministry, they used no other ceremony than the laying on of hands. . . . Though there is no fixed precept concerning the laying on of hands, yet as we see that it was uniformly observed by the apostles, this careful observance ought to be regarded by us in the light of a precept. And it is certainly useful, that by such a symbol the dignity of the ministry should be commended to the people, and he who is ordained reminded that he is no longer his own but is bound in service to God and the Church. Lastly, it is to be observed that it was not the whole people but only pastors who laid hands on ministers, though it is uncertain whether or not several always laid their hands. (IV.3.16)

In spite of this commendation of the laying on of hands, however, Calvin did not adopt it in actual practice in the church in Geneva because of what he regarded as superstitious views about it that had grown up in the medieval church.[10] There, when a new minister was required, the other ministers selected and examined a suitable candidate. If they approved of him, they submitted him to the City Council for their consent and finally to the people. "As to the manner of introduction, since the ceremonies of time past have been perverted into much superstition, because of the weakness of the times, it will suffice that a declaration be made by one of the ministers denoting the office to which ordination is being made;

[9] See Elsie Ann McKee, *John Calvin on the Diaconate and Liturgical Almsgiving* (Geneva: Librairie Droz, 1984).

[10] See Calvin, *Institutes of the Christian Religion* IV.19.31.

then that prayers and petitions be made, in order that the Lord give him grace to discharge it."[11]

A broadly similar procedure was followed in other Reformed churches, varying only in detail. Thus, for example, within the congregation of Flemish weavers who sought refuge in England around 1548 under Valerand Pullain (ca. 1509–57), the ministers and elders first submitted nominees to the congregation, who chose either one of these or someone else to be examined by them. If he was found satisfactory, he was ordained by the ministers, and the imposition of hands was used. When a minister was required by the English exiles at Geneva during the reign of Queen Mary, the practice was for the congregation to appoint two or three candidates to be examined by the elders and other ministers. The examiners indicated who they thought was the most suitable, and a period of at least eight days was allowed for inquiries and objections. If no objections were made, the candidate was presented at a Sunday morning service by a minister, who was to preach about his duty, and in the afternoon the "election" took place. There was no imposition of hands, but the minister who had preached was to pray "as God shall move his herte" prior to the election, and afterward "geveth thankes to God with his request of suche thinges as shall be necessarie for his office." On their return to England during the reign of Queen Elizabeth I, the Puritans tried unsuccessfully to secure changes in the Anglican practice so that it might conform more closely to this pattern.[12]

In Scotland under John Knox (ca. 1514–72), the procedure adopted was that which had been used by the exiles at Geneva for whom Knox had been pastor. There was also in Scotland the office of superintendent, which seems to have been set up not as a type of permanent episcopacy but simply as a temporary expedient to

[11] "Draft Ecclesiastical Ordinances September & October 1541," in *Calvin: Theological Treatises*, ed. J. K. S. Reid, Library of Christian Classics 22 (Philadelphia: Westminster Press, 1954), 59–60, n. 11.

[12] For both Pullain's *Liturgia sacra* and the practice of the Genevan exiles, see W. D. Maxwell, *John Knox's Genevan Service Book* (Edinburgh: Oliver & Boyd, 1931 = London: Faith Press, 1965), 165–74. For the English Puritans, see Paul F. Bradshaw, *The Anglican Ordinal: Its History and Development from the Reformation to the Present Day*, ACC 53 (London: SPCK, 1971), 37–54.

organize the Presbyterian system, to take charge of vacant parishes, and to ordain suitable ministers for them, although superintendents had no power of ordination inherent in their office but acted under the commission of the General Assembly of the Church. In 1569, Knox drew up a rite for their "election" based on a form composed by the Polish reformer John á Lasco (1499–1560) for exiled foreign congregations in London in 1550. Following the pattern of his rite, after the examination of the candidates came a substantial prayer asking for the gift of the Holy Spirit and ending with the Lord's Prayer, followed by a shorter prayer of blessing. Knox's version of these drew mainly on á Lasco's, including addressing the prayer to Christ rather than to the Father, but was also influenced by the original form of the prayer and blessing composed by the German Reformer Martin Bucer (1491–1551), on which á Lasco himself had drawn and which had also formed the primary source of the first Anglican ordination rites of 1550.[13]

> O Lord, to whom all power is given in heaven and in earth, Thou that art the Eternal Son of the Eternal Father, who hast not only so loved Thy Church that, for the redemption and purgation of the same, thou has humbled thyself to the death of the cross, and thereupon hast shed Thy most innocent blood to prepare to Thyself a spouse without spot, but also, to retain this Thy most excellent benefit in recent memory, hast appointed in Thy Church Teachers, Pastors, and Apostles, to instruct, comfort, and admonish the same: look upon us mercifully, O Lord, Thou that only art King, Teacher, and High Priest to thy own flock: and send unto this our brother, who, in thy name, we have charged with the chief care of thy Church, within the bounds of L., such portion of thy Holy Spirit, as thereby he may rightly divide thy word, to the instruction of thy flock, and to the confutation of pernicious errors and damnable superstitions. Give unto him, good Lord, a mouth and wisdom, whereby the enemies of thy truth may be confounded, the wolves expelled and driven from Thy fold, Thy sheep may be

---

[13] English translation of Bucer's text in E. C. Whitaker, *Martin Bucer and the Book of Common Prayer*, ACC 55 (Great Wakering: Mayhew-McCrimmon, 1974), 175–83; and, with analysis, in Puglisi 2:39–53. See also ibid. 2:75–85, for John á Lasco's rite, and 2:95–101, for the adaptation of á Lasco's rite by Puritan exiles from England in the Netherlands. For the Anglican ordination rites, see below, pp. 163–65.

fed in the wholesome pastures of Thy most holy word, the blind and ignorant may be illuminated with Thy true knowledge: finally, that, the dregs of superstition and idolatry which yet rested within this realm being purged and removed, we may all not only have occasion to glorify Thee our only Lord and Saviour, but also daily to grow in godliness and obedience of thy most holy will, to the destruction of the body of sin, and to the restitution of that image to the which we were once created, and to the which, after our fall and defection, we are renewed by participation of Thy holy Spirit, whom, by true faith in thee, we do profess as the blessed of Thy Father, of whom the perpetual increase of thy graces we crave, as by Thee our Lord King, and only Bishop we are taught to pray, "Our Father," etc.

God, the Father of our Lord Jesus Christ, who hath commanded His Gospel to be preached to the comfort of His elect, and hath called thee to the office of a watchman over His people, multiply His graces with thee, illuminate thee with His Holy Spirit, comfort and strengthen thee in all virtue, govern and guide thy ministry to the praise of His holy name, to the propagation of Christ's kingdom, to the comfort of His Church, and, finally, to the plain discharge and assurance of thy own conscience, in the day of the Lord Jesus, to whom, with the Father, and with the Holy Ghost, be all honour, praise, and glory, now and ever. So be it.[14]

Unlike á Lasco's rite, an imposition of hands did not accompany this blessing. Instead, a handshake was exchanged afterward between the one elected and the other ministers and elders present "in sign of their consent" (apparently inspired by Galatians 2:9, "the right hand of fellowship"). The inclusion of the elders in this action is an indication of their greater prominence in the government of the church here than they had under Calvin. Later imposition of hands was restored for the ordination of both ministers and superintendents under pressure from King James VI, and the elders participated in this too. In 1610 episcopacy was introduced, again under pressure from the King, and new ordination rites for bishops and ministers were published in 1620, being a compromise between the former practice and the Anglican rites. An attempt in

[14] Text from *The Book of Common Order of the Church of Scotland*, ed. G. W. Sprott, 2nd ed. (Edinburgh: Blackwood, 1901), 13–30.

1636 to impose the Anglican rites *in toto* was unsuccessful: episcopacy was rejected and Presbyterianism established.[15]

The Westminster Assembly in 1645, though continuing to give elders a place in church government, moved more in the direction of continental Calvinism and did not accord them a special role in ordination: ordained ministers alone were to examine the candidate and perform the imposition of hands. After the examination, the ordinand was to be sent to the congregation where he was to serve in order to preach on three days and have his suitability judged by them. Representatives of the congregation were then to appear before the presbytery to declare their assent or objections. If they assented, the ordination was to take place in their church and a solemn fast kept by the congregation beforehand. At least three or four of the presbytery were to attend the ordination service. One of them was to preach a sermon on the duties of minister and people, questions were to be asked of both ordinand and congregation, and then while the ministers laid hands on the candidate, a short prayer or blessing on the following lines was to be said by one of them.

> Thankfully acknowledging the great mercy of God, in sending Jesus Christ for the Redemption of his People, and for his ascension to the right hand of the Father, and then pouring out his Spirit, and giving gifts to Men, Apostles, Evangelists, Prophets, Pastors, and Teachers, for the gathering and building up of his Church, and for fitting and enclining this man to this great Work; To entreat him to fill him with his Holy Spirit, to give him (whom in his Name we thus set apart to this holy Service) to fulfill the Work of his Ministry in all things, that he may both save himselfe and the People committed to his charge.[16]

---

[15] See Puglisi 2:87–95; Duncan Shaw, "The Inauguration of Ministers in Scotland 1560–1620," *Records of the Scottish Church History Society* 16 (1966): 35–62; *Scottish Liturgies of the Reign of James VI*, ed. G. W. Sprott (Edinburgh: Blackwood, 1901), 111–31. For the later practices of the Church of Scotland, see Gordon Donaldson, "Scottish Ordinations in the Restoration Period," *Scottish Historical Review* 33 (1954): 169–75; W. R. Foster, *Bishop and Presbytery: The Church of Scotland 1661–1688* (London: SPCK, 1958).

[16] *Propositions Concerning Church Government and Ordination of Ministers* (1647), 15–26.

The service ended with a charge to the minister and the people, a prayer commending him and them to God, a psalm, and a blessing. These same basic elements continued to be found in all later rites of Reformed churches.

THE CHURCH OF ENGLAND

Exceptionally among the churches of the Reformation, the term "priest" was retained for an ordained minister in some Lutheran churches—for example, those of the Scandinavian countries— and in the Church of England. The Church of England was also unique in not regarding election of the candidates by the people as an essential requirement of a true ordination. Even in these cases, however, it can be argued that this did not signal a rejection of the Reformation doctrine as such but only a desire to make as little change as possible in external forms. The first ordinal of the Church of England, published in 1550, the year after the appearance of the first *Book of Common Prayer*, provided rites for the ordination of deacons, priests, and bishops, and was based primarily on the rite composed by Bucer that was mentioned earlier in connection with Knox in Scotland.[17] Although his was only a single rite, Bucer did suggest that it might be carried out "more solemnly and at greater length" when a bishop was ordained, and simplified for a deacon, and this is basically what the Anglican rites did, supplementing Bucer's text with a number of features adapted from the former medieval practice. The rites were preceded by a preface, which stated that ministers should be admitted "by public prayer with imposition of hands." The main elements in the rite for deacons, which was the simplest of the three, were: a sermon, the presentation of the candidates, the litany, the eucharistic liturgy of the word up to the end of the Epistle, an examination of the ordinands, and the imposition of hands by the bishop with the words, "Take thou authority to execute the office of a Deacon in the Church of God committed unto thee: in the name of the Father, the

---

[17] For further details of Anglican ordination rites, see Bradshaw, *The Anglican Ordinal*; E. P. Echlin, *The Story of Anglican Ministry* (Slough: St. Paul Publications, 1974); Hans-Jürgen Feulner, *Das "anglikanische Ordinale": eine liturgiegeschichtliche und liturgietheologische Studie* (Neuried: Ars Una, 1997); Puglisi 2:111–46.

Son, and the Holy Ghost. Amen." This was followed by the giving of the New Testament (rather than the gospel book, as in medieval times). The Eucharist then continued from the gospel onward (which one of the new deacons read), and concluded with a special collect before the blessing. It is clear from this that the litany (which included a special petition and concluding collect for the ordinands) was understood to be the requisite "public prayer," which preceded and was distinct from the formal commissioning for ministry with imposition of hands.

The rite for priests was similar, except that it came after the gospel and included an English version of *Veni Creator Spiritus* from the medieval rite, a lengthy exhortation to the ordinands, a period of silent congregational prayer, and another substantial prayer before the laying on of hands. In Bucer's rite this prayer had contained a petition for the gift of the Holy Spirit on those being ordained, but the Anglican rite removed that petition from the prayer entirely, so that once again the "public prayer" for them was principally the litany. As in the medieval rite, priests joined with the bishop in performing the imposition of hands. This was accompanied by a formula beginning with the words from John 20:22-23, "Receive the Holy Ghost," which had been used at the second imposition of hands in the medieval rite, and followed by, "and be thou a faithful dispenser of the word of God, and of his holy sacraments." The newly ordained then received a Bible as well as the chalice and paten formerly given, though with different words: "Take thou authority to preach the word of God, and to minister the holy sacraments in this congregation."

Following medieval precedent, the rite for bishops was described as the form of "consecrating" a bishop, instead of "ordering," as in the other two rites. It was rather more elaborate than the others, and did include a complete prayer for the candidate before the laying on of hands, which drew on material from the medieval service. In accordance with tradition, the imposition of hands was performed by all the bishops present, after which the gospel book was laid upon the new bishop's neck. He then received the pastoral staff.

When these rites were revised in 1552 because of protests from some extreme Protestants, all directions about how the candidates were to be vested were removed from them, and the *traditio instru-*

mentorum was modified: priests received the Bible alone, and bishops did not have the Bible laid on their necks but given to them and were not presented with the pastoral staff. No major changes were made to the rites at subsequent revisions of the *Book of Common Prayer*, with which the ordinal was now bound up, apart from an alteration to the wording of the preface to the ordinal in 1662 to make episcopal ordination explicitly a *sine qua non* for admission to ministry in the Church of England. At the same time, opportunity was taken to clarify, by a number of minor changes to the rites, that bishops and priests constituted separate orders of ministry and not merely different degrees within the same ministry.

BAPTIST AND CONGREGATIONALIST CHURCHES

These may be classed together since they have a common origin in seventeenth-century English Separatism. Both viewed ordination as the recognition by the local congregation that a person had been called by God to the ministry and already had the necessary gifts and graces, and as the setting apart of that person to function as a minister within the congregation. According to the *Savoy Declaration* of 1658, a modification to suit congregational polity of the *Westminster Confession of Faith* of 1646, in a section titled "The Institution of Churches, and the Order Appointed in Them by Jesus Christ,"

> 11. The way appointed by Christ for the calling of any person, fitted and gifted by the Holy Ghost, unto the office of pastor, teacher or elder in a church, is, that he be chosen thereunto by the common suffrage of the church itself, and solemnly set apart by fasting and prayer, with imposition of hands of the eldership of that church, if there be any before constituted therein. And of a deacon, that he be chosen by the like suffrage, and set apart by prayer, and the like imposition of hands.

However, it went on to indicate that the imposition of hands was not essential, and, in fact, Congregationalists generally abandoned it and later often substituted the giving of the right hand of fellowship.

> 12. The essence of this call of a pastor, teacher or elder unto office consists in the election of the church, together with his acceptation of it, and separation by fasting and prayer. And those who are so chosen, though not set apart by imposition of hands, are rightly

constituted ministers of Jesus Christ, in whose name and authority they exercise the ministry to them so committed. The calling of deacons consisteth in the like election and acceptation with separation by prayer.

On the other hand, it was a very different matter if the process of election were to be dispensed with:

15. Ordination alone without the election or precedent consent of the church, by those who formerly have been ordained by virtue of that power they have received by their ordination, doth not constitute any person a church-officer, or communicate office-power to him.

And while preaching was an essential aspect of the office of the pastor and teacher, it was not exclusive to it.[18] Ironically, what this tended to leave as exclusive to the ordained was presidency at the Lord's Supper, thus resulting in a strange parallel with the ordination of priests in the Roman Catholic Church!

13. Although it be incumbent on the pastors and teachers of the churches to be instant in preaching the Word, by way of office; yet the work of preaching the Word is not so peculiarly confined to them, but that others also gifted and fitted by the Holy Ghost for it, and approved (being by lawful ways and means in the providence of God called thereunto) may publicly, ordinarily and constantly perform it; so that they give themselves up thereunto.

The provisions of sections 11 and 13 were repeated almost verbatim in the *Second London Confession* drawn up by the Baptists in 1677 and in the *Confession of Faith* of 1689, chapter 26, paragraphs 9 and 11, although using the terms *bishop, elder,* and *pastor* as synonyms for the same office and making no mention of teacher. Most Baptist and Congregational churches subsequently continued to practice the formal ordination of pastors, but there have been those who have argued that any form of distinctive ministry was in danger of

[18] On the struggles that had taken place earlier among Puritans in England over this question, see Richard L. Greaves, "The Ordination Controversy and the Spirit of Reform in Puritan England," *Journal of Ecclesiastical History* 21 (1970): 225–41.

compromising belief in the priesthood of all believers. In any case, no exclusive rights are conferred by the act of ordination, and not only lay preaching but also lay presidency at the Eucharist is possible. Although strict congregational polity would require a minister to be ordained again each time that he was called to a new congregation, it eventually gave way in both Baptist and Congregational churches to an ordination involving wider church representatives, not just a single congregation, and was recognized throughout the denomination (the minister simply being inducted into the new charge if he moved from one congregation to another).[19]

JOHN WESLEY AND THE METHODIST TRADITION

John Wesley (1703–91) did not intend to set up a formal structure of ministry in opposition to that of the Church of England, but he did perform actions to initiate his assistants/itinerant preachers into their role, ranging from a simple prayer in some cases to a formal commissioning in others, which sometimes included the imposition of hands and the giving of a Bible. When the English bishops would do nothing about providing a bishop for America, he went further and in 1784 ordained two men as deacons on one day and as presbyters or "elders" the next day to serve there, and "set apart" Dr Thomas Coke, an Anglican priest, as "superintendant" [sic]. Later he ordained other elders for Scotland and eventually for England. His justification for these actions was that, as a result of having read many years earlier Edward Stillingfleet's *Irenicum* (London, 1661) and Peter King's *An Enquiry into the Constitution, Discipline, Unity and Worship of the Primitive Church* (London, 1691), he believed bishops and priests differed only in degree and not in order and that as the spiritual *Episcopos* of the Methodist societies he had the right to ordain preachers for them. He adapted the Anglican ordination rites for this purpose. The main changes were the omission of the preface, the deletion of all directions about

[19] For Baptist churches, see Ernest A. Payne, *The Meaning and Practice of Ordination among Baptists: A Report Submitted to the Council of the Baptist Union of Great Britain and Ireland* (London: Carey Kingsgate, 1957); Robert Torbet, *The Baptist Ministry: Then and Now* (Philadelphia: Judson, 1953). On the history of English Congregationalism in general, see R. Tudur Jones, *Congregationalism in England, 1662–1962* (London: Independent Press, 1962).

vesture, the substitution of the terms "elder" and "superintendant" for "priest" and "bishop," and "ordain" for "consecrate" in the rite for superintendants, and the omission the phrase from John 20:23, "whose sins . . . ," at the imposition of hands on elders. The rite for the diaconate was retained, with deacons being given a Bible instead of the New Testament.[20]

These services provided the basis of the ordination rites of Methodists in the United States, although in the course of time they underwent various changes. In 1792 the Methodist Episcopal Church replaced the name "superintendant" with "bishop" and "The Lord pour upon thee the Holy Spirit" was substituted for the imperative "Receive the Holy Ghost" at the imposition of hands on elders. In the nineteenth century the same change was made in the rite for bishops, and "consecrate" also replaced "ordain" in that rite to make it clear that the episcopate was not a separate order. Other Methodist churches rejected the office altogether, preferring an elected "President of Conference," and some also dispensed with the diaconate. The Methodist Episcopal Church and the Methodist Episcopal Church, South, also severed the link between ordination rites and the celebration of the Eucharist during the nineteenth century. Although the 1944 ordinal of the reunited Methodist churches marked a more cautious turn (with the restoration of elements deleted in the heyday of Protestant liberalism and the 1964 rite being even more conservative), the connection to the Eucharist was not reinstated. Orders for the consecration of deaconesses emerged in the late nineteenth century, with the first authorized service of the Methodist Episcopal Church in 1908 borrowing the deaconess prayer from the fourth-century *Apostolic Constitutions*.[21]

---

[20] See further A. B. Lawson, *John Wesley and the Christian Ministry: The Sources and Development of His Opinions and Practice* (London: SPCK, 1963); J. K. Mathews, *Set Apart to Serve: The Meaning and Role of Episcopacy in the Wesleyan Tradition* (Nashville: Abingdon Press, 1985); Puglisi 2:150–61.

[21] See further A. C. Outler, "The Ordinal," in *Companion to the Book of Worship*, ed. W. F. Dunkle and J. D. Quillian (Nashville: Abingdon Press, 1970), 103–33; G. F. Moede, *The Office of Bishop in Methodism: Its History and Development* (Nashville: Abingdon Press, 1964); and for commentary on the 1964 rite, Puglisi 3:195–202.

In Britain, Wesley's services continued to be printed in subsequent editions of *The Sunday Service* despite the fact that there were no superintendents or deacons there and, in any case, the Methodist Conference of 1792 had forbidden the practice of ordination and substituted a simple reception into Full Connexion by the Annual Conference. This was done largely in order to regulate the admission of ministers to Methodism, which was becoming somewhat chaotic. It was not until 1836 that formal ordination with imposition of hands at the Conference was restored in the Wesleyan Methodist Church, and in 1848 a rite of ordination containing elements from all three of Wesley's rites but especially from those for elders and superintendents was adopted for the purpose. Its main features were extemporized prayer, the reading of a number of prescribed passages of Scripture, a token election (the admission to Connexion having taken place earlier in the day), the exhortation to the candidates and their examination from the rite for elders (with some minor changes), the bidding from the rite for superintendents, a period of silent prayer and the collect (slightly emended) from the rite for elders. Then came the prayers before the imposition of hands from both rites, the imposition of hands itself performed by the president of the Methodist Conference together with other ministers and accompanied by a formula adapted from the rite for elders, and the giving of a Bible. The service concluded with the final collect from the rite for superintendents and the Lord's Supper followed.[22] Minor changes were made in 1883, including the addition of the English version of *Veni Creator Spiritus* from the Anglican rite.[23] The non-Wesleyan Methodist ordinations were generally of the same kind, except that Primitive Methodists were ordained at the District Meeting instead of the Conference and, apart from the United Methodist Free Churches, "election" was played down, being dropped altogether in the rite of the United Methodist Church that was formed in 1913. After the reunion of British Methodists in 1932, the Wesleyan

---

[22] *Order of Administration of the Lord's Supper and Baptism . . . Together with the Ordination Service: As Used by the Wesleyan Methodists* (London: John Mason, 1848), 91–118.

[23] *The Book of Public Prayers and Services for the Use of the People Called Methodists* (London: Wesleyan-Methodist Book-Room, 1883), 269–79.

Methodist rite was adopted with minor alterations in the 1936 *Book of Offices.*[24]

All this emphasis on formal rites of ordination, however, did not preclude the persistence of lay preaching within Methodism just as much as within the Baptist and Congregationalist traditions.

CONCLUSION

In reaction to the complexities of the medieval rites of ordination and to what James Puglisi has called the "over-sacramentalization" of ordination in medieval theology,[25] the sixteenth-century Reformers attempted to return to what they saw as the simplicity of New Testament practice and teaching. Yet even this did not bring about complete agreement among them. How many of the words for ministers found in the New Testament were titles of actual offices? How many of them were intended to be permanent institutions? How many were merely synonyms for the same ministry?

Nor did what they found in its pages always dictate what they adopted. Thus, while those of the Reformed tradition were convinced that election was the *sine qua non* of ministerial appointment according to the New Testament, they did not view the equally scriptural gesture of the imposition of hands as enjoying the same status and were happy to dispense with it where they believed it would give an erroneous impression. On the other hand, the bishops of the Church of England, although aware that election by the people had been practiced in the primitive church, denied that this was always essential and, in the words of John Whitgift, Archbishop of Canterbury from 1583 to 1604, "now in this state of the church it were most pernicious and hurtful."[26]

---

[24] *The Book of Offices, Being the Orders of Service Authorized for Use in the Methodist Church* (London: Methodist Publishing House, 1936). See also Puglisi 3:176–85. On the history of the Methodist rite in Britain, see further A. R. George, "Ordination," in *A History of the Methodist Church in Great Britain*, vol. 2, ed. Rupert Davies, A. R. George, and Gordon Rupp (London: Epworth Press, 1978), 143–58.

[25] Puglisi 2:25.

[26] *The Works of John Whitgift*, vol. 1, ed. John Ayre, Parker Society (Cambridge: Cambridge University Press, 1851), 368.

Equally, the inherent ambiguity of what the Reformers read in the New Testament failed to provide a clear guide to practice. It was not obvious to everyone, for example, who should be responsible for examining the candidates and who should participate in the laying on of hands, and different conclusions were reached on those matters in different churches. Similarly, although all the Reformers saw prayer as being part of the process of appointment in the New Testament, this did not always lead them to adopt an ordination prayer as such, but it appears to have been thought sufficient for ordinations to take place within the general context of prayer. In Luther's rite it is the congregation that first prays for the gift of the Holy Spirit and the presiding minister may simply recite the Lord's Prayer in conjunction with the imposition of hands. In the same way, the essential prayer of the Anglican rites for deacons and priests is the litany with its congregational responses. In those rites that did include an ordination prayer and where imposition of hands was practiced, the two were rarely simultaneous, but the laying on of hands was often done in conjunction with a subsequent blessing or a commissioning formula. While the Reformers may have recognized that both prayer and the imposition of hands were parts of New Testament practice, they did not conclude that the two necessarily went together. Although records of early Reformed ordination practice are frequently very sketchy, it appears to have been the Westminster Assembly that first restored the association of the imposition of hands with the principal prayer of the rite.

Chapter 9

The Roman Catholic Church from the Council of Trent to the Present

THE COUNCIL OF TRENT

In response to the claims made by the Reformers, discussion of the sacrament of holy orders began at the Council of Trent in 1562 in its twenty-third session, with the final decree, consisting of four short chapters and eight canons, being promulgated in 1563. It is important to recognize not only the aspects of traditional teaching that this document defended and affirmed but also the areas in which it refrained from passing judgment or entering into debate. In other words, it should be seen as dealing with specific issues that had arisen and required a response, not as a complete and definitive statement of the Roman Catholic doctrine of ordination.[1]

The first chapter insisted that there existed in the church a new, visible, and external priesthood, into which the Old Testament priesthood had been changed. Christ instituted this priesthood and delivered to the apostles and their successors "the power of consecrating, offering, and administering his body and blood, and likewise the power of remitting and of retaining sins." The relevant canon condemned the Reformation view that all that Christ had instituted was the office and ministry of preaching the Gospel and that therefore those who did not preach were not priests. Nevertheless, attempts were made during the prior deliberations of the

---

[1] English translations of the decree of the Council of Trent from *The Church Teaches: Documents of the Church in English Translation*, translated by J. F. Clarkson et al. (St. Louis: Herder, 1955), 329–32; Latin text in Heinrich Denzinger–Adolfus Schönmetzer, *Enchiridion Symbolorum*, 32nd ed. (Freiburg: Herder, 1963), nos. 1763–78. A fuller commentary on the decree can be found in Kenan B. Osborne, *Priesthood: A History of the Ordained Ministry in the Roman Catholic Church* (New York: Paulist Press, 1988), 248–79. See also A. Duval, "The Council of Trent and Holy Orders," in *The Sacrament of Holy Orders* (Collegeville, MN: Liturgical Press, 1962), 219–58.

Council to add to this denial some positive statement about the place of preaching in relation to the priesthood but nothing came of this. In other sessions of the Council, however, considerable emphasis was given to this aspect of the ordained ministry. In the fifth session, held in 1546, the preaching of the Gospel had been called "the principal duty of bishops," and priests who had a pastoral charge were required at least on Sundays and feasts "to feed the people committed to them with wholesome words" either by preaching themselves or by means of others who were competent (chapter 2). A later session added the catechizing of children every Sunday and feast; and parish priests were required to preach daily during Advent and Lent, or at least on three days in the week, or whenever the bishops deemed it necessary (Session 24, chapter 4). Because of this broader vision of the priesthood, the Council also ordered the establishment of seminaries in every diocese in order that priests might be appropriately trained for their ministry (Session 23, chapter 18).

In the second chapter of the decree on the sacrament of holy orders the existence of seven orders was defended with the claim that, while only priests and deacons were explicitly mentioned in the New Testament, "from the very beginning of the church" the names of subdeacon, acolyte, exorcist, reader, and doorkeeper "are known to have been in use." Although acknowledging that the subdiaconate was regarded as a major order "in the writings of the Fathers and of the sacred councils," it did not pass a judgment on this matter.

This was followed in the next chapter by a defense of ordination as a sacrament instituted by Christ, and not just "a kind of rite of choosing ministers of the word of God and of the sacraments," in the words of the third canon. It asserted that "it is very clear from the testimony of Sacred Scripture, from apostolic tradition, and from the unanimous agreement of the Fathers, that grace is conferred through holy ordination, which is effected by words and external signs." No attempt was made, however, to resolve the question as to what exactly those essential words and actions were, given the diversity of views on the sacramental form and matter that still existed among theologians, although it might be significant that the chapter ended with the quotation of 2 Timothy 1:6-7, which mentions the imposition of hands. On the other hand, the only action specifically named in the accompanying canons is the anointing, which is said to be "required." This was to counter the criticism of the Reformers, who had particularly attacked this ceremony as drawn from the Old Testament priesthood and not from the New Testament ministry of the word.

In the final chapter the Council asserted that "in the sacrament of orders, just as in baptism and confirmation, a character is imprinted, which can neither be blotted out nor taken away," and therefore a person who had once been ordained a priest could never again become a layman. It did not, however, venture to define the nature of that "character." It denied that all Christians were priests or endowed with equal spiritual power, and then went on to speak of the specific powers of bishops. But it did not attempt to resolve the still disputed question of whether or not they constituted a separate order, or whether the episcopal power of jurisdiction derived from papal appointment or directly from God. These matters had constituted the major topics of debate during the session,[2] but failure to reach agreement on them meant that they left virtually no mark on the final text. It simply stated:

> Besides the other ecclesiastical grades, the bishops who have succeeded the apostles belong in a special way to the hierarchical order; and placed (as the Apostle says) by the Holy Spirit to rule the Church of God (cf. Acts 20, 28), they are superior to priests, and can confer the sacrament of confirmation, can ordain the ministers for the Church, and they have the power to perform very many other functions that those of an inferior grade cannot.

It concluded by reaffirming the established mediaeval view that, provided that the ritual act had been correctly performed, an ordination was valid even if other conditions were not met: "neither the consent, call or authority, neither of the people, nor of any secular power or public authority, is necessary to the extent that without it the ordination is invalid."

---

[2] See M. McGough, "The Immediate Source of Episcopal Jurisdiction: A Tridentine Debate," *Irish Ecclesiastical Record* 86 (1956): 82–97; 87 (1957), 91–109; 88 (1957), 306–23; Seamus Ryan, "Episcopal Consecration: Trent to Vatican II," *Irish Theological Quarterly* 33 (1966): 133–50, here at 136–40.

Although not immediately influential when it first appeared, Durandus' thirteenth-century pontifical eventually became the model for the first printed pontifical of 1485, commissioned by Innocent VIII and drawn up by his master of ceremonies, Agostino Piccolomini, and John Burchard of Strasbourg.[3] It reproduced its source almost word for word, apart from the insertion of more much detailed ceremonial directions, but three differences from Durandus' archetype in the rite for bishops are worth noting:

1. Reference to the election of the candidate and attestation of his worthiness are removed from the beginning of the rite and replaced with the reading of the papal mandate for his consecration, thus reflecting what had become the real source of episcopal appointments by this time.[4]

2. The more detailed directions about the imposition of the gospel book not only preserved Durandus' instruction that it was to be open but required that it was to be placed with the help of the assisting bishops "on the neck and shoulders of the elect in such a way that the lower part of the book shall touch the neck of the elect's head, the text remaining downwards, which one of the elect's chaplains kneeling behind him shall hold up continuously until the book itself is to be delivered to the elect in [his] hands."[5]

3. *Veni Sancte Spiritus* is replaced by *Veni Creator Spiritus*, as in the rite for priests, a practice that was apparently already common

---

[3] *Explicit Pontificalis Liber magna diligentia Reverendi in Christo Patris Domini Augustini Patricii de Picolominibus, Episcopi Pientini et Ilcinensis, ac venerabilis viri Domini Iohannis Burckardi . . . correctus et emendatus* (Rome: Stephan Planck, 1485). See also Marc Dykmans, *Le Pontifical romain révisé au XVe siècle*, ST 311 (Vatican City: Biblioteca Apostolica Vaticana, 1985).

[4] See further Sharon L. McMillan, *Episcopal Ordination and Ecclesial Consensus* (Collegeville, MN: Liturgical Press, 2005), 203–12, 218–20.

[5] This arrangement is illustrated in woodcuts from 1520 and 1572, the latter differing from the former in that while the book touches the neck, it is held away from the head: *Pontifical Services III, Illustrated from Woodcuts of the XVIth Century*, with notes by F. C. Eeles, ACC 8 (London: Longmans, Green & Co., 1908), 36–37, figures 34 and 35.

in a number of churches as several of the manuscripts of the Pontifical of Durandus list it as an alternative in the margin.

Further versions were produced in the years that followed, with the first truly "official" pontifical being published by Clement VIII in 1595 and imposed by him on the Western church as a whole in 1596,[6] at least theoretically putting an end to medieval variation. Even though this appeared after the Council of Trent, it shows no signs of influence from that quarter. In 1645 under Urban VIII a further revision of the pontifical took place, and again under Benedict XIV in 1752, and Leo XIII in 1888, with a version with minor corrections appearing under John XXIII in 1961/62.[7] In no case, however, was any significant change made to the ordination rites.

POST-TRIDENTINE THEOLOGY

In the centuries after the Council of Trent, large numbers of theologians wrote about the sacrament of holy orders without, however, contributing much of lasting significance to the debate. One of the more important and influential figures was the Jesuit scholar Robert Bellarmine (1542–1621), writing only twenty years after the Council's discussion of the subject. Two assertions in particular stand out from his work, both of them taking a firm position in what were highly controversial areas. The first was that, although there were only seven orders, the ordination of a bishop was most certainly a sacrament, because there were two grades of priesthood; the second was that, in spite of having argued that the imposition of hands was the external sign of ordination in the New Testament, he concluded that the two powers of priesthood were conferred by two separate ceremonies: the delivery of the chalice and paten conferred the power to celebrate the Eucharist and the imposition of hands conferred the power to forgive sins.[8]

---

[6] *Pontificale Romanum, editio princeps (1595–1596)*, ed. Manlio Sodi and Achille Maria Triacca (Vatican City: Libreria Editrice Vaticana, 1997), 40–117.

[7] For details of the various editions, see Martin Klöckener, *Die Liturgie der Diözesansynode*, Liturgiewissenschaftliche Quellen und Forsuchungen 68 (Münster: Aschendorff, 1986), 324–29.

[8] Robert Bellarmine, *De sacramento ordinis*, book 1, chaps. 2, 5, and 9; in *Roberti Bellarmini Opera Omnia*, vol. 5, ed. Justinus Fèvre (Paris: Ludovicum Vivès, 1870–74), 22–24, 26–28, 31–33.

In this period Catholic theology was more concerned with the defense of papal privileges than with developing a theology of the episcopate. Nevertheless, there were some theologians who saw the importance of understanding episcopal consecration as the means by which each bishop shared in the universal jurisdiction of bishops as a body, especially Italian theologians in the eighteenth century who were concerned to defend the status of titular bishops, which had been severely attacked by some at the Council of Trent, and this theology of episcopal collegiality continued to be maintained by some theologians into the nineteenth century. Unfortunately, however, the preoccupation of the First Vatican Council with papal infallibility in 1870 led to the eclipse of that way of thinking and to the dominance of the view that bishops receive their jurisdiction directly from the pope.[9]

THE TWENTIETH CENTURY

It was only in the twentieth century that aspects of the theology of orders that had been controversial since medieval times received official definition in the Roman Catholic Church. In his 1943 encyclical *Mystici Corporis*, Pius XII rather surprisingly stated in passing that bishops did receive their jurisdiction directly from the pope, thus appearing to treat that much debated question as already resolved.[10] Perhaps equally surprisingly, in his 1944 apostolic constitution *Episcopalis consecrationis*, he ended centuries of debate by declaring that the bishops who participated in the ordination of a bishop were themselves co-consecrators and not merely assistants to the presiding bishop. After noting that in some places the assisting bishops only joined in saying *Accipe Spiritum Sanctum* at the laying on of hands, following the directions in the pontifical, while in others, including Rome itself, they also said in a low voice the

---

[9] See Ryan, "Episcopal Consecration: Trent to Vatican II," 140–49.

[10] *Mystici Corporis* 42, in AAS 35 (1943), 212. Seamus Ryan, "Vatican II: The Re-Discovery of the Episcopate," *Irish Theological Quarterly* 33 (1966): 209, n. 3, protested that "it can scarcely be contended that Pius XII wished to propose this as formal teaching. A question debated for centuries and left open by two councils cannot be taken as solved by an apparently incidental reference to be found in the form of a relative clause in a papal encyclical."

prayer beginning *Propitiare* with its following preface, he declared that:

> Although only one bishop is required and suffices for the validity of an episcopal consecration when the essential rites are performed, nevertheless the two bishops who from ancient institution and according to the prescription of the Roman Pontifical are present at a consecration, being themselves consecrators and thus in future to be called co-consecrators, ought with the consecrator not only to touch the head of the elect with both hands, saying *Accipe Spiritum Sanctum*, but, having made at a suitable time the mental intention of conferring episcopal consecration together with the consecrating bishop, also to recite the prayer *Propitiare* with the whole following preface and likewise for the duration of the rest of the rite to read in a low voice everything else that the consecrator reads or sings, with the exception of the prayers prescribed for blessing of the pontifical vestments, which are put on in the rite of consecration.[11]

In 1947 in another apostolic constitution, *Sacramentum ordinis*, he decreed that the essential "matter" and "form" of the ordination of bishops, priests, and deacons in the Roman Pontifical were the imposition of hands and the central petition of the original Roman ordination prayers that expressed "the power of order and the grace of the Holy Spirit," and that at least in future the *traditio instrumentorum* was not necessary for the validity of the ordination.[12] It is rather astonishing that it took until this late date for this declaration to be made. The texts of a wide range of ancient Eastern ordination rites had been published by Jean Morin as early as 1655, and these had shown that the imposition of hands and prayer were the only constant elements in those rites.[13] Although more recent scholarship might want to view the essentials of ordination more widely than this particular minimalist definition, it did restore focus on the epicletic and pneumatological dimensions of ordination (in

---

[11] Latin text in AAS 37 (1945): 131–32.

[12] Ibid., 40 (1948): 5–7.

[13] Jean Morin, *Commentarius de sacris Ecclesiae ordinationibus, secundum antiquos et recentiores, Latinos, Graecos, Syros et Babylonios* (Paris, 1655; 2nd ed., Antwerp, 1695 = Farnborough: Gregg, 1969), new and expanded edition by Giuseppe Assemani (Rome, 1756).

recognizing an invocation of the Holy Spirit rather than an imperative formula as constituting the central words) and paved the way for the drastically simplified rites for bishops, priests, and deacons that appeared in 1968. In order to bring the Roman Pontifical into line with the statements in these two apostolic constitutions, the Sacred Congregation of Rites issued a decree in 1950 specifying a set of variations to the rubrics, which were to be inserted in future editions;[14] these were later incorporated into the 1962 edition.

It was, however, historical research in the decades preceding the Second Vatican Council that made a significant contribution to the resolution of another major issue at the Council, the relationship of the episcopate to the presbyterate. While the majority of theologians in the period since the Council of Trent had inclined to the view that the episcopate did constitute a separate order, the discovery of the existence of medieval papal bulls permitting some presbyters to perform ordinations[15] seemed to suggest that the power to ordain was conferred with the presbyterate and not simply on bishops, and this led to considerable consternation among theologians.[16] On the other hand, the discovery that many bishops in the patristic period had passed directly from the diaconate to the episcopate without being ordained as presbyters seemed to show on the contrary that episcopal consecration itself was a sacramental act and not merely a higher degree of the presbyterate. The theological reflection on the role of the bishop and the sacrament of order in general that resulted from these historical discoveries among scholars such as Bernard Botte, Yves Congar, and Joseph Lécuyer widened the horizons of the debate with an increasing appreciation of the patristic tradition and laid the groundwork for the reappraisal of the episcopate in the teaching of the Second Vatican Council.[17]

Progress was also made over the question of the relationship of the laity to the ordained. Because the concept of the priesthood of

[14] Latin text in AAS 42 (1950): 448–55.

[15] See above, p. 145.

[16] For details, see Ryan, "Vatican II: The Re-Discovery of the Episcopate," 212–16.

[17] See David N. Power, *Ministers of Christ and His Church* (London: Chapman, 1969), 124–26.

the faithful was such a major element in the doctrine of the Protestant churches, it had tended to be ignored in official Roman Catholic teaching during the centuries after the Council of Trent. However, the emergence of a more positive theology of the laity among Roman Catholic theologians in the middle of the twentieth century led to a reappearance of the image in papal documents. The first signs of it occur in the encyclical *Mediator Dei*, issued in 1947. Here, while continuing to condemn what were seen as Protestant errors in relation to priesthood, Pius XII nevertheless affirmed that the faithful do offer the eucharistic sacrifice along with the priest:

> The fact, however, that the faithful participate in the Eucharistic Sacrifice, does not mean that they also are endowed with priestly power. It is very necessary that you make this quite clear to your flocks. For there are today, Venerable Brethren, those who, approximating to errors long since condemned, teach that in the New Testament by the word "priesthood" is meant only that priesthood which applies to all who have been baptized; and hold that the command by which Christ gave power to His Apostles at the Last Supper to do what He Himself had done, applies directly to the entire Christian Church, and that thence, and thence only, arises the hierarchical priesthood. Hence they assert that the people are possessed of a true priestly power, while the priest only acts in virtue of an office committed to him by the community. . . .
>
> By the waters of Baptism, as by common right, Christians are made members of the Mystical Body of Christ the Priest, and by the "character" which is imprinted on their souls, they are appointed to give worship to God. Thus they participate, according to their condition, in the priesthood of Christ. . . .
>
> In this most important subject it is necessary, in order to avoid giving rise to a dangerous error, that we define the exact meaning of the word "offer." The unbloody immolation at the words of consecration, when Christ is made present upon the altar in the state of a victim, is performed by the priest and by him alone, as the representative of Christ and not as the representative of the faithful. But it is because the priest places the divine Victim upon the altar that he offers it to God the Father as an oblation for the glory of the Blessed Trinity and for the good of the whole Church. Now the faithful participate in the oblation, understood in this limited sense, after their own fashion and in a twofold manner, namely, because they not only offer the Sacrifice by the hands of the priest,

but also, to a certain extent, in union with him. It is by reason of this participation, that the offering made by the people is also included in liturgical worship.[18]

In an allocution to the cardinals, *Magnificate Dominum*, on November 2, 1954, the pope restated much of what he had said on this subject in *Mediator Dei* but attempted to define the difference between the priesthood of the faithful and the ministerial priesthood more clearly: "the 'priesthood' common to all the faithful, high and reserved as it is, differs not only in degree, but in essence also, from priesthood fully and properly so called, which lies in the power of offering the sacrifice of Christ Himself, since the priest fully and properly so called bears the person of Christ, the supreme High Priest."[19]

THE SECOND VATICAN COUNCIL

The idea that the priesthood of the faithful and the ministerial priesthood differed in essence was taken up by Vatican II, which asserted that, in spite of this difference, the two priesthoods "are nonetheless interrelated: each of them in its own special way is a participation in the one priesthood of Christ." Thus, what united them was that it was Christ's priesthood in which they both participated; what distinguished them was not that their participation was just at two different levels or degrees of the same reality but that it was by two quite distinct modes. "The ministerial priest, by the sacred power he enjoys, teaches and rules the priestly people; acting in the person of Christ, he makes present the Eucharistic sacrifice, and offers it to God in the name of all the people. But the faithful, in virtue of their royal priesthood, join in the offering of the Eucharist. They likewise exercise that priesthood in receiving the sacraments, in prayer and thanksgiving, in the witness of a holy life, and by self-denial and active charity" (*Lumen Gentium* 10).[20] While some theologians have reacted positively to this

---

[18] Latin text in AAS 39 (1947): 521–95, here at 553–56; English translation from *Mediator Dei: Encyclical Letter of Pope Pius XII on the Sacred Liturgy* (Washington, DC: National Catholic Welfare Conference, 1947), secs. 82–83, 88, 92.

[19] Latin text in AAS 46 (1954): 666–77, here at 669; English translation from *American Ecclesiastical Review* 132 (1955): 52–63, here at 55.

[20] See also *Presbyterorum Ordinis* 2; *Apostolicam Actuositatem* 3.

explanation of the relationship between the two kinds of priesthood, others have claimed that it remains ambiguous and so requires further exploration and elucidation.

The Second Vatican Council took another major step in its definition of the nature of the ordained ministry. Rather than focusing exclusively on its priestly dimension, as medieval theologians and Trent had done, the Council instead spoke of the ordained as participating in the threefold office of Christ as prophet, priest, and king, in their teaching, liturgical, and pastoral functions respectively (*Lumen Gentium* 21, 25–29). This way of understanding Christian ministry not only broadened the traditional concept of the purpose of ordination but also rooted it christologically, in the ministry of Jesus himself. The idea of the *triplex munus* of Christ had its origin in patristic thought and had been revived in some Reformation works and above all in John Calvin's *Institutes* (II.15). It had first been taken over by German-speaking Roman Catholic theologians from their Lutheran counterparts in the eighteenth century and was also employed by John Henry Newman, who apparently derived it from Calvin. It was increasingly adopted by twentieth-century Roman Catholic theologians and eventually found a place in the 1943 encyclical of Pius XII, *Mystici Corporis*.[21] The Council not only applied the concept to the ordained ministers but extended it to the laity too, as sharers in their own way in the threefold functions of Christ (*Lumen Gentium* 31, 34–36).[22]

Finally, the Council settled the centuries-old debate about the relationship between bishops and presbyters by affirming that the episcopate was indeed a distinct order from the presbyterate: "the Sacred Council teaches that by episcopal consecration the fullness of the sacrament of Orders is conferred, that fullness of power, namely, which both in the Church's liturgical practice and in the language of the Fathers of the Church is called the high priesthood, the supreme power of the sacred ministry" (*Lumen Gentium* 21). As for priests, "although they do not possess the highest degree of

---

[21] AAS 35:200. For the earlier history of the *triplex munus*, see Peter J. Drilling, "The Priest, Prophet and King Trilogy: Elements of its Meaning in *Lumen Gentium* and for Today," *Église et Théologie* 19 (1988): 179–206.

[22] See further Osborne, *Priesthood*, 310–13, 317–24, 339–40; Susan K. Wood, *Sacramental Orders* (Collegeville, MN: Liturgical Press, 2000), 12–19.

the priesthood, and although they are dependent on the bishops in the exercise of their power, nevertheless they are united with the bishops in sacerdotal dignity" and "constitute one priesthood with their bishop although bound by a diversity of duties" (*Lumen Gentium* 28).[23]

In accordance with a recommendation in *Lumen Gentium* 29, Pope Paul VI issued a *motu proprio* in 1967, *Sacrum diaconatus ordinem*, that restored the possibility of following the ancient practice of ordaining to the diaconate men who would not subsequently go on to ordination as priests but remain as permanent deacons.

THE 1968 RITES OF ORDINATION

The Constitution on the Sacred Liturgy of the Second Vatican Council in 1963 had already specified that in the revision of the ordination rites "the address given by the bishop at the beginning of each ordination or consecration may be in the mother tongue" and that "when a bishop is consecrated, the laying of hands may be done by all the bishops present,"[24] but it was apparent to many that the rites were in need of much more major surgery than that. However, as Bernard Botte, who was secretary to the group charged with the revision of these rites, later observed, because the Council had wanted the people to be catechised on holy orders through the rites and prayers, the radical solution of restoring the rites to their fifth-century state by suppressing the later secondary elements had to be set aside and a different method adopted.[25]

[23] See also *Presbyterorum Ordinis* 2, 7. On the Council's teaching on the episcopate, and especially its collegial character, see further Ryan, "Vatican II: The Re-Discovery of the Episcopate," 217–42; Osborne, *Priesthood*, 324–33.

[24] *Sacrosanctum Concilium* 76. Jan M. Joncas, "Recommendations Concerning Roman Rite Ordinations Leading to the Reform Mandated in *Sacrosanctum Concilium* 76," *Ecclesia Orans* 9 (1992): 307–39, presents a detailed account of the large number of suggestions for changes to rubrics and text that had been made from the initial official consultations prior to Vatican II onward that resulted in this final meager permissive version.

[25] Bernard Botte, *From Silence to Participation* (Washington, DC: Pastoral Press, 1988), 134. A more detailed account of the process of revision is recorded by Annibale Bugnini, *The Reform of the Liturgy 1948–1975* (Collegeville, MN: Liturgical Press, 1990), 707–16.

Rites for deacons, priests, and bishops (this last now called an ordination once again) were produced in 1968, prefaced with a rite for
admission to candidacy for ordination, replacing the previous rite
of tonsure.[26] All three rites shared a common structure. Set within
the Eucharist, following the ministry of the word (for which a wide
choice of readings was provided), their main elements comprised:

- the presentation of the candidates to the presiding bishop and
  a declaration of assent to them made by the congregation,
  the presentation of a candidate for the episcopate being performed by two priests representing the diocese for which he
  was to be ordained, rather than, as formerly, by two bishops
  representing the college to which he was being admitted[27]
- a homily by the bishop, or the reading of a model address,
  concerning the duties of particular order, and a brief examination of the candidates, ending with a promise of obedience to
  the bishop in the case of deacons and priests
- the prayer of the people, comprising a bidding, the litany of
  the saints, and collect
- the imposition of hands in silence on each ordinand
- the ordination prayer
- the delivery of symbols of office
- the kiss

The newly ordained then fulfilled the liturgical functions of
their order in the Eucharist: deacons assisted with the preparation
of the eucharistic elements and with administering communion;
priests concelebrated the Eucharist with their bishop; bishops did
the same with the other bishops and priests who had taken part in
their ordination; and if the ordination had taken place in the
cathedral of a new bishop, he might be invited to preside and some

[26] *De Ordinatione Diaconi, Presbyteri et Episcopi, Editio typica* (Vatican City:
Typis Polyglottis Vaticanis, 1968); English translation: *Ordination of Deacons,
Priests and Bishops, Study Edition* (Washington, DC: United States Catholic Con-
ference, 1979).

[27] See the comments by McMillan, *Episcopal Ordination and Ecclesial Consensus*, 256–58, who also regrets the loss of the traditional separate selection-
presentation unit in the ordination of a bishop (see 252–56).

priests of his diocese were to concelebrate with him and the other bishops present.

Most of the texts were revised versions of traditional ones from the former pontifical. Although those rites had inherited from Durandus a statement of the duties of deacons and priests, a parallel statement needed to be supplied in the case of bishops, and similarly while a public examination already existed for bishops, versions for deacons and priests did not. Thus, the existing forms were improved and new ones composed.[28] While the traditional examination of a bishop had focused on testing doctrinal orthodoxy, the new versions in all three rites instead took the form of promises about the way the candidates would fulfill their office.

The ordination prayers for deacons and priests followed the original Roman ordination prayers with only minor changes, but that for bishops was taken from the corresponding prayer in the ancient *Apostolic Tradition*,[29] its substitution having been proposed by Botte as preferable to the narrow cultic focus of the Roman prayer.[30] It should also be remembered that he and most other scholars at the time thought that the *Apostolic Tradition* embodied the practices of the early church in Rome. Its adoption was defended in the apostolic constitution that accompanied the promulgation of the rites on the grounds that it was "still used, in large part, in the ordination rites of the Coptic and West Syrian liturgies" and so it would "witness to the harmony of tradition in East and West concerning the apostolic office of bishops." In reality, however, it is the more expanded version of that prayer in the fourth-century church order *Apostolic Constitutions* that is used in those rites, and in the West Syrian case only for the consecration of a patriarch. Only the central section of the ordination prayer for bishops was said by all the bishops together as co-consecrators, and not the rest of the prayer, as had previously been directed by the 1944 apostolic constitution, *Episcopalis consecrationis*.[31]

[28] Botte, *From Silence to Participation*, 136–37.

[29] See above, pp. 61–62.

[30] Botte, *From Silence to Participation*, 134–35. See also Bugnini, *The Reform of the Liturgy*, 713–15.

[31] For the disquiet at that former practice felt by the commission preparing the rites, see Bugnini, *The Reform of the Liturgy*, 710.

The imposition of hands continued the traditional practice in which the bishop alone laid his hand on deacons, the bishop and priests did so on priests, and all the bishops present did so on a new bishop. The older practice of two deacons (rather than two bishops) holding the open gospel book over the head (and not the neck and shoulders) of a candidate for the episcopate during the ordination prayer was restored. The symbols of office given to the newly ordained were mainly the traditional ones: a deacon received the stole, dalmatic, and gospel book, a priest the stole, chasuble, and paten and chalice (but without the formula bestowing power to celebrate mass and now containing the people's offering of bread and wine to be used in the ordination Eucharist), and a bishop the gospel book, ring, miter (this without any spoken formula), and pastoral staff, after which he was ritually seated if being ordained within his own cathedral. The anointing of the hands of priests and of the head of bishops (but not their hands) was also retained and placed after the ordination prayer in the case of bishops and after the vesting in the case of priests, with formulae making it clearer that the action was explicatory of what had already been bestowed in ordination rather than the conferral of any additional power. It had originally been intended to omit the *Veni Creator Spiritus* that had previously been associated with this action, as its retention in the new location could imply that the Holy Spirit had not yet been received, but an intervention by the Pope resulted in the hymn being kept in the rite for bishops and placed at the very beginning.[32] On the other hand, the option of singing it or Psalm 110 during the vesting and anointing of priests was still permitted in the rite for priests.

In 1972 in a *motu proprio* of Pope Paul VI, *Ministeria quaedam*, the tonsure, minor orders, and the subdiaconate (for all of which no revised rites had been produced) were suppressed. In their place were two "ministries"—lector and acolyte—conferred not by "ordination" but by "institution."[33] The rites for both take place after the ministry of the word in the Eucharist, or during a service of the

---

[32] Botte, *From Silence to Participation*, 138. See also Bugnini, *The Reform of the Liturgy*, 715–16, for the reasons that had been advanced for its omission.
[33] Latin text in AAS 64 (1972): 529–34.

word, and consist of a bidding, a prayer, and the delivery of a symbol of the office.

THE 1990 RITES OF ORDINATION

Soon after the publication of the 1968 rites, dissatisfaction was expressed with some aspects of them, and the ordination prayer for priests in particular came in for criticism on the grounds that it focused too much on the Old Testament priesthood and not enough on the priesthood of Christ. Work even started on the preparation of a second edition in 1974, but it did not progress far because the ecclesiastical climate was not favorable to further revision at that time.[34] Nevertheless, with longer experience of their use it became clear that the rites would benefit from a number of minor improvements, and so a revised version was authorized in 1990.[35] The principal changes were:

- the addition of a general introduction to all the rites on the theology of ordination and the structure and possible adaptations of the rites, and also of specific introductions to each of them on the nature of the particular order being conferred (drawing to a great extent on *Lumen Gentium*), the roles of the various ministers in the rite and the manner of its celebration
- the rearranging of the rites in descending rather than ascending order—bishop, priests, deacons—in line with ancient practice
- changes and additions to the questions put to the candidates in the rites for priests and deacons: the question concerning the ministry of the word is placed before instead of after the one concerning the administration of the sacraments in the rite for priests and a further question about praying without ceasing added; and a commitment to celibacy is inserted in

[34] See Bugnini, *The Reform of the Liturgy*, 721–23.

[35] *De Ordinatione Episcopi, Presbyterorum et Diaconorum, Editio typica altera* (Vatican City: Libreria Editrice Vaticano, 1990); English translation: *Rites of Ordination of a Bishop, of Priests, and of Deacons* (Washington, DC: United States Catholic Conference of Catholic Bishops, 2003). See Wood, *Sacramental Orders*, xii–xiv, for the process leading up to this, and for a theological commentary and critique of the rites, 28–63, 86–116, 143–65; also Puglisi 3:21–42.

the rite for deacons (except, of course, for those who are married), in accordance with the directive issued in a *motu proprio, Ad pascendum,* by Pope Paul VI in 1972, something that had already been done in the 1978 English edition of the Roman Pontifical

- many small but quite significant changes to the ordination prayers for priests and deacons, now called "prayers of ordination" rather than as before "prayers of consecration": they reduce the language that portrayed ordination as an elevation in status or honor,[36] use Old Testament typology in a more restrained way, link the ordained priesthood more directly to the priesthood of Christ, and specify in greater detail its sacramental ministry[37]

Among other minor changes are the removal of explicit mention of the *Veni Creator Spiritus* in the rite for priests, retaining only Psalm 110 "or a similar song"; the reintroduction of a formula to be said at the giving of the miter at the ordination of a bishop; and making presidency at the ordination Eucharist in his own cathedral no longer something the new bishop may be invited to do but instead something that "it is most fitting" that he does.[38] The rite of admission to candidacy for ordination in a slightly modified form is placed in an appendix to the Pontifical.

CONCLUSIONS

The new rites are unquestionably a major improvement on those in the 1962 Pontifical, especially in their simplification and clarity. Nevertheless, because there has been a strong tendency to retain

---

[36] Something that had been criticized in the 1968 rites by, among others, Mary Collins, *Worship: Renewal to Practice* (Washington, DC: Pastoral Press, 1987), 137–73. For an analysis of the extent to which the 1990 rites have overcome this, see Jan Michael Joncas, "The Public Language of Ministry Revisited: De Ordinatione Episcopi, Presbyterorum et Diaconorum 1990," *Worship* 68 (1994): 386–403.

[37] For a more detailed study of the changes in the prayers, see Wood, *Sacramental Orders*, 97–105, 154–58.

[38] For a more complete listing of the changes in the rites, see Puglisi 3:30–31, n. 45.

historic texts and ceremonies as much as possible and only make a limited number of innovations, there remain several areas where the rites may be thought to be somewhat unbalanced or reflective of some questionable medieval understandings of ordination.

Thus, while the introductory material, rightly or wrongly, makes considerable use of the threefold nature of the ministry adopted in *Lumen Gentium*, this is not consistently carried through in the rites themselves. It has been argued that the rite for a bishop concentrates more on the aspect of governance than on preaching the Gospel (partly as a result of using the prayer from the *Apostolic Tradition*, which does not mention the latter function) and the rite for priests more on the sacerdotal dimension of the office than on its pastoral functions (partly because all the symbols of office that are given relate to the former).[39]

It is also to be regretted that in every case the imposition of hands is performed in silence, detached from the ordination prayer itself, even when the rite is being used for only one person, and even though in the 1962 Pontifical it had remained in the middle of the prayer in the case of deacons. The rites thus continue to portray the imposition of hands and the prayer as two distinct ritual acts, just as has also been the case in the practice of many of the Reformation churches, rather than as two aspects of the same reality as was the case in early Christian practice.

Finally, the 1990 version in particular marks a great advance in recognizing a role for the laity in the rites, and for the local church in the ordination of its bishop.[40] Not only are all ordinations preferably to be celebrated on a Sunday or holyday "when a large number of people can attend," as in the 1968 rites, but the laity are given their traditional place in assenting to the candidates and participating in the litany. Directive 7 in the new General Introduction adds the following: "While the laying on of hands is taking place the faithful should pray in silence. They take part in the prayer of ordination by listening to it and by affirming and concluding it through their final acclamation." Unfortunately, this directive is

[39] See Wood, *Sacramental Orders*, 51–52, 56–57, 95–96, 103, 105.

[40] On this latter point, see the comments of McMillan, *Episcopal Ordination and Ecclesial Consensus*, 267–70.

not included in the text of the rites themselves, and in other ways ordination still appears to be viewed as largely a clerical affair. For example, the bishop's address at the ordinations of priests and deacons continues to refer to the congregation present as "the relatives and friends" of the ordinands, rather than as members of the church actively involved in the sacramental act. Nor are they included in the exchange of the kiss at the end. Thus the rites do not bring out the full significance of the part that belongs to the Christian community in the act of ordination. What Susan Wood has said of the ordination of bishops is true *mutatis mutandis* of all ordinations:

> Ordination is both epiclesis and human choice. It is not necessary to choose between them. The Spirit is present in both the ordaining bishops and the community. The laying on of hands by the ordaining bishops and the assent by the people represent a recognition prompted by the presence of the Spirit within the bishops and within the community to recognize the Spirit within the one who is ordained. At the same time it is a prayer for that Spirit to dwell within this person that he may govern in the Spirit. Hervé-Marie Legrand reminds us that modern writers have a tendency to restrict the action of the Spirit solely to the laying on of hands by the bishop, while, in reality, the Spirit is active at every moment in the election-ordination. This supports a theology of apostolic succession as both a succession of ministers who have received the laying on of hands and a succession of apostolic communities which have retained the apostolic faith. The key lies in the relationship between the minister and the community. These are not two separate and unrelated successions, but one succession in which the minister is in communion with the community, articulating, personifying and representing the apostolic faith of that community, and the community recognizing itself in its minister.[41]

---

[41] Wood, *Sacramental Orders*, 43. The reference to Legrand is to his article, "Theology and the Election of Bishops in the Early Church," *Concilium: Election and Consensus in the Church* (New York: Herder and Herder, 1972), 31–42, here at 38.

Chapter 10

Other Modern Ordination Rites

A number of churches made some changes to their ordination services earlier in the twentieth century, but it was the combined influence of the liturgical and ecumenical movements on the churches that was the main catalyst for widespread revision of ordination rites in the last quarter of the century. They were also influenced to varying extents by the parallel revision of the rites of ordination by the Roman Catholic Church, as described in the previous chapter. Not surprisingly, therefore, the most notable feature of those revised rites has been a movement toward both a common ritual structure and a shared understanding of the nature of ordination between the various Christian churches. This convergence in understanding can also be seen in the section on ministry in the World Council of Churches' 1982 document, *Baptism, Eucharist and Ministry*.[1] Although it appeared too late to exercise any direct influence on many of the revised forms, it nonetheless provides a useful snapshot of the measure of agreement that had been reached in the main Christian churches, despite the fact that certain aspects of what it had to say did not gain universal acceptance and were challenged by some of the churches in their official responses to it.[2]

THE CHURCH OF SOUTH INDIA

One of the most significant developments in modern ordination rites was the publication in 1958 of the ordinal of the church of South India, which had been formed in 1947 as a union of Anglican,

---

[1] Geneva: World Council of Churches, 1982.

[2] The responses are published in full in *Churches Respond to BEM*, ed. Max Thurian, Faith and Order Papers 129 and 132 (Geneva: World Council of Churches, 1986), and in summary form in *Baptism, Eucharist and Ministry 1982–1990: Report on the Process and Responses*, Faith and Order Paper 149 (Geneva: World Council of Churches, 1990), 74–88, 120–30.

Congregational, and Presbyterian churches. These rites were also substantially copied by the united churches of North India, Pakistan, and Bangladesh. Under the influence of the contemporary practice of the Church of Scotland, which followed the pattern laid down by the seventeenth-century Westminster Assembly, the imperative formula accompanying the imposition of hands characteristic of Anglican rites was abandoned in favor of an ordination prayer with the imposition of hands being performed during its central petition, which was an invocation of the Holy Spirit on the ordinand for the particular ministry being conferred. A novel expedient, however, was employed when there was more than one candidate: instead of the whole prayer being repeated over each person, or the imposition of hands being separated from the prayer, the prayer was said collectively over all, and when the central petition was reached, that alone was repeated for each ordinand while hands were laid on him, after which the rest of the prayer was said. In accordance with ancient tradition, the bishop alone laid hands on deacons, the bishop and presbyters did so on presbyters, but in the case of a bishop not only other bishops but presbyters too join in the imposition of hands.

A different prayer is provided for each of the three orders—bishops, presbyters, and deacons—that attempts to articulate the understanding of the particular office's nature. These prayers are set within a similar clear and simple ritual structure:

- the presentation of the candidates and the assent of the people, followed by the liturgy of the word
- the examination of the candidates
- a period of silent prayer and the English version of *Veni Creator Spiritus*
- the ordination prayer with imposition of hands
- concluding ceremonies—the delivery of a Bible (and in the case of a bishop the pastoral staff), the giving of the right hand of fellowship, and the declaration that the candidates are ordained
- the celebration of the Eucharist

The rites are preceded by a preface that states there are three essential elements in ordination—election by the people (the presentation of the candidates in the service representing the last step in this process), prayer, and the imposition of hands.[3]

The prayer used for presbyters will serve as an example of the form and style of the ordination prayers that were adopted:

The Bishop, standing together with the Presbyters, says:
We glorify thee, O God, most merciful Father, that of thine infinite love and goodness towards us thou didst choose a people for thine own possession to be a royal priesthood and a holy nation, and hast given thine only Son Jesus Christ to be our great High Priest and the Author of eternal salvation. We thank thee that by his death he has overcome death and, having ascended into heaven, has poured forth his gifts abundantly upon thy people, making some apostles, some prophets, some evangelists, some pastors and teachers, for the building up of his Body the Church, until his coming again in glory; and we humbly beseech thee,
The Bishop lays his hand upon the head of each person to be ordained in turn, the Presbyters also laying on their right hands; and the Bishop repeats the following words: SEND DOWN THY HOLY SPIRIT UPON THY SERVANT . . . WHOM WE, IN THY NAME AND IN OBEDIENCE TO THY MOST BLESSED WILL, DO NOW ORDAIN PRESBYTER IN THY CHURCH, COMMITTING UNTO HIM AUTHORITY TO MINISTER THY WORD AND SACRAMENTS, TO DECLARE THY FORGIVENESS TO PENITENT SINNERS, AND TO SHEPHERD THY FLOCK.
The people each time repeat: **Amen.**
And the Bishop continues, praying for all those ordained:
Give them grace, we beseech thee, O Lord, to offer with all thy people spiritual sacrifices acceptable to thee. Enrich them in all utterance and all knowledge, that they may proclaim the gospel of thy salvation. Make them watchful and loving guardians over thy flock, as followers of the Good Shepherd who gave his life for the sheep. Enable them in all things to fulfill their ministry without reproach in thy sight; so that, abiding steadfast to the end, with all thy faithful servants they may be received into thine eternal joy: through Jesus Christ our Lord, who livery and reigneth and is

---

[3] See further Paul F. Bradshaw, *The Anglican Ordinal: Its History and Development from the Reformation to the Present Day*, ACC 53 (London: SPCK, 1971), 172–90.

worshipped and glorified with thee, O Father, and the Holy Spirit, one God, world without end. **Amen.**[4]

ANGLICAN

The South India ordinal subsequently provided the model for the ordination rites published in 1968 as part of the unsuccessful attempt at Anglican-Methodist unity in England,[5] and through that document for revised ordination rites within the Anglican Communion, as well as for the British Methodist rite of 1975. It should be noted, however, that not all Anglican provinces have followed the South India pattern. Some have merely adopted a very conservative revision of the 1662 ordinal, and even those that have modeled their rites on the South India version have made a number of changes. All have made some alterations in the prayers and other texts, including the adoption of "you" rather than "thou" language for addressing God (except for the Church in Wales, 1984), and the substitution of "priest" for "presbyter" (although some provinces retain the latter as an alternative). New Zealand (1989) in particular has included rich imagery in its ordination prayers and an interesting central petition that replaces the more usual "Send down your Holy Spirit upon your servant N." with "through your Holy Spirit . . . empower your servant N." The US Episcopal Church (1979) and the Scottish Episcopal Church (1984, amended 2006) went further still and abandoned the South India prayer for a bishop altogether in favor of a version of the ordination prayer for a bishop from the *Apostolic Tradition*, following the lead given by the 1968 Roman Catholic rites.

Even the basic structure of the South India rites has not escaped some adjustment in the Anglican revisions. The provision for priests to participate with bishops in the imposition of hands on a new bishop has been rejected, as has the giving of the right hand of fellowship and declaration after ordination; sometimes a special greeting of the newly ordained is added instead and sometimes

---

[4] *The Ordinal: Orders for the Ordination of Deacons, the Ordination of Presbyters, the Consecration of Bishops* (Madras: Published for the Church of South India by Oxford University Press, 1958; 2nd ed., 1962).

[5] The Anglican-Methodist Unity Commission, *Anglican-Methodist Unity: 1 The Ordinal* (London: SPCK/Epworth, 1968).

the customary giving of the peace in the eucharistic rite is made to serve that purpose. Some provinces have placed the presentation after the liturgy of the word instead of before it; and some have restored a litany to the prayer of the people prior to the ordination prayer (sometimes substituting it for the English version of *Veni Creator Spiritus*), or inserted it earlier in the rite, after the presentation. Variation also exists with regard to the persons who are to perform the presentation (reflecting different understandings of the relationship between bishop, clergy, and people), with regard to the vesture of the ordinands and the point in the rite at which they are to put it on (before the service or after the ordination prayer), as well as with regard to the way in which the newly ordained are to participate in the Eucharist that follows.

Some provinces give a New Testament instead of a Bible to deacons and some omit *Veni Creator Spiritus* from that rite in accordance with older tradition; some give a chalice and paten as well as the Bible to priests, or at least make that an option; some allow for the giving of a pastoral staff (and sometimes other episcopal insignia) to a new bishop, though others make no mention of it; and some even permit the anointing of both priests and bishops. The 2007 rites of the Church of England add the option of washing the feet of new deacons as a parallel ceremony to those anointings, and permit the giving of the Bible to be deferred until the end of the Eucharist as part of the dismissal. The Episcopal Church in the United States, Scotland, and South Africa (1988) have also reinstated the ancient ritual seating of the new bishop as the conclusion of the ordination rite. In some cases the rites are still printed in "ascending" sequence—deacon, priest, bishop—but many provinces have restored the older reverse order. Although the South India arrangement for repeating the central petition of the ordination prayer when more than one person is to be ordained has met with some criticism, as tending to create the impression of three separate prayer units, it has been retained in every version except South Africa, where the imposition of hands, with its own formula, always follows the ordination prayer, even when there is only one ordinand.[6]

---

[6] For examples of rites produced in the 1970s and 1980s, see *Modern Anglican Ordination Rites*, ed. Colin O. Buchanan, Alcuin/GROW Liturgical Study 3

From the variety of ordination prayers used in the different churches of the Anglican Communion, the prayer for priests from the US Episcopal Church must suffice as a typical example:

> *The Bishop then says this Prayer of Consecration*
> God and Father of all, we praise you for your infinite love in calling us to be a holy people in the kingdom of your Son Jesus our Lord, who is the image of your eternal and invisible glory, the firstborn among many brethren, and the head of the Church. We thank you that by his death he has overcome death, and, having ascended into heaven, has poured his gifts abundantly upon your people, making some apostles, some prophets, some evangelists, some pastors and teachers, to equip the saints for the work of ministry and the building up of his body.
> *Here the Bishop lays hands upon the head of the ordinand, the Priests who are present also laying on their hands. At the same time the Bishop prays*
> Therefore, Father, through Jesus Christ your Son, give your Holy Spirit to N.; fill *him* with grace and power, and make *him* a priest in your Church.
> *The Bishop then continues*
> May *he* exalt you, O Lord, in the midst of your people; offer spiritual sacrifices acceptable to you; boldly proclaim the gospel of salvation; and rightly administer the sacraments of the New Covenant. Make *him* a faithful pastor, a patient teacher, and a wise councilor. Grant that in all things *he* may serve without reproach, so that your people may be strengthened and your Name glorified in all the world. All this we ask through Jesus Christ our Lord, who with you and the Holy Spirit lives and reigns, one God, for ever and ever.
> *The People in a loud voice respond* **Amen.**[7]

METHODIST

The ordination rites of the British and American United Methodist churches typify the practices now adopted in worldwide Methodism. As indicated above, the 1975 "Ordination of Ministers also

---

(Bramcote: Grove Books, 1987). For analysis of the American rites of 1979 and the English rites of 1980, see Puglisi 3:137–73. Among the most recent revisions are the Church of Ireland, *Book of Common Prayer* (Dublin: Columba Press, 2004) and the Church of England, *Common Worship: Ordination Services* (London: Church House Publishing, 2007).

[7] The Episcopal Church, *The Book of Common Prayer* (New York: Church Hymnal Corporation, 1979), 533–34.

called Presbyters" of the British Methodist Church[8] adhered closely to the South India pattern via the 1968 proposed Anglican-Methodist ordinal, locating the laying on hands by the President of Conference and other ministers during the central petition of the prayer and repeating this section for each ordinand. Ordination takes place at the annual conference, but prior to this the authenticity of the call to ordination is tested at local, district, and connexional levels, both before training and throughout it, and the ordinands undergo a period of probation. The ordination rite followed the liturgy of the word and consisted of the presentation of the candidates, the assent of the congregation, examination, silent prayer with concluding collect, the English version of *Veni Creator Spiritus*, and the ordination prayer. The rite ended with the President of Conference giving the newly ordained a Bible (the formula that accompanied it in earlier rites being turned into a prayer after the action) and the celebration of the Eucharist followed. A rite for the *Ordination of Deacons and Deaconesses* was adopted in 1989, and in 1999 a revised service for the "Ordination of Presbyters, usually called Ministers" was produced that followed the same basic pattern as the previous rite, although with some new language and the inclusion of a short litany after the silent prayer and a restored formula at the giving of the Bible. Its ordination prayer is as follows:

> Lord our God, we give you thanks and praise. You are the light and life of your people in every age, calling us to declare your acts of mercy and love. You sent your Son Jesus Christ to be our Saviour. He called the apostles to witness to his words and deeds, his life, death and resurrection. Through him you have made your Church a royal priesthood for the glory of your name. In the power of the Holy Spirit you strengthen and shepherd your people, by sending apostles and prophets, pastors, evangelists and teachers, in a succession of truth and grace. By the same Spirit you have called these your servants to be Ministers in your Church. Increase in them the gifts of your grace for their life and ministry.
>
> *The prayer continues as the President lays her/his hands upon the head of each ordinand in turn, other ministers also laying their right hands on the ordinand. The President says over each one:*

---

[8] *The Methodist Service Book* (London: Methodist Publishing House, 1975), G1–5. For analysis of the rite, see Puglisi 3:185–93.

Father, send the Holy Spirit upon N. for the office and work of a Presbyter in your Church.

Each time the President says these words, all answer: **Amen.**

When hands have been laid on all of them, the President continues:

Gracious God, as you call and ordain these your servants to this ministry, we ask you to fulfill in them the work you have begun. Grant them unfailing love for those people among whom you appoint them as pastors and teachers. May they boldly proclaim your truth and faithfully celebrate your sacraments. Give them wisdom and patience in their witness and service. Sustain and strengthen them at all times, giving faith and perseverance to all who believe in you through their word. May they be counted worthy at the last to enter into the joy of their Lord. We ask this through Jesus Christ our Lord, who lives and reigns with you, in the unity of the Holy Spirit, one God for ever and ever. **Amen.**[9]

The US United Methodist Church authorized a new ordinal in 1979.[10] It had a similar outline structure to the British rite but with separate forms for bishops, elders, and deacons. In the case of the diaconate, the service moved directly from the examination to the imposition of hands, which was performed by the bishop prior to the ordination prayer. In the case of elders there was silent prayer and (optionally) a version of the hymn *Veni Creator Spiritus* before the ordination prayer, and a modified form of the South India method of performing the imposition of hands was adopted: in the middle of the ordination prayer the bishop simply said each candidate's name while, together with other elders, laying hands on him/her. The "Consecration of Bishops" had the presentation of the candidates and a period of silent prayer for them before the liturgy of the word. This was followed by the examination, a second period of silent prayer, the optional hymn, and the "Prayer of Consecration," which was modeled on the corresponding prayer in the ancient *Apostolic Tradition* mediated through the version used for bishops in the 1979 rite of the US Episcopal Church. The South

[9] *The Methodist Worship Book* (Peterborough: Methodist Publishing House, 1999), 297–312.

[10] *An Ordinal, The United Methodist Church: Adopted for Official Alternative Use by the 1980 General Conference* (Nashville: United Methodist Publishing House, 1979). For commentary, see Puglisi 3:203–23.

India method of laying on hands by all the bishops was adopted when there was more than one candidate. All three rites ended with the giving of a Bible (though this was optional in the case of deacons and elders), a charge spoken by the presiding bishop, and the exchange of the peace. The celebration of the Eucharist usually (though not always) followed, during which the newly ordained participated according to their order.

In 1988, provision was made for laypersons to share in the imposition of hands, and the 1996 general conference took the more radical step of allowing probationary members for the orders of deacon and elder to exercise their full ministry within the congregation to which they were appointed without ordination, mandating a new rite of commissioning for that and thereby affecting the character of ordination itself. These changes were embodied in provisional liturgical texts in 1998.[11] Although discouraging the practice, the rites still permitted laypeople to join in the laying on of hands, and they directed that other deacons should do so at the ordination of new deacons. In the current version of the text published in 2012 and approved for 2013–16 use, where probationary deacons and elders are now described instead as "provisional members," the bishop extends his or her hands over them at their commissioning while saying a short prayer, and this is followed by an invocation of the Holy Spirit said to each one individually while the bishop stands behind and lays both hands on their shoulders. At the ordination of elders and of deacons, a substantial prayer is used, followed by an individual imposition of hands on each one accompanied by a very short invocation of the Holy Spirit and followed by an imperative formula bestowing authority to exercise their ministry. In the case of elders, it reads as follows:

> *The bishop, with hands extended over those being ordained, prays.*
> We praise you, eternal God, because you have called us to be
> a priestly people, offering you acceptable worship through Jesus
> Christ, Apostle and High Priest, Shepherd and Bishop of our souls.

---

[11] General Board of Discipleship, *Services for the Ordering of Ministry in the United Methodist Church: Provisional Texts* (Nashville: United Methodist Publishing House, 1998). See further John E. Harnish, *The Orders of Ministry in the United Methodist Church* (Nashville: Abingdon Press, 2000).

We thank you that, by dying, Christ has overcome death and, having ascended into heaven, has poured forth gifts abundantly on your people, making some apostles, some prophets, some evangelists, some pastors and teachers, to equip the saints for the work of ministry, to build up Christ's body, and to fulfill your gracious purpose in the world.

Give to these, your servants, the grace and power they need to serve you in this ministry. Make them faithful pastors, patient teachers, and wise counselors. Enable them to serve without reproach, to proclaim the gospel of salvation, administer the sacraments of the new covenant, to order the life of the church and to offer with all your people spiritual sacrifices acceptable to you; through Jesus Christ our Lord.

Representatives from the laity, the ecumenical church, and the order of elders who are to join in the laying on of hands stand with the bishop. When the bishop lays hands on the head of the candidate, others may lay hands on the candidate's back or shoulders. Family members and friends may be invited to stand where they are for silent prayer during the laying on of hands for each ordinand.

The bishop lays both hands on the head of each candidate, praying:

Father Almighty (Almighty God), pour upon *Name* the Holy Spirit, for the office and work of an elder in Christ's holy church.

All audibly affirm the action, saying, **Amen.**

Immediately the ordinand places hands on a Bible as the bishop lays both hands on the hands of the ordinand and says:

Name, take authority as an elder to preach the Word of God, to administer the Holy Sacraments, and to order the life of the Church in the name of the Father, and of the Son, and of the Holy Spirit.

All audibly affirm the action, saying, **Amen.**[12]

An elder's stole and/or chalice and paten may be presented to each one and the chalices and patens used for the Eucharist that then follows. In the case of deacons, a deacon's stole and/or a towel, pitcher, and basin may be given. The consecration of bishops adheres closely to the earlier form and strongly insists that only bishops participate in the imposition of hands.

[12] General Board of Discipleship, *Services for the Ordering of Ministry in the United Methodist Church* (Nashville: United Methodist Publishing House, 2012).

LUTHERAN

Ordination rites in Lutheran churches throughout the world today can generally be characterized as consisting of the following basic elements: presentation of the candidate, exhortation to the candidate and/or the assembled congregation, examination of the candidate and the taking of vows, intercessory prayer, and imposition of hands. The rite is usually located within a eucharistic celebration. Perhaps one of the most distinctively Lutheran features is the frequent inclusion of a statement or oath by the candidate of doctrinal allegiance to the Augsburg Confession and sometimes to other confessions included in the *Book of Concord*.

Two families of current rites can be distinguished. One is closely related to the service composed by Luther, and rites from this family include those of the German churches. Here the prayer directly associated with the imposition of hands (sometimes informally called the ordination prayer) is the Lord's Prayer, as it was for Luther, usually followed by another prayer for the outpouring of the Holy Spirit, together with a declaration of ordination during a further laying on of hands. The German rite of 1982 provides three alternative forms of prayer for the Spirit, of which this is one:

> Almighty God, merciful Father, we thank you for calling this brother/sister to serve your Church through the ministry that announced reconciliation. We pray: give him/her the Holy Spirit so that he/she will announce adequately your word and serve your community by the administration of your sacraments according to your will. Save him/her from temptation and doubt. Grant him/her the courage and assurance necessary for witnessing your salvation to the world. Keep your Church and all its servants in your truth until the day that your kingdom will be fulfilled in glory. Through Jesus Christ, our Lord.[13]

The other family owes more to ecumenical influences and is comparable to the 1968 Roman Catholic rite, though in English-speaking churches the influence of Anglican rites is also apparent. Here the imposition of hands takes place during petition for the Holy Spirit within a substantial ordination prayer, and such rites

---

[13] Translation from Puglisi 3:65. For analysis of the German rites, see ibid. 3:43–72.

tend also to include the vesting of the newly ordained, the presentation of symbols of office, an exhortation to the congregation, and the acclamation of assent to the candidate by the congregation. The rite of the Evangelical Lutheran Church in America (ELCA) would be the most conspicuous example of this group, where associating the imposition of hands with the imperative formula "receive the Holy Spirit . . . ," as earlier American rites did, has been abandoned. A first version of this rite was published in 1982 by a joint commission of the three Lutheran churches that were to unite to form the ELCA in 1988,[14] and a further revision, involving only minor changes, was authorized in 2009. Among its features that were new to American Lutheranism were the use of a litany for the prayer of the people, and its placement in close proximity to the laying on of hands, and the transfer of the congregational acclamation of assent to the newly ordained on behalf of the whole church to the end of the rite (although it remained after the examination in the rite for the installation of a bishop). Its ordination prayer (called simply the "Thanksgiving") is as follows:

The presiding minister leads the assembly in giving thanks.
The Lord be with you.
And also with you.
Let us give thanks to the Lord our God.
It is right to give our thanks and praise.
    Holy God, holy and mighty, holy and immortal, we bless you for your infinite love in Christ our Lord, in whom we have redemption and forgiveness of sins according to the riches of his grace. We thank you that by his death your Son overcame death, and that, raised by your mighty power, he gives us new life. We praise you that, having ascended into heaven, Christ pours out his gifts abundantly on the church, making some apostles, some prophets, some pastors and teachers, to equip your people for their work of ministry for building up the body of Christ.

---

[14] *Occasional Services: A Companion to the Lutheran Book of Worship* (Minneapolis: Augsburg Publishing House, 1982), 192–203. For earlier rites used by the American Lutheran churches, see Puglisi 3:72–88, and for analysis of the 1982 rite, ibid. 3:88–106.

The presiding minister lays both hands on the head of each ordinand. Other ordained pastors who are participating in the laying on of hands place one hand on the ordinand.

Following a time of silent prayer, the presiding minister continues, praying for each ordinand in turn.

Eternal God, through your Son, Jesus Christ, pour out your Holy Spirit upon *name* and fill *her/him* with the gifts of grace for the ministry of word and sacrament. Bless *her/his* proclamation of your word and administration of your sacraments, so that your church may be gathered for praise and strengthened for service. Make *her/him a* faithful pastor, patient teacher, and wise counselor. Grant that in all things *she/he* may serve without reproach, that your people may be renewed and your name be glorified in the church; through Jesus Christ, our Savior and Lord, who lives and reigns with you and the Holy Spirit, one God, now and forever. **Amen.**[15]

In both families of rites it is usual for other ministers to join the presiding minister in the imposition of hands, but whatever the location of that action, the importance of the inclusion within the rite of a hymn or hymns invoking the Holy Spirit, very often some version of *Veni Creator Spiritus*, should not be overlooked. In the Lutheran contexts this is frequently understood as an integral part of the prayer of the people for the ordinand(s). In most Lutheran churches a separate rite for introduction into a particular parish or other ministry is provided. This is usually termed "installation." Entry by an ordained pastor (presbyter) into the episcopal office is also marked by a distinct liturgical rite. While this may follow the form of ordination, as in Sweden, it is not generally understood as being an ordination to another order of ministry. Some churches call it "episcopal consecration," but others use the term "installation" or even "induction." In some cases, bishops from other churches with which the church is in communion are invited to join in the laying on of hands.

REFORMED

An early attempt to revise ordination rites came in 1970, when the Cumberland Presbyterian Church, the US Presbyterian Church,

---

[15] *Evangelical Lutheran Worship: Occasional Services for the Assembly* (Minneapolis: Augsburg Fortress, 2009).

and the US United Presbyterian Church produced a common form of service "for Ordination and Installation" of ministers of the word, elders, and deacons.[16] However, in 1994 the Presbyterian Church published a further interim revision that, among other changes, reflected gender-inclusive language,[17] with a final text appearing in 1999. Within the context of the normal Sunday order of service, the moderator presents the candidate to the congregation at the beginning and then after the liturgy of the word makes a statement about the nature of ordination. After this the whole congregation makes a reaffirmation of the baptismal covenant, including the thanksgiving over the water, which may optionally end with the anointing of the ordination candidate. The moderator then conducts the examination of the candidate, and an elder asks the congregation for their acceptance and support. The ordination prayer follows immediately. A choice of two forms is provided for elders and deacons, and three for ministers of the word and sacrament. In the first two for ministers, all present may join in the substantial central portion of the prayer while the ministers and elders lay hands on the candidate, and an alternative version of the last part is provided for occasions when the minister is also being installed. In the third, the moderator alone says the words of the second half of the prayer while hands are laid on the candidate; the candidate may then offer a prayer, and all present may say a concluding prayer. The moderator declares that the candidate is ordained (and installed); a welcome and a charge to the newly ordained follow; "appropriate" symbols of office may be presented, and if the minister is also being installed, a charge may also be given to the congregation. A new minister may preside at the Eucharist that follows. As an example, the first form of the ordination prayer for a minister proceeds thus:

> The Lord be with you.
> **And also with you.**
> Let us give thanks to the Lord our God.
> **It is right to give our thanks and praise.**

---

[16] *The Worshipbook—Services* (Philadelphia: Westminster Press, 1970), 89–95.

[17] *Book of Interim Ordination Rites* (Louisville: Presbyterian Publishing House, 1994).

Gracious and eternal God, with joy we give you all thanks and praise. Throughout the ages you have been faithful to your covenant people whom you have called out of bondage and redeemed to be your own. In every time and place you have chosen servants from among your people to point the way to salvation. We are grateful for ancestors in the faith who followed without fear, placing their trust in you alone. We give you thanks for judges and monarchs who ruled in righteousness and peace. We praise you for prophets and apostles who spoke your bold words of mercy and of truth. We thank you for pastors and teachers who have nurtured your people in faith and faithfulness. Above all we praise you for Jesus Christ, who came not to be served, but to serve, and to give his life to set others free. Anointed by your Holy Spirit, he proclaimed your reign on earth, revealing your saving love in all he said and did.

Those gathered around the candidate lay hands on him/her.
All present may pray together:

Gracious God, pour out your Spirit upon your servant N., whom you called by baptism as your own. Grant *him/her* the same mind that was in Christ Jesus. Give *him/her* a spirit of truthfulness rightly to proclaim your Word in Christ from pulpit, table, and font, and in the words and actions of daily living. Give *him/her* the gifts of your Holy Spirit to build up the church, to strengthen the common life of your people, and to lead with compassion and vision. In the walk of faith and for the work of ministry, give to your servant N., and to all who serve as pastors among your people, gladness and strength, discipline and hope, humility, humor, and courage, and an abiding sense of your presence.

The laying on of hands is completed.
The moderator continues:

Gracious God, pour out your Spirit of power and truth upon the whole church, that we may be for you a holy people, baptized to serve you in the world. Sustain the church in ministry. Ground us in the gospel, secure our hope in Christ, strengthen our service to the outcast, and increase our love for one another. Show us the transforming power of your grace in our life together, that we may be effective servants of the gospel, offering a compelling witness in the world to the good news of Christ Jesus our Lord. **Amen.**[18]

[18] Presbyterian Church (USA), *Book of Occasional Services* (Louisville: Geneva Press, 1999), 5–118.

The practices of other Reformed churches, including the Church of Scotland and the United Reformed Church in England and Wales, are broadly similar. At the ordination of a minister in the Church of Scotland, the Presbytery clerk gives an account of the steps leading to the appointment, and the moderator makes a statement about the nature of ordination and examines the candidate. The moderator says the ordination prayer and others join him/her in laying hands on the candidate during its petition for the Holy Spirit. The Lord's Prayer, a declaration that the new minister is ordained, and the exchange of the right hand of fellowship follow. Symbols of ministry (Bible, pitcher, and communion vessels) are presented to the new minister and laid on the Holy Table with appropriate words. A charge is given to the minister and to the congregation, prayers are offered, and the Eucharist may follow, at which the new minister may preside.[19]

Although the United Reformed Church provides full texts for the ordination and induction of ministers of word and sacraments, these do not have to be followed verbatim. The service includes the presentation of the candidate, who makes a brief statement about his/her call, followed by a statement on behalf of the local synod, outlining the steps that have led to the call. After the reading of the Basis of Union and questions put to the ordinand, the members of the local church and synod are asked for their support, and the ordination prayer is then said, during which hands are laid on the candidate by those appointed by the synod. The presiding minister makes a declaration that the person is ordained, the right hand of fellowship is given by appointed representatives, and symbolic gifts may be presented. The celebration of the Lord's Supper is optional.[20]

CONGREGATIONALIST AND BAPTIST

Neither of these traditions requires the use a prescribed text for the ordination of their ministers, and hence all that is possible in both cases is a description of typical practice. So, for example, in

[19] Panel on Worship of the Church of Scotland, *Ordinal and Service Book*, Interim Edition 2 (Edinburgh: Church of Scotland, 2005), 6–21.

[20] *Worship: from the United Reformed Church* (London: United Reformed Church, 2004).

the form produced by the United Church of Christ in the United States in 1986,[21] which congregations and associations usually take as the basis from which to plan and adapt a service, the main elements are: greeting, presentation (including a statement about the church's belief and the nature of ordination), exhortation, examination of the candidate, acclamation of assent by the people, laying on of hands by those appointed (which in practice increasingly means the whole congregation) either in silence or during a hymn, ordination prayer, declaration that the new minister is ordained, presentation of a Bible, and a greeting by the leaders on behalf of the people. The ordination may be incorporated within a service of the Word or of the Word and Sacrament. If the latter, the new minister may preside and give the blessing.

Similarly, at a typical Baptist ordination the candidate is presented by the chairman of the deacons to the congregation and, after receiving vows from the candidate, the presiding minister declares him/her fit to be ordained. There follows a blessing of the candidate and the ordination prayer, accompanied by the imposition of hands by ministers and in many cases by representative laity also. Charges are given to the candidate and to the congregation, and often a Bible is delivered to the candidate. The presiding minister welcomes the candidate into the ministry, and the Lord's Supper follows, presided over by the new minister.

CONCLUSIONS

Despite the claim made at the beginning of this chapter that modern ordination rites exhibit a convergence both in form and in theology, it will be obvious that while this may be true in broad terms, in matters of wording and of ceremonial detail there are still considerable variations, some of which reflect significant differences in the understanding of ordination and hence of ecclesiology both from church to church and in some cases within churches.

Although from their beginnings the Reformation churches recognized that ordination was not an action to be performed by ordained ministers alone but also observed by a congregation of

[21] United Church of Christ, *Book of Worship* (New York: United Church of Christ, Office for Church Life and Leadership, 1986), 400–411.

laypeople, the extent of active lay involvement in the rite still remains an open question between those churches today. There is a similar divergence with regard to the part to be played by the particular community in which the newly ordained is to minister over against laypeople representing the wider church.

One particular case in point is the presentation of ordinands at the beginning of the rite. Those traditions that generally hold their ordination services in a centralized location, be it a metropolitan or diocesan cathedral or a national conference, thus give clear expression to the universal character of the ordained ministry. However, if it is not counterbalanced in the presentation by elements that show how such ministries are rooted and embodied in specific Christian communities, it can give the impression of a belief in "absolute ordination," which was so roundly rejected in early Christianity. If, for example, those who present the ordinand, whether ordained or laypersons, have no connection to the place where his or her ministry is to be exercised, that will increase that impression, especially if no mention is made of that place in the presentation; if the presenters are all ordained ministers themselves, that will suggest admission to a particular clerical order rather than response to the need of a specific community; if the layperson participating in the presentation is the spouse of the ordinand, in order that he or she might feel more involved, that will reinforce the notion that ordination is a personal affair rather than a representation of the community. Nor is the situation necessarily remedied merely by the inclusion of an acclamation of assent to the candidates by the assembled congregation, whether at the presentation or after they have heard the responses to the examination questions. However suitable that might be for its own sake, for ordinations taking place in a centralized setting that congregation is not the local community in which the ministry will be exercised. And if such an acclamation of assent is deferred until the end of the whole rite, that will only add to the sense that ordination is largely an exclusively clerical action rather than one involving the whole church. If, on the other hand, the presentation includes some expression as to how the candidate has arrived at this point—an attestation of suitability from those responsible for his or her selection, testing, and training, for instance, or the reading of a mandate for ordination from those in authority—that will provide a link between the liturgical action and the process that preceded it.[22]

Although a formal or public examination of candidates for the diaconate and presbyterate was not a part of the practice of the early or medieval traditions, it was introduced in the case of a bishop in Western medieval practice, and from there the churches of the Reformation adopted it for all ministers, as part of their determination to ensure that such men possessed the requisite qualities and were of sound doctrine and to demonstrate this to the congregation. Similar examinations have now rightly become the standard practice of all traditions, so that the clergy and laity present, who represent the church, may hear a public declaration of the faith and intentions of those whom it is believed that God is calling to ordained ministry. The nature of the questions posed will naturally vary from church to church, as they reflect the particular concerns of each of those churches and the particular character of the ministry to which it is believed that they are called.[23]

The prayer of the people has been a much neglected part of the ordination rite in many denominations in years gone by, as attention was focused instead on what were seen as the principal ritual gestures and authoritative words. Even today, when the importance of the active participation of the people in the act of ordination is gradually being acknowledged, this prayer is sometimes separated by other intervening elements (or at least a good deal of physical movement) from the ordination prayer proper said by the presiding minister, with which it should naturally form one continuous act of prayer. Sometimes the desire to include both a litany and silent prayer and a version of the now well-established hymn, *Veni Creator Spiritus*, creates something of an overload. While the hymn may be a late-comer to ordination rites, its explicit invocation of the Holy Spirit makes it particularly appropriate for the purpose. On the other hand, the use of a litany is not only ancient but informative, as it sets prayer for the ministerial candidates within the wider context of the church's intercession.

---

[22] On the role of the local church, see further Puglisi 3:227–37.
[23] See further Puglisi 3:237–40.

As with the prayer of the people, so too, the central importance of an ordination prayer (rather than an imperative or indicative formula commissioning those being ordained) is now being increasingly recognized. That ordination is expressed through an *epiklesis* of the Holy Spirit does not imply any less certainty that what is sought will be bestowed on the one being ordained. As the World Council of Churches' *Baptism, Eucharist, and Ministry* states:

> it is the risen Lord who is the true ordainer and bestows the gift. . . . Although the outcome of the Church's *epiklesis* depends on the freedom of God, the Church ordains in confidence that God, being faithful to his promise in Christ, enters sacramentally into contingent, historical forms of human relationship and uses them for his purpose. Ordination is a sign performed in faith that the spiritual relationship signified is present in, with and through the words spoken, the gestures made and the forms employed.[24]

The ordination prayer traditionally not only makes petition for the requisite gifts and graces for the fruitful exercise of the particular ministry but also offers praise and thanksgiving to God for that ministry, as it has come down from Christ. In both these aspects it articulates what the church believes about the nature and functions of Christian ministry. It is therefore desirable that it sets the particular ministry within the ecclesiological framework of the calling of the whole people of God, of Christ's gifts to the church and of the biblical "types" on which the ordained ministry is shaped, as well as delineates the functions that the one being ordained will exercise in collaboration with other ministers among and together with God's people in order that all may be brought to salvation.

When we come to the sign of the laying on of hands, two principal questions emerge. The first is its relationship to the prayer. Although, as we have seen, in early Christianity hands were laid on those being ordained while the prayer for them was being said, that is not always what happened in later practice. Partly as a result of ordaining more than one person at a time and partly as a consequence of viewing the ritual gesture as something quite inde-

---

[24] *Baptism, Eucharist, and Ministry*, section on ministry, paras. 39 and 43.

pendent of the prayer, the two tended to become separated. Even now, the need to ordain several candidates at the same services creates difficulties in attempting to restore ancient practice. Repeating the whole prayer over each of them appears impractical unless the prayer is very short, and then it is robbed of the richness and gravitas it ought to possess. The solution adopted by many from the precedent set in the Church of South India—saying the prayer only once but repeating its central petition over each candidate while laying hands on that person and then continuing with the rest of the prayer over them all—is also not without its weaknesses. It can easily appear that it is not one unified prayer but three separate orations, one before the hand-laying, one short prayer over each candidate, and a further final prayer afterward. Moreover, laying on hands only while one short sentence is said can easily give the impression that a medieval understanding of "matter" and "form" has been adopted and that ordination is thought to be effected by a particular verbal formula rather than by God acting in response to the prayer of the church. Extending the length of the petitions made over each person, minimizing the disruption between the parts of the prayer by reducing any physical movement by candidates or by those performing the imposition of hands, and attempting to connect the various parts by repeated congregational responses (for example, "Come, Holy Spirit") can, however, ameliorate this problem, even if it cannot eliminate it entirely.

The second question raised by the laying on of hands is that of who should be involved. As our survey has shown, there is considerable diversity between the churches over this matter. This is one of the crucial points in the service where a particular ecclesiology may appear to be symbolized, even if the intention is otherwise. If the presiding minister alone performs the action, this may be thought by some not to be representative of the whole church but instead implying a more hierarchical model than they wish to espouse (even though the prayer that the gesture accompanies is the prayer of the church and not of the minister personally). If other ministers join in the action, are they sharing equally with the presiding minister ("co-consecrators" or "concelebrants") or are they signifying their assent to the new member of their ministerial order? The symbolism is ambivalent. If, in a desire to be inclusive, laypeople are also invited to take part in the action, does this imply the adoption of a congregational polity or merely confuse the distinctive roles of ordained and laypeople in liturgical celebration? And if ministers of other churches are invited to lay on hands as well, might this not appear to symbolize a degree of unity and mutual recognition of ministries that the various churches do not actually share? As will be obvious, this is a delicate area in which great care is needed and where merely intending to symbolize one thing may not be sufficient to prevent others from reading into it a quite different meaning. It is also worth noting that if more than a representative few participate in the action, the physical movement involved is likely to cause a serious interruption to the flow of the prayer.

What will also be evident from our survey is a widespread trend to introduce a variety of secondary symbolic acts after the ordination prayer and imposition of hands, such as the vesting of the newly ordained, the delivery of items intended to denote the specific liturgical functions of that ministry, and even the anointing of their heads or hands. Awareness of the consequences of the proliferation of such ceremonies in the medieval rites should serve as a warning in this area. It is easy for such dramatic elements to overshadow what is truly central in the rites or even to be confused with them. In order to avoid this, if they are to be adopted, they need to be clearly distanced from the prayer and imposition of hands and shown by the words that are used to be explicatory of what has already been received rather than the bestowal of further authority or powers. The presentation of the bread and wine to be used in the corporate eucharistic celebration in the current Roman Catholic rite is a good example of a transformation of a ritual that previously was seen in a more personal way.

Concluding the ordination rite with an act of reception by the church is another moment with ecclesiological significance. To quote *Baptism, Eucharist, and Ministry* once more,

> Ordination is an acknowledgment by the Church of the gifts of the Spirit in the one ordained, and a commitment by both the Church and the ordinand to the new relationship. By receiving the new minister in the act of ordination, the congregation acknowledges the minister's gifts and commits itself to be open towards these gifts. Likewise those ordained offer their gifts to the Church and commit themselves to the burden and opportunity of new author-

ity and responsibility. At the same time, they enter into a collegial relationship with other ordained ministers. (44)

But this then raises the question of who should be involved in this act of reception. Are the newly ordained to be received by the presiding minister alone, by the other members of their ministerial order who are present, by ordained ministers alone, or by the laity as well? Ecclesiologically, much hangs on the decision that is made. Similarly, the part to be played by the new ministers in the Eucharist that follows—or even more significantly, whether or not there is to be a Eucharist—also says something about the relationship between those ministers and others and about the relationship of their ministry to the Eucharist. As *Baptism, Eucharist, and Ministry* observed, "a long and early Christian tradition places ordination in the context of worship and especially of the eucharist. Such a place for the service of ordination preserves the understanding of ordination as an act of the whole community, and not of a certain order within it or of the individual ordained" (41). In particular, if the ordination takes place in the church in which the newly ordained person is to be the chief minister (for instance, a bishop in his or her own cathedral, a presbyter in the congregation in which he or she will take charge), there would be something rather strange about them not presiding over the eucharistic celebration but instead being the recipient of the presidency of another.

It seems appropriate to end these considerations with a further observation from *Baptism, Eucharist, and Ministry* that ought to find suitable liturgical expression in rites of ordination:

All members of the believing community, ordained and lay, are interrelated. On the one hand, the community needs ordained ministers. Their presence reminds the community of the divine initiative, and of the dependence of the Church on Jesus Christ, who is the source of its mission and the foundation of its unity. They serve to build up the community in Christ and to strengthen its witness. In them the Church seeks an example of holiness and loving concern. On the other hand, the ordained ministry has no existence apart from the community. Ordained ministers can fulfill their calling only in and for the community. They cannot dispense with the recognition, the support and the encouragement of the community. (12)

Index

gospel book, imposition of, 69–71, 83, 90–91, 117–18, 125, 131, 164–65, 175, 186

grave digger, 137

Gregorian Sacramentary, 106

Gregory Nazianzen, 56

Gregory of Tours, 109

Gregory VII, Pope, 135

Gryson, Roger, 74

Gy, Pierre–Marie, 65, 87

Halleux, André de, 26

hazzan, 7

high priest, 1, 4, 14, 30, 42–43, 62–63, 67–68, 70, 94, 113–16, 121, 141, 143, 182; Jesus as, 2, 14–15, 41–43, 160, 193, 199

Hippolytus, *see Apostolic Tradition*

Hoffman, Lawrence, 7, 65

house church, 21–22, 28–29

Hugh of St Victor, 137

Ignatius of Antioch, 20, 32–34, 38, 40, 67

Innocent III, Pope, 139

Innocent VIII, Pope, 175

Irenaeus, 10, 36–37, 40–41

Jacobite rite, *see* Syrian Orthodox Church

Jerome, 39–40, 54–55, 143

John the Deacon, 107

John XXIII, Pope, 176

jurisdiction, power of, 144–45, 174, 177

Justinian, Emperor, 134

Justin Martyr, 34, 41

King, Peter, 167

kiss, ritual, 83, 102–3, 117, 124, 129–31, 184, 190

Kleinheyer, Bruno, 120

Knox, John, 159–60, 163

laity, 30, 39, 43–44, 50, 74, 78, 103, 117, 140, 150, 153, 179–80, 182, 189, 199, 207–9, 211–13

Laodicea, Council of, 54, 56

Lasco, John á, 160–61

Lateran Council, 135, 138

lector, *see* reader

Lécuyer, Joseph, 179

Legrand, Hervé–Marie, 190

Leofric Missal, 120

Leo I, Pope, 107, 135

Leonine Sacramentary, *see* Verona Sacramentary

Leo XIII, Pope, 176

Levite, 1–4, 12, 30, 40, 42–43, 67, 112, 114, 123–24

librarian, 119, 137

litany, 89–90, 93, 111, 120, 127, 129–31, 138, 163–64, 171, 184, 189, 195, 197, 202, 209

Lombard, Peter, 138, 145

Luther, Martin, 151–56, 171, 201

Lutheran rites, 154–57, 201–3

ma'amadoth, 5

Maier, Harry, 28–29

Maronite rite, 82, 87, 89, 91–94, 98, 100, 102, 104–5

Martimort, Aimé Georges, 74

Maurus, Rabanus, 141

Melchizedek, 2, 14

Melkite rite, 82, 90, 92, 94, 96–98, 100–1, 104

Methodist rites, 167–70, 194, 196–200

metropolitan, 82

minor orders, 47–49, 57, 73, 78, 84, 86, 119, 128, 136–38, 140, 146, 186

Missale Francorum, 106, 119, 125, 129–31

Morin, Jean, 178

Mozarabic rite, *see* Spanish rite

Munier, Charles, 118

Newman, John Henry, 182
Nicaea, Council of, 51, 54, 134
Novatian, 50

obedience, promise of, 146, 184
omophorion, 103
Optatus of Milevis, 43
Ordinals of Christ, 137
ordines Romani, 72, 106–7, 110
Origen, 43, 67

Palladius, 70
papal ordination, 71, 108–9, 118, 125
Paphnutius, Bishop, 134
pastor, 20, 157–58, 160, 162, 165–66,
    193, 196–98, 200, 202–3, 205
patriarch, 82, 185
Paul VI, Pope, 183
people, prayer of the, 89–90, 184,
    195, 202–2, 209–10
Petri, Laurentius, 155
Philo of Alexandria, 40
Philostorgius, 84
Piccolomini, Agostino, 175
Pius XII, Pope, 177, 180, 182
Polycarp, 31, 60
pontificals, 82, 117–18, 120, 125–31,
    142–43, 146, 175–79, 188–89
Porter, Harry Boone, 124
Presanctified, Liturgy of the, 104
Presbyterian rites, *see* Reformed rites
presbyteros, 18–19, 21, 28, 38; *see also*
    elder
presentation of candidates, 129–31,
    163, 184, 192, 195, 197–98, 201,
    204, 206–8
priesthood, 1–4, 14–15, 41–45, 55,
    62–63, 65, 72, 77, 96–98, 102,
    118, 121, 141–44, 149, 150–53,
    167,172–74, 176, 179–83, 187–89
prophet, 9–10, 12, 21–22, 24–28, 32,
    35, 37, 42, 46, 72, 79, 96, 101, 157,
    162, 182, 193, 196–97, 200, 202, 205

psalmist, 117–19
Pseudo–Dionysius, 70, 85, 87,
    91–93, 103
Puglisi, James, 170
Pullain, Valerand, 159

rabbi, 7, 65
Ratcliff, Edward, 59, 71
Ratold, Sacramentary of, 120
reader, 6, 34, 43, 47–49, 53, 73–76,
    78–79, 81–82, 103, 107, 117, 119,
    136, 173, 186
Reformed rites, 158–63, 170, 203–6
right hand of fellowship, 161, 165,
    192, 194, 206
Roman Catholic rites, 183–90, 194,
    201, 212
Romano–Germanic Pontifical, 126,
    129–31, 146
Roman rite, 81, 106–17, 125–31

sacristan, 119
Sarapion of Thmuis, 58, 79–81, 99
Savoy Declaration, 165
scribe, 119
seating of a bishop, 35, 49, 60, 68–
    69, 83, 102–3, 128, 186, 195
Segelberg, Eric, 61
Severian of Gabala, 70
Shepherd of Hermas, 27–28, 34
Socrates, church historian, 80
South India, Church of, 191–94,
    197–98, 211
Spanish rite, 117, 119–20, 123–24
Statuta ecclesiae antiqua, 117–19, 125
Stewart–Sykes, Alistair, 35–36, 46,
    60, 66
Stillingfleet, Edward, 167
subdeacon, 43, 47–49, 53, 73–76, 78–
    79, 81–82, 100, 103, 106–7, 117,
    119, 134–35, 138, 148, 173, 186
superintendent, 154, 156, 159–60,
    167–69